Postcard History Series

# McMinn County

**On the Front Cover:** Three McMinn County courthouses have occupied the public square in Athens since 1822. A two-story brick structure was built in 1828 and lasted until 1873, when age and damages it received during the Civil War necessitated its replacement. The courthouse pictured here was completed in 1874 at a cost of $30,000. For the first time, accommodations were made for all courts and clerks, as well as for the tax collector, register of deeds, trustee, sheriff, and storage for public records. The building was remodeled with concrete floors, modern plumbing, and electrical service in 1928 and was enlarged with an extension of both east and west wings. On Election Day in November 1964, a fire that started near the cupola severely damaged the old courthouse, although all county records were saved. With much controversy, the building was razed to make room for the present courthouse, which opened in 1966. (Courtesy McMinn County Historical Society.)

**On the Back Cover:** The café inside the Athens Bus Station served both the weary bus traveller as well as many Athens citizens who dropped in for a good meal and news from visitors. (Courtesy the Don Reid collection.).

POSTCARD HISTORY SERIES

# *McMinn County*

*Joe Guy*
*with postcards from the collection of Don Reid*

ARCADIA
PUBLISHING

ISBN 978-0-7385-8573-4

Published by Arcadia Publishing
Charleston, South Carolina

Printed in the United States of America

Library of Congress Control Number: 2009940204

For all general information contact Arcadia Publishing at:
Telephone 843-853-2070
Fax 843-853-0044
E-mail sales@arcadiapublishing.com
For customer service and orders:
Toll-Free 1-888-313-2665

Visit us on the Internet at www.arcadiapublishing.com

*For Don Reid. We miss you, buddy.*

# Contents

# Acknowledgments

In 2004, my friend Don Reid, a well-respected local attorney, invited me to his office, where he showed me his fantastic old postcard collection. Any time spent with Don was always a great time, and we discussed publishing a book together. A few years passed as I followed other book projects, and every time we saw each other around the county courthouse, we always talked about getting together on a postcard book.

In the spring of 2009, we talked again, and this time decided we would focus on the project before either of us could get distracted by something else. We met in June, discussed the book, and agreed on coauthoring it, and Don left me with two volumes of his postcards. I had already been in contact with Maggie Bullwinkel at Arcadia Publishing, and within a few weeks, I had sent her our proposal with samples of Don's cards. On the evening of August 25, I received an e-mail from Maggie letting us know the book had been approved for publication. I was elated and made myself a mental note to call Don the following day to make sure he had seen the good news. But I never got to tell him.

Sadly, Don Reid passed away that night. His death came as a shock to his family, to his friends, and to his community. Grieving myself and being at a loss at what to do with the book, I was immediately encouraged by Don's wife, Linda, and the rest of his family to finish the project. Linda was kind enough to supply additional postcards, and within a few months, the book was completed.

It has been a difficult journey for Linda and the Reid family, for Don's friends, and for myself, and if not for the continued encouragement and assistance of many people, this book would not have been possible. I want to thank Linda Reid for her patience and assistance, Etowah historian Durant Tullock for his help with the history on the Etowah section, Patsy Duckworth for her help with the history of North Athens, and Maggie Bullwinkel at Arcadia for her patience and guidance. And thank-you to my wife and sons for their enduring support for all the things I am blessed to be able to do.

But most of all, I thank Don. He was a great friend that left us much too quickly. I hope his excitement at sharing his card collection and his love of McMinn County and its history will live on through the pages of this book. As Don was fond of saying, "It's a great day."

Unless otherwise noted, all images are from the collection of Don Reid.

# INTRODUCTION

McMinn County, Tennessee, was founded in 1819 on land previously owned by the Cherokee Indian Nation. Situated in Southeast Tennessee, McMinn County is halfway between Knoxville and Chattanooga, halfway between Atlanta and Bristol, and halfway between New York and Miami. For its citizens, it remains a rural county of mountain ridges with deep hollows and wide-creek valleys; its different topography also defining the different people who, for 150 years, have called McMinn County home.

But it is the towns that are often pictured in old postcards, which are featured in this book. The cards themselves come from the collection of the late Don Reid and feature many long-forgotten scenes from Athens, Englewood, and Etowah. Athens, the county seat, was founded in 1822 at the center of the county and remains the largest town. Englewood came about as a mill town, with two communities combining at a railroad junction. Etowah was founded in 1906 as a one-sided railroad boomtown. All three have different histories, different people, and different stories to tell.

Many of the businesses and buildings in these postcards are long gone. I hope, as I know Don would have, that you enjoy this journey through McMinn County as it once was.

# *One*

# Athens
## The Old Downtown

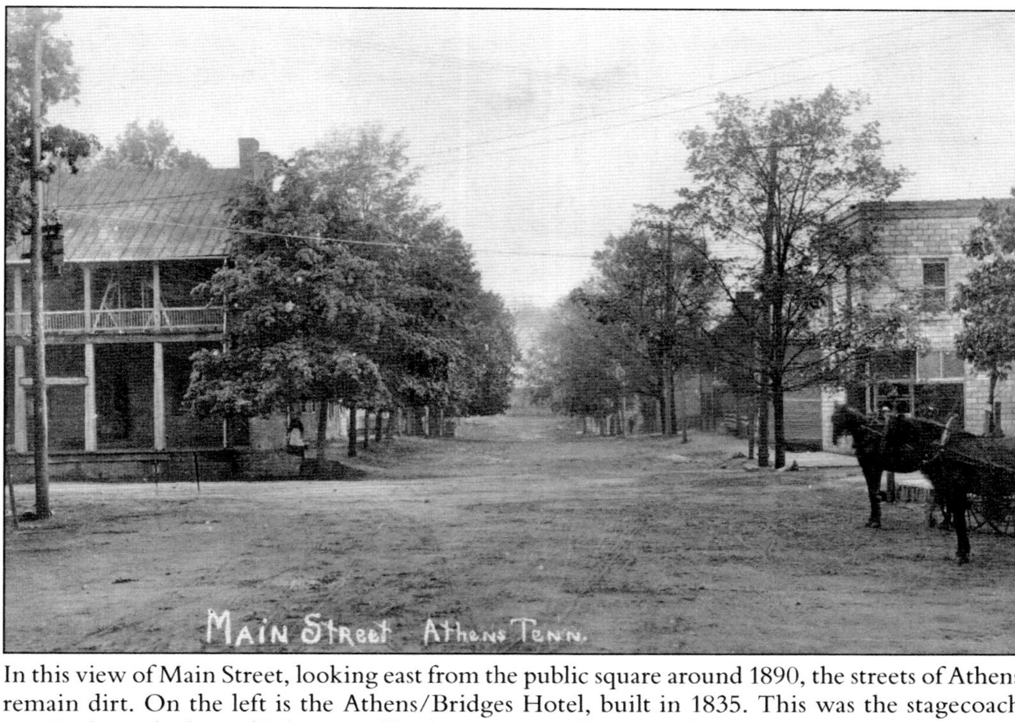


In this view of Main Street, looking east from the public square around 1890, the streets of Athens remain dirt. On the left is the Athens/Bridges Hotel, built in 1835. This was the stagecoach stop in the early days of Athens, and both James K. Polk and Andrew Jackson stayed at the hotel during their presidential campaigns. Most notably, it was the headquarters of Gen. John Ellis Wool during the Cherokee Removal of 1836–1837, when it was operated by James Bridges. The *Athens Post*, forerunner to the modern *Post-Athenian*, was published in a small building behind the Athens Hotel by Sam Ivins of New Jersey, who lived across the street. The Rice House, likely the oldest building in the downtown area that still stands today, is also visible down the street on the right.

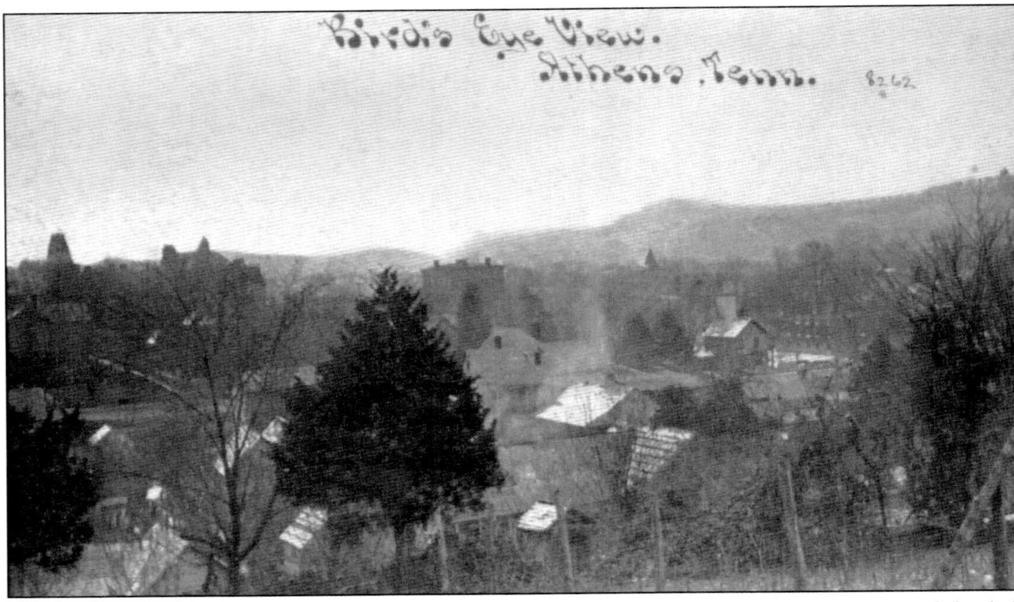


From a series of photographs taken around 1880–1890, this view is from the top of the hill above where the East Tennessee and Georgia, and later Southern, Railroad Depot was located. The hill was utilized during the Civil War as an artillery emplacement and was involved in at least one skirmish with attacking Confederate cavalry in August 1864, when artillery on this hill exchanged fire with another emplacement on Van Dyke Hill to the south. Old College, constructed in 1857 and the forerunner of today's Tennessee Wesleyan College, is located at the center of the picture.

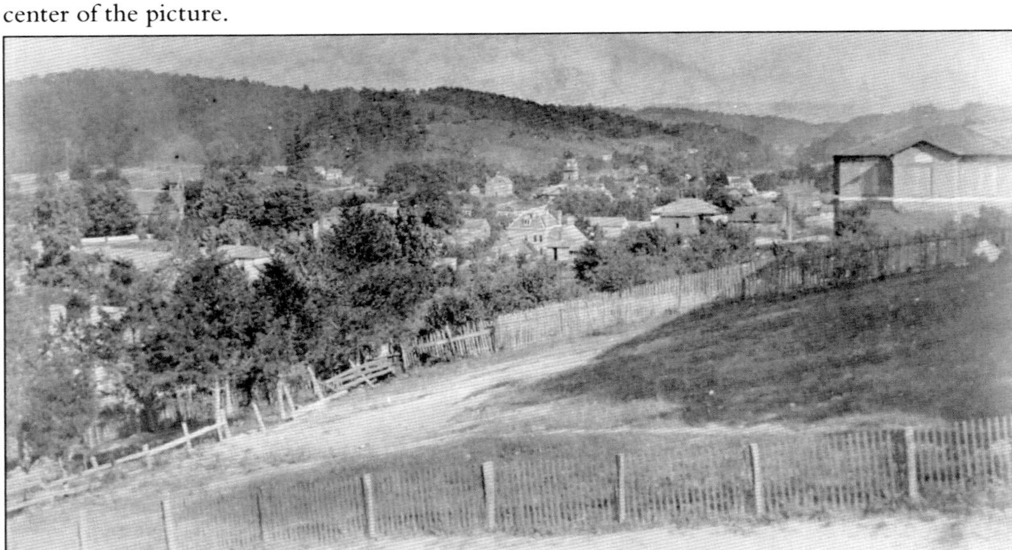

Another view from Fort Hill, now Depot Hill, shows Athens in the distance. Just to the right of center is the McMinn County Jail, and on the hill farther to the right is the Forrest Hill School. In the distance beyond the jail, the cupola of the courthouse is visible, and just to the left is Athens Roller Mills on the bank of Eastanaulee Creek. Mars Hill Church's roof and steeple are visible at middle left. Far in the distance is Starr Mountain, on top of which intersect the county lines of McMinn, Monroe, and Polk Counties. (Courtesy McMinn County Historical Society.)

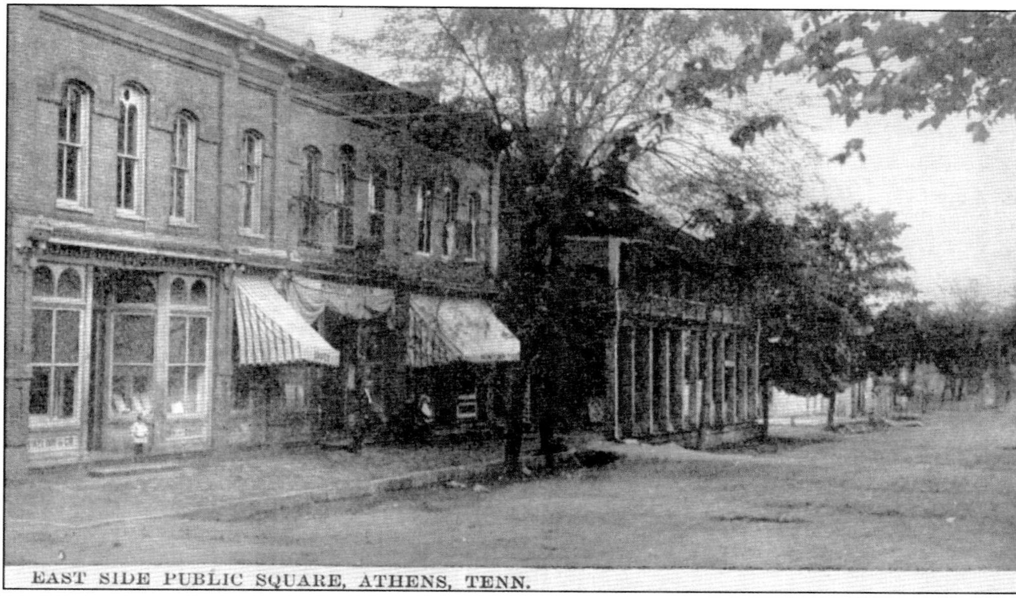

Jackson Street is seen here looking south on the public square, with the Athens Hotel at the end of the block. McKeldin and Company Dry Goods occupied the store on the right for many years. This was also the second location of the Proffitt's Clothing Stores that eventually spread across the southeast before being acquired by Belk. Except for the Athens hotel, all of these 19th-century brick stores remain. All were connected by large steel doors that opened into the adjacent buildings, forming an early indoor shopping mall for McMinn County patrons.

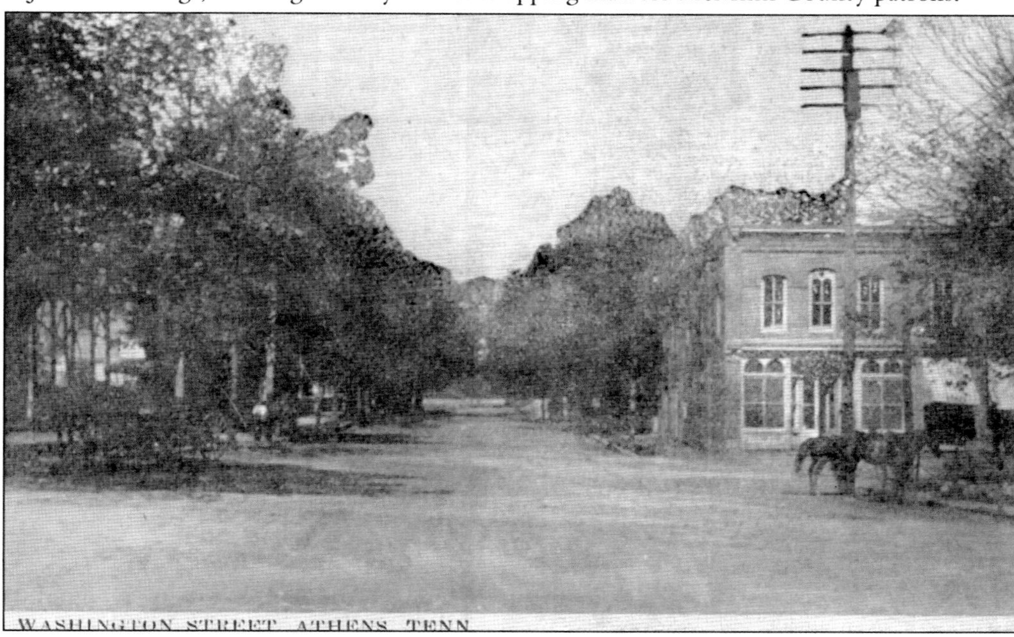

Here is a view down Washington Street looking east from the public square around 1890. McKeldin and Company Dry Goods is visible on the right, and barely visible on the left is the McGauhey Tin Shop. A few horses are tied on the right while their riders visit the courthouse, and a buggy waits on the left outside the Hotel Magill.

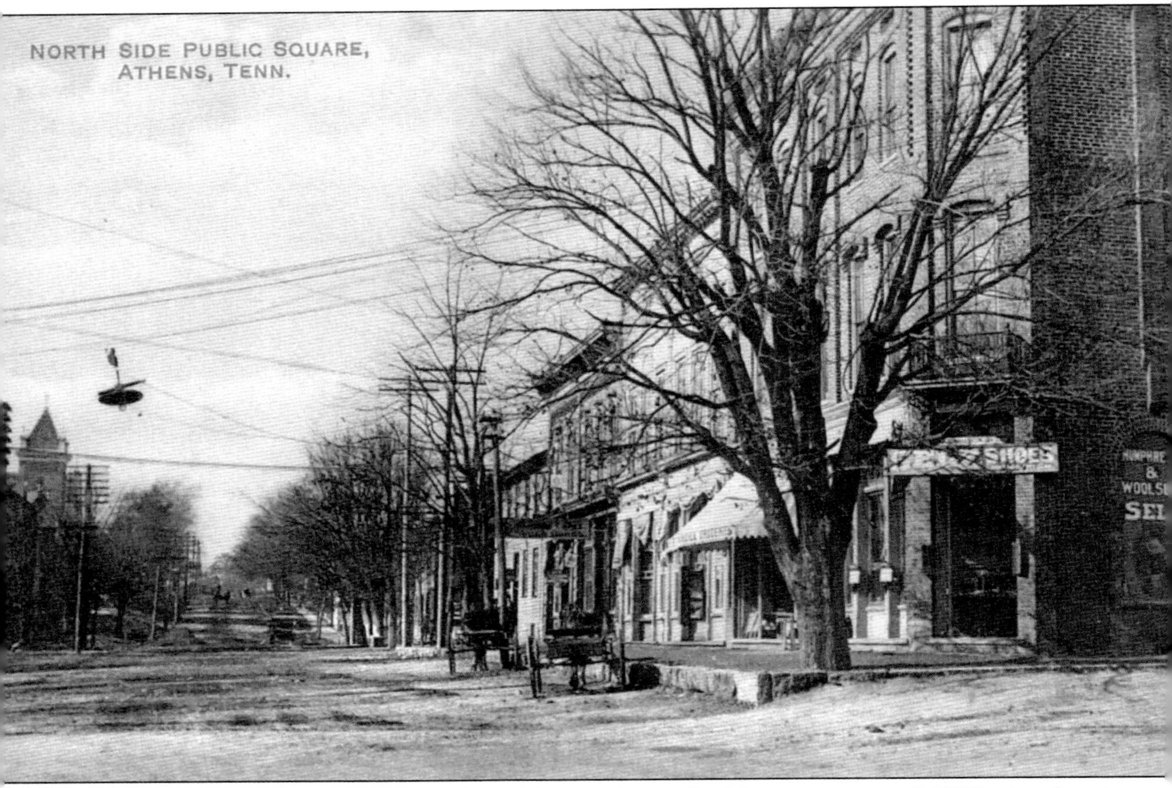


This postcard features a view of Washington Street looking west around 1900. An electric streetlight hangs over the intersection of Washington and Jackson Streets, but the streets are still dirt. The Hotel Magill stands on the near right corner with a grocery and shoe store in its storefront. Next is the Hornsby Building and then the A. C. Robeson building, constructed in the 1860s, which is the only building still standing. At the end of the block stands the Mathews house on "Atlee Corner," and just beyond is the Grubb house on "Grubb Corner." On the left is James Crow's Grocery Store with the spire of the Methodist Church, built in 1878, in the distant left. At this location, in an earlier building, Parson William Brownlow preached on his East Tennessee Methodist circuit. Brownlow would later be one of the strongest and most outspoken Union men in the South and was later elected governor. This Methodist congregation split over slavery prior to the Civil War, with the Union-leaning Methodists maintaining this site and the Confederate-leaning Methodists occupying a site north of town. The split remained until the mid-1900s.

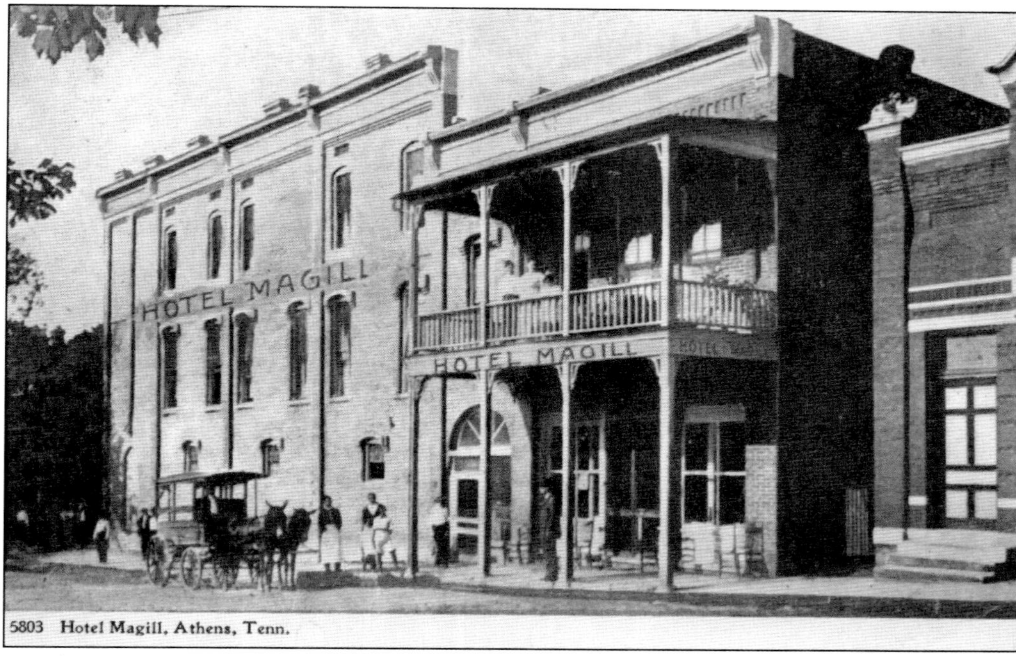


Another early-1900s view of the Hotel Magill and Annex Hotel shows a partial view of the new First National Bank building. J. Harvey Magill was the proprietor of these hotels, as well as one in Niota and the more famous White Cliff Springs Hotel on the summit of Starr Mountain on the east side of the county. Magill's talents in advertising and hotel management ensured his success.

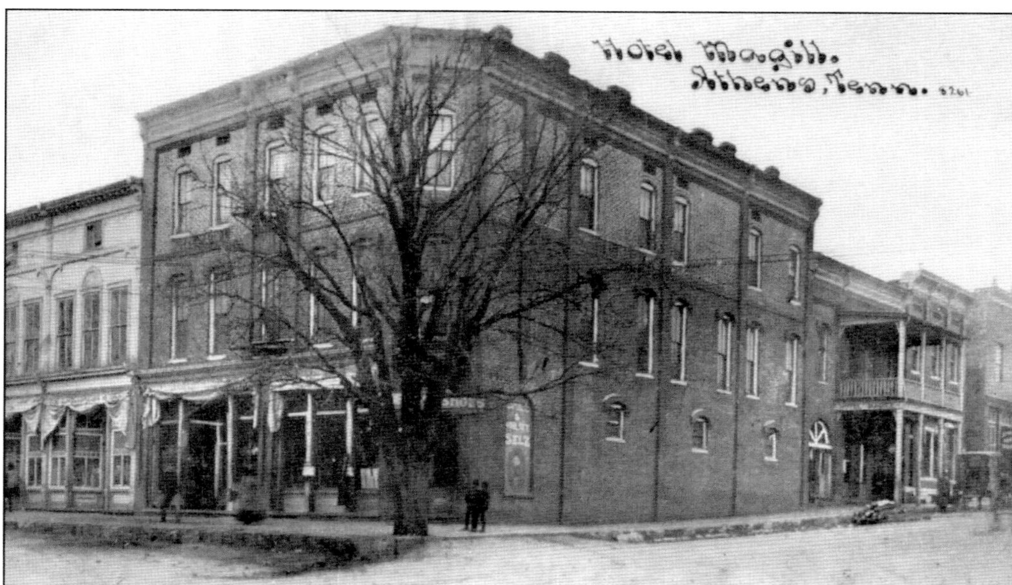


A good view of the Hotel Magill is seen here on the corner of Jackson and Washington Streets. The portico attached to the rear of the building covered the entrance to the Annex Hotel. The storefront on the far right would later be replaced by the First National Bank building, which later became the first location of Athens City Hall.

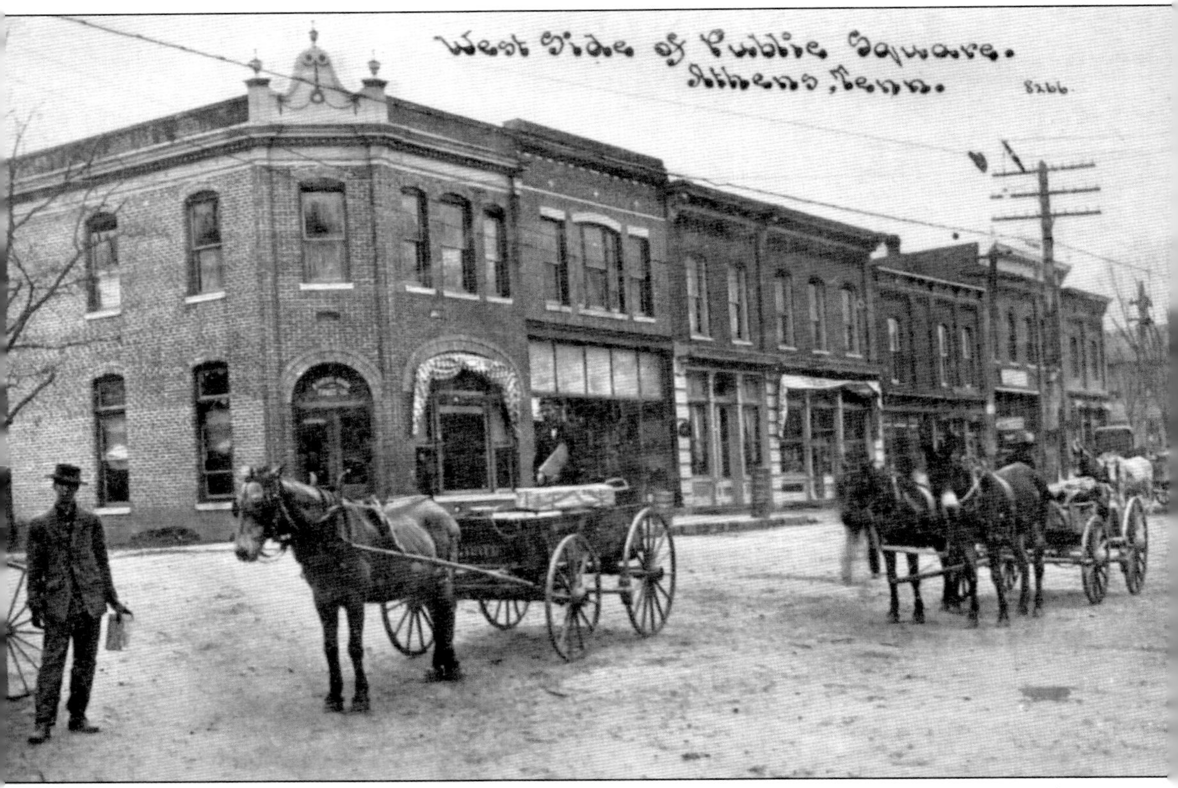


Here is White Street looking north on the public square around 1900. Athens Bank and Trust occupies the near corner, with James Crow's store on the far end of the block and the Grubb house on the far right. Dr. James S. Vaughn's dentist office was located on the top floor of the bank building. The plank walkway in front of these buildings covers the White Street Ditch, a deep wash that was once an Athens landmark. When Athens allowed saloons on its streets, many cases of drunken patrons falling into the ditch were recorded in old newspapers. Wagons loaded with goods stand in the street, indicating perhaps this was "court day," a good time for farmers to come into town to sell wares and produce.

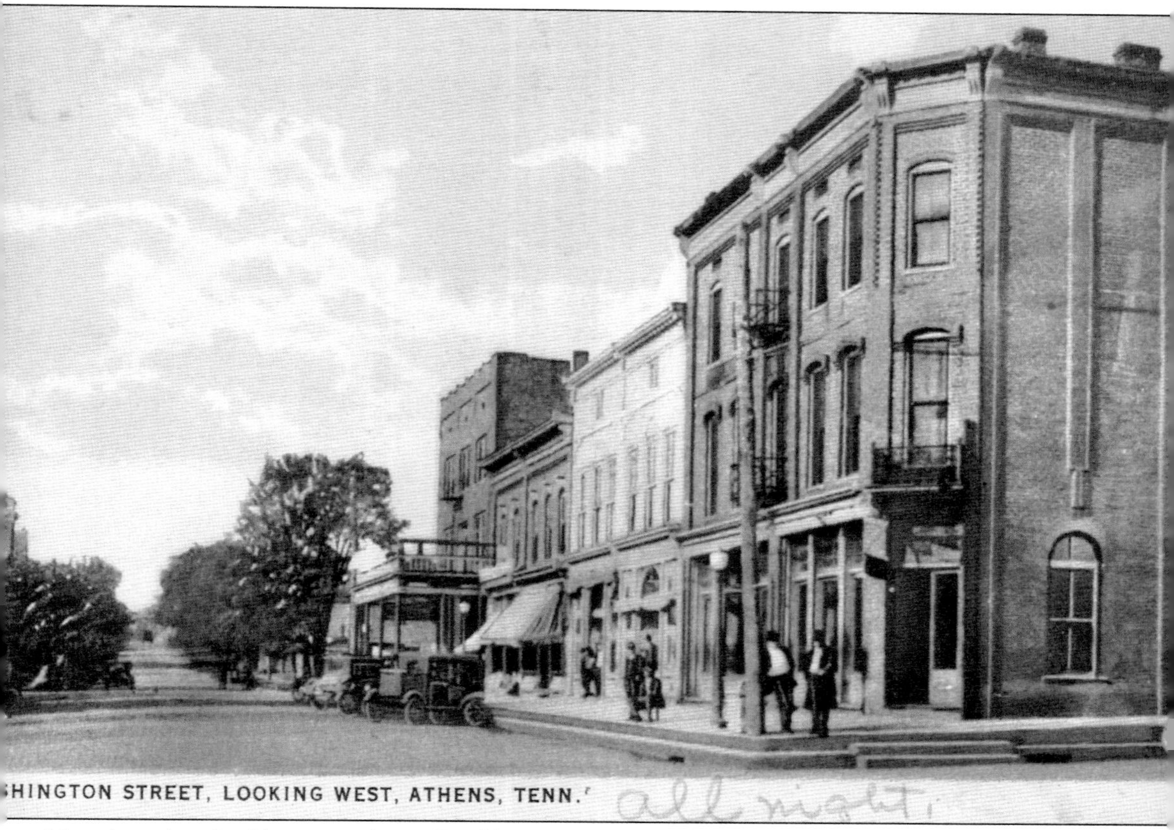


Here is a view looking west down Washington Street in the 1920s. The Mathews house has been replaced by the Foree Hotel, and the concrete sidewalks and streets show the downtown improvements of the late 1920s. By this time, Model A cars replaced most horses and wagons. In 1915, Miles Riddle opened a drugstore in the Hotel Magill storefront. Riddle's, and later Riddle and Wallace, remained an Athens downtown business for more than 90 years.

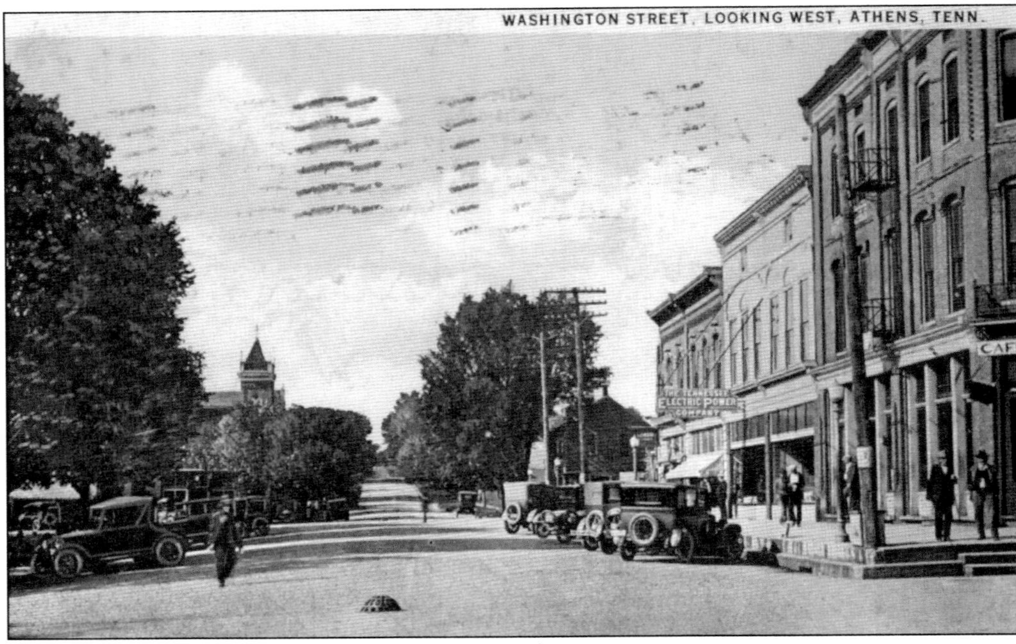


This is a view looking west down Washington Street in the early 1930s. The Foree Hotel is gone, destroyed by fire on April 6, 1929. The Grubb house is visible, and a café has replaced the shoe store in the Hotel Magill. Athens's streets have been improved with large, metal drainage grates being installed, and the East Tennessee Electric Power Company has established an office midway down the block.

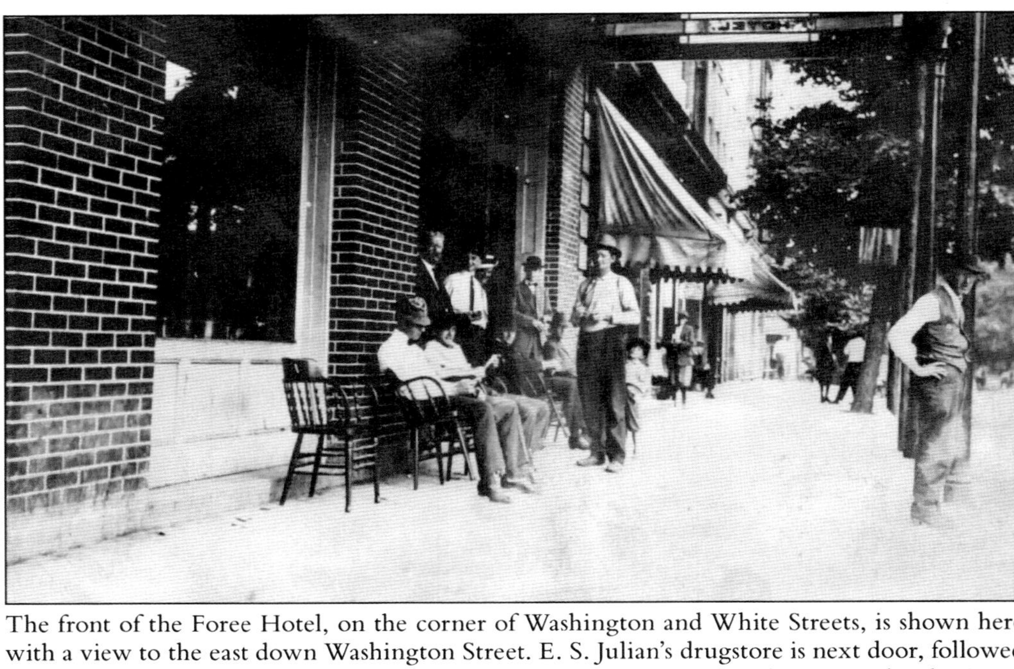

The front of the Foree Hotel, on the corner of Washington and White Streets, is shown here with a view to the east down Washington Street. E. S. Julian's drugstore is next door, followed by Miles Riddle's drugstore. At times, Athens had more drugstores than any other business. (Courtesy McMinn County Historical Society.)

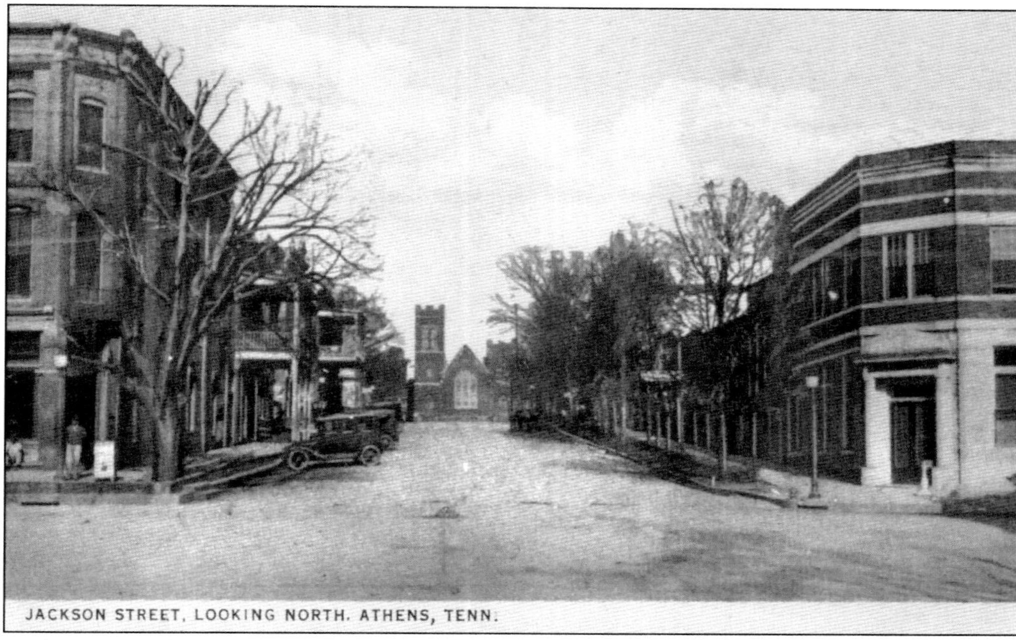


In this postcard, the view is looking north up Jackson Street sometime after 1926, when the First National Bank relocated to its new, more spacious building on the right corner. Beside the bank and up the street stands the first Athens Fire Department Station. Trees still line Jackson Street in this postcard, framing the picturesque setting of Trinity Methodist Church, built in 1909, at the center of the picture.

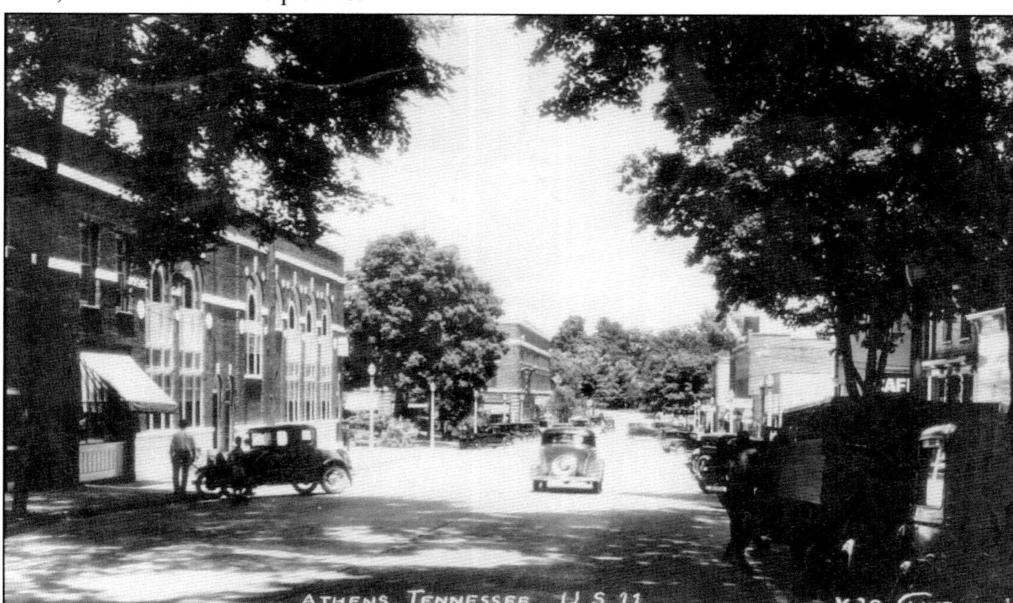


This is Madison Avenue looking west in a postcard dated 1940. On the left is the Citizen's Bank Building, and on the right, hidden behind the trees, is the bus station and café. The tree to the left center is on the corner of the courthouse square, and just across the street is the Robert E. Lee Hotel.

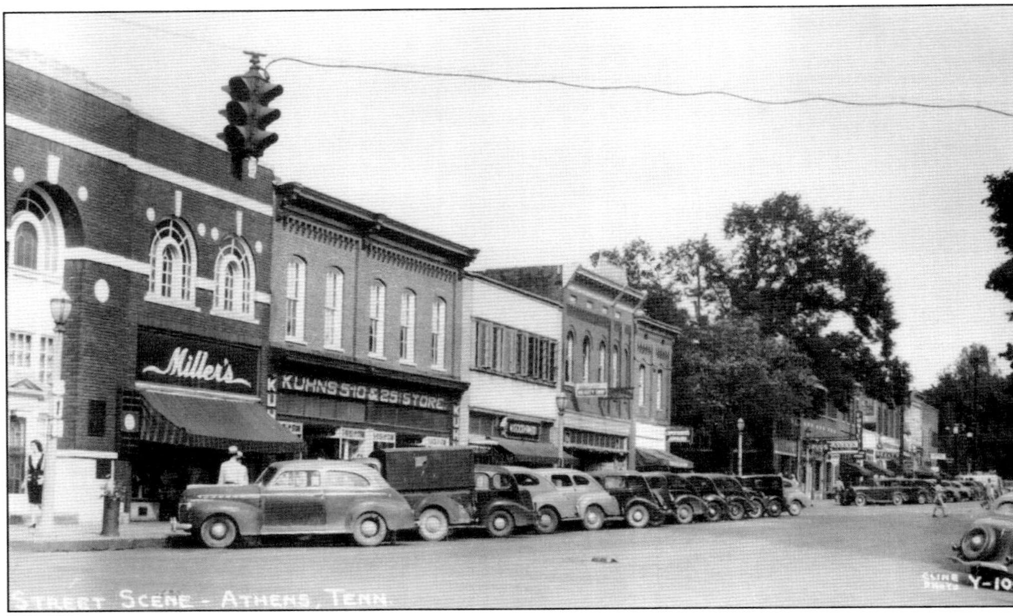


This postcard from the 1940s shows a clear view of the west side of the public square along White Street that some citizens still recall from their childhood. Citizen's National Bank anchors the near corner, with Miller's Department Store, Khun's Department Store, M. Goodfriends Clothing Store, Firestone, and Copenhaver Jewelry in the old James Crow building. Goodfriends, established on the south side of the public square in 1915, later gave rise to the Goody's Family Clothing Corporation. Still farther up the street, the Grubb home still stands on the corner.

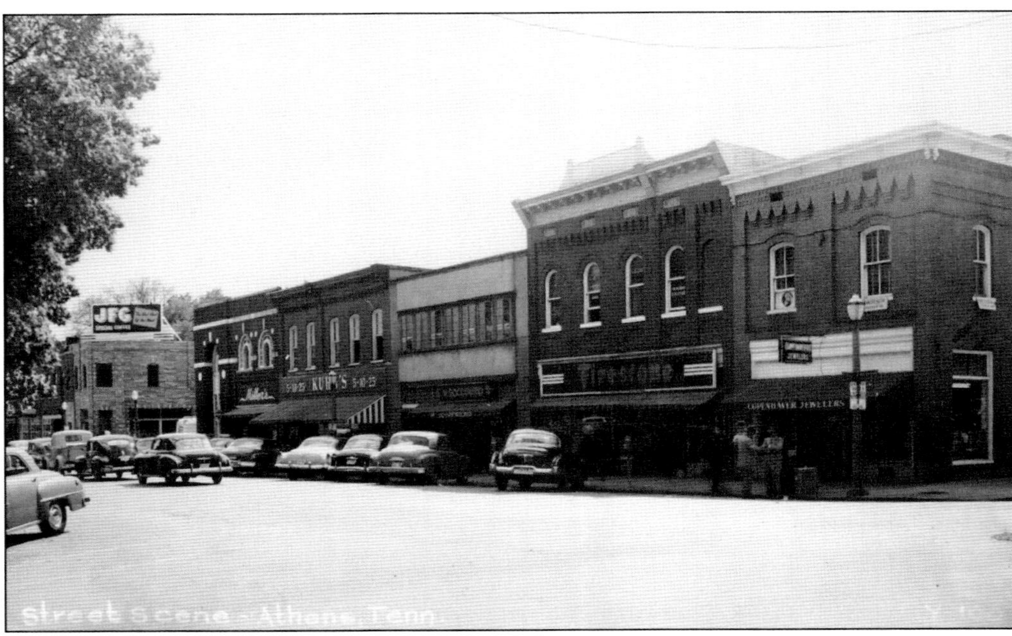


Another view of the west side of the public square from the opposite end of White Street shows the same stores pictured before. On the far left, the bus stop and café are visible under the JFG Coffee sign.

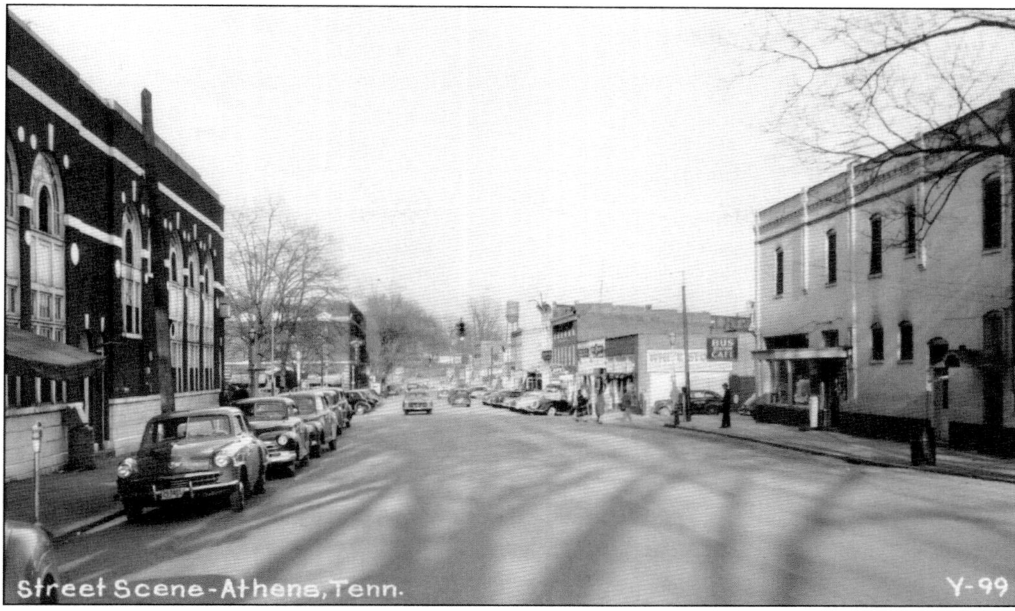


In a view looking east down Madison Avenue in the 1950s, evidence of recent fire at the bus station is visible on the right. Athens's first White Store sits on the corner of White Street and Madison Avenue at the center right, with the brick offices of Madison Hall standing in the middle of the block, followed by Cherokee Hardware in the old Bayless and Moody Hardware Building. Madison Hall was owned by attorney E. B. Madison, and courts were held in the upper hall when the second courthouse was under construction in 1874.

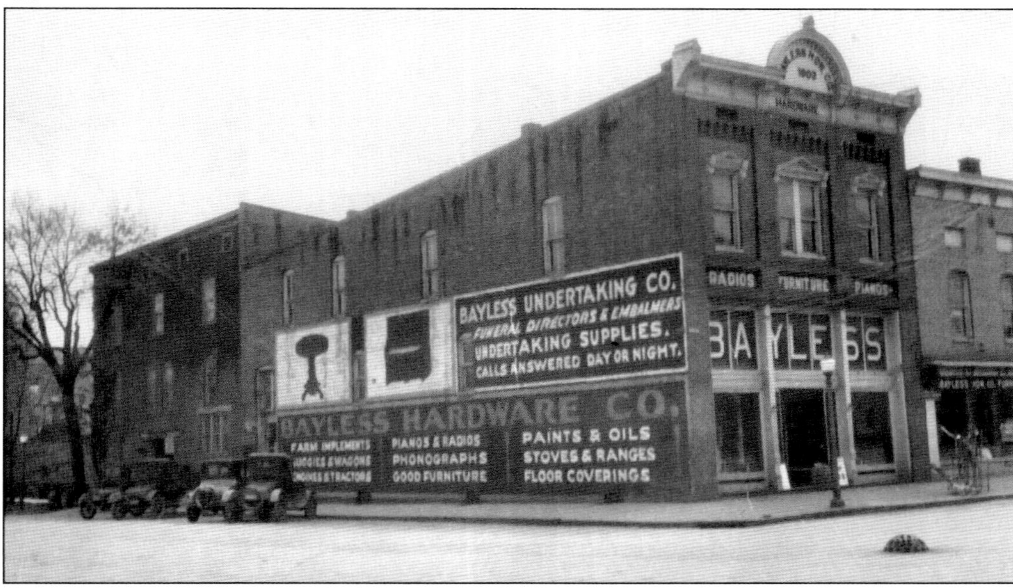


Called Cleage Hall when it was first built in 1835, this building long held stores of various types. After a terrible fire in 1880, the structure was rebuilt and became Bayless and Moody Hardware in 1905. Under the slogan "Everything From Cradle to Grave," the business truly offered anything from baby cribs to an embalming and casket service. (Courtesy McMinn County Historical Society.)

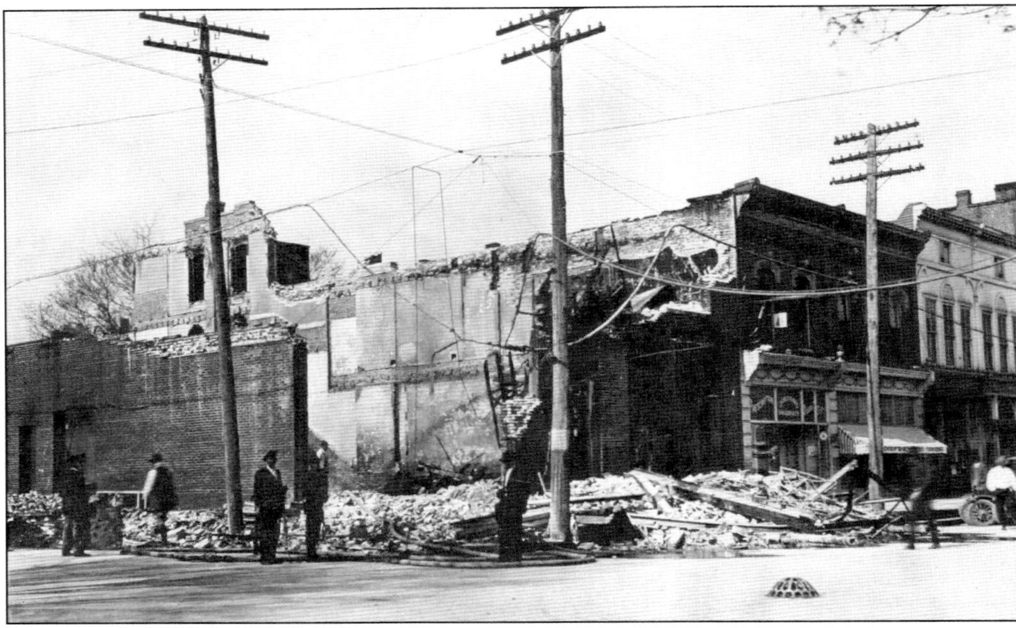

The Foree Hotel is shown here just after the devastating fire of 1929. Several people were injured when they jumped from the second and third floors, but no one was killed. The Foree family planned to rebuild, but eventually the site was sold for the construction of a new movie theater, the Strand. (Courtesy McMinn County Historical Society.)

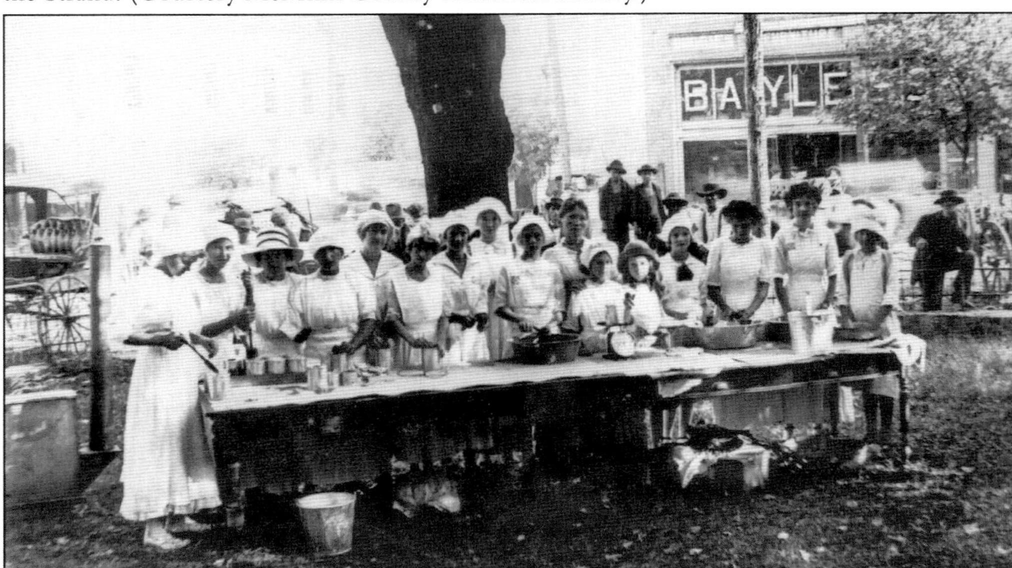

In the early decades of the 20th century, home-demonstration agents were employed by the State of Tennessee to bring new skills in housekeeping and home-goods marketing to rural areas of the South. Here a home-demonstration club meets on the front lawn of the McMinn County Courthouse to demonstrate canning techniques. In this photograph, taken around 1920, horse-drawn buggies are visible in the background, as is Bayless and Moody Hardware. (Courtesy McMinn County Historical Society.)

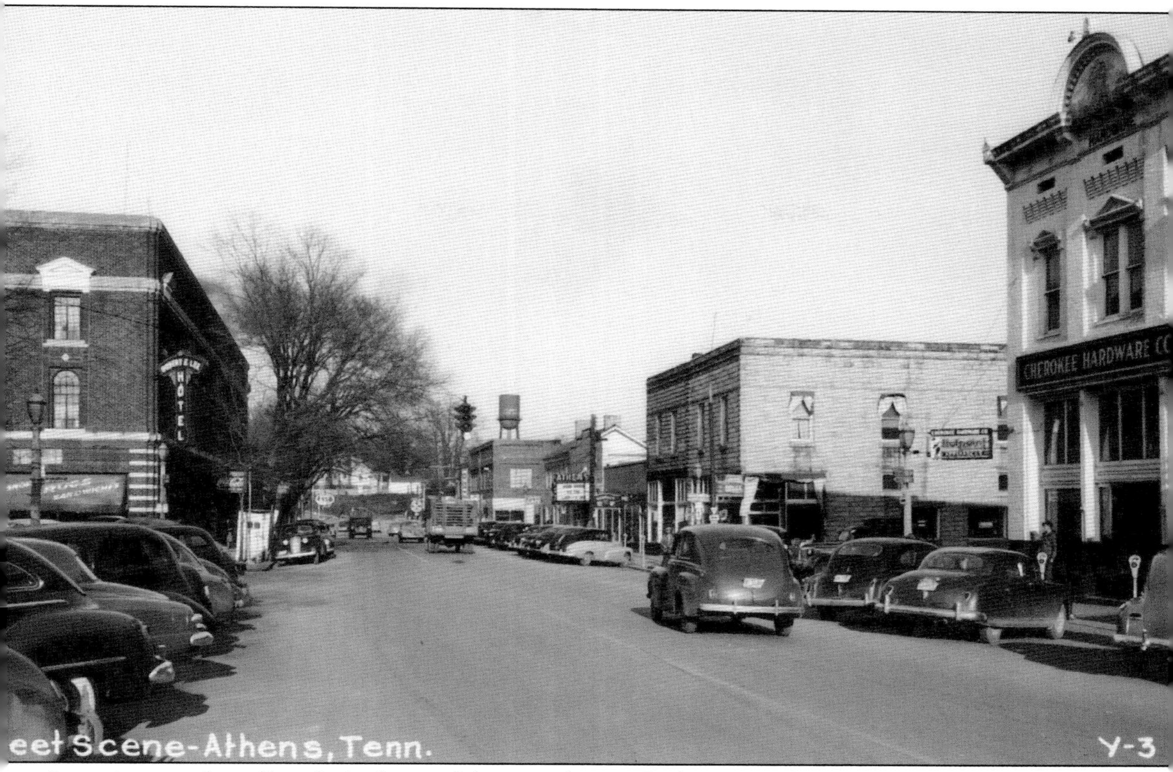


In a picture taken directly in front of the courthouse, looking east down Madison Avenue in the 1940s, the Robert E. Lee Hotel stands on the left with Cherokee Hardware, which replaced Bayless and Moody, on the left. To the right center, in the former location of the Ivins house, stands the Athens Theatre, one of three movie houses once operating downtown. More than one young boy caught his mother's wrath for patronizing this area of Athens, then considered to be seedy.

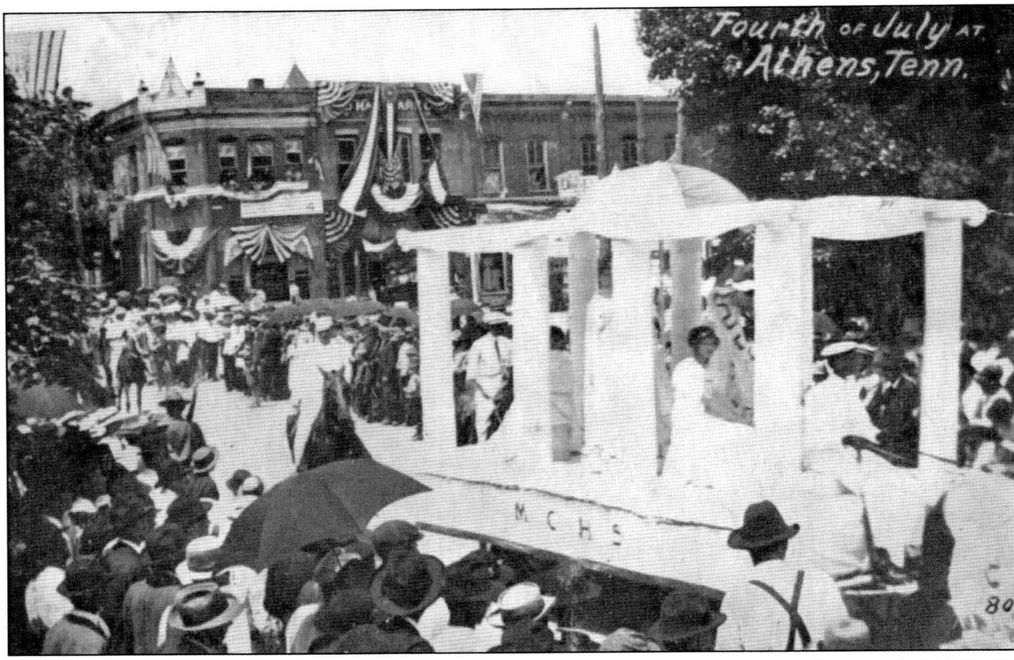


A Fourth of July parade is featured in this postcard from the early 1900s. The float reads "MCHS." It was likely put together by the staff and students at McMinn County High School. The Athens Bank building and Reed's Hardware are both decorated with festive bunting, and many citizens turned out for the celebration.

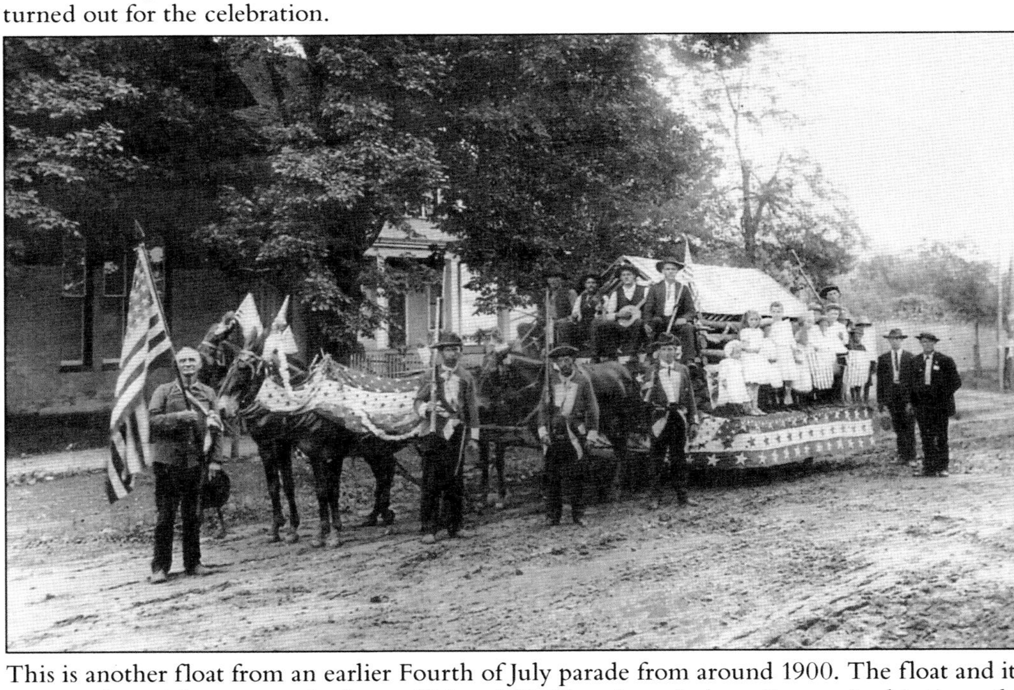

This is another float from an earlier Fourth of July parade from around 1900. The float and its costumed participants pose in front of Mars Hill Church on Jackson Street. At this time, the street was still unpaved, and no buildings had yet been built on the corner of Jackson and Horsby Streets, just beyond the back of the float. (Courtesy McMinn County Historical Society.)

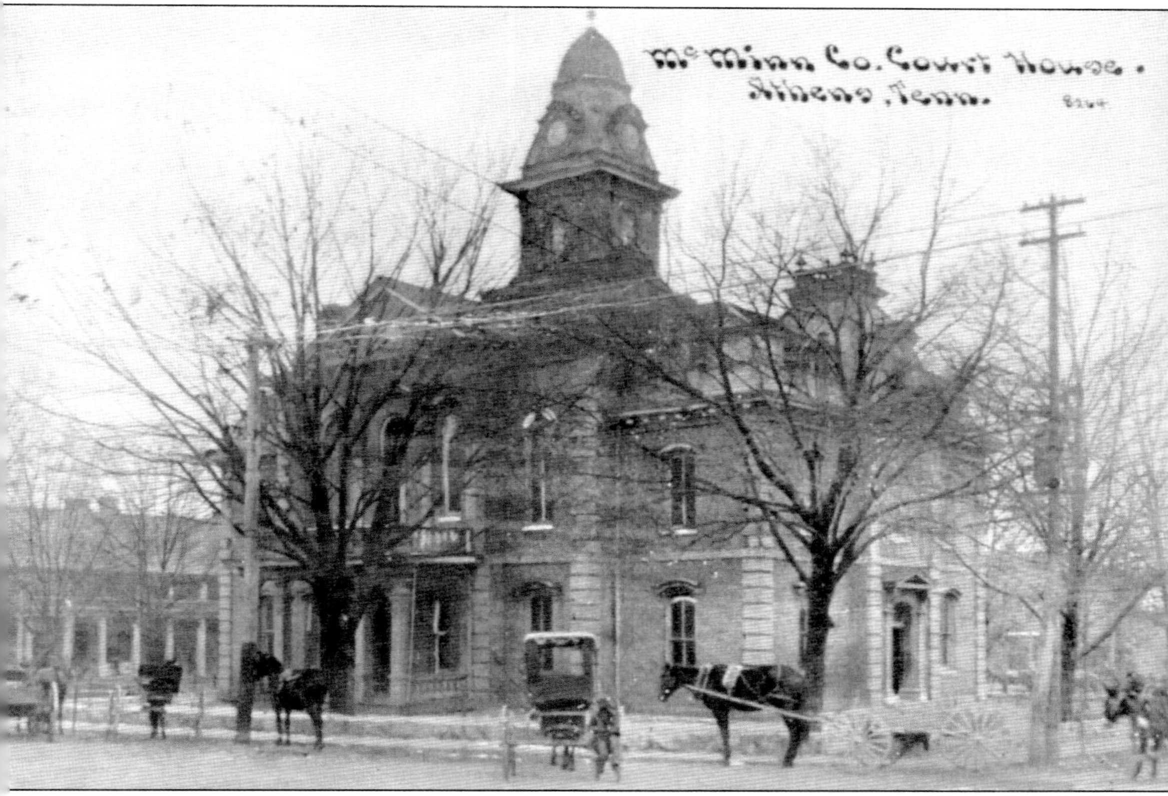


The public square in Athens has been home to four courthouses. The first was a log structure built in 1823 on the north side of the square, followed by a 40-by-60-foot brick building constructed in 1828 on the square itself. The John Walker murder trial in 1834, which ultimately laid the legal groundwork for the Cherokee Removal of 1836–1838, was held in that courthouse. The building was damaged during the Civil War, requiring the construction of the fourth McMinn County Courthouse in 1874, seen here in a southeasterly view. Horses, wagons, and buggies are tied around the courthouse, likely during a December session of Quarterly Court. This building remained until 1964, when it was damaged by fire. The Athens Hotel can be seen on the left.

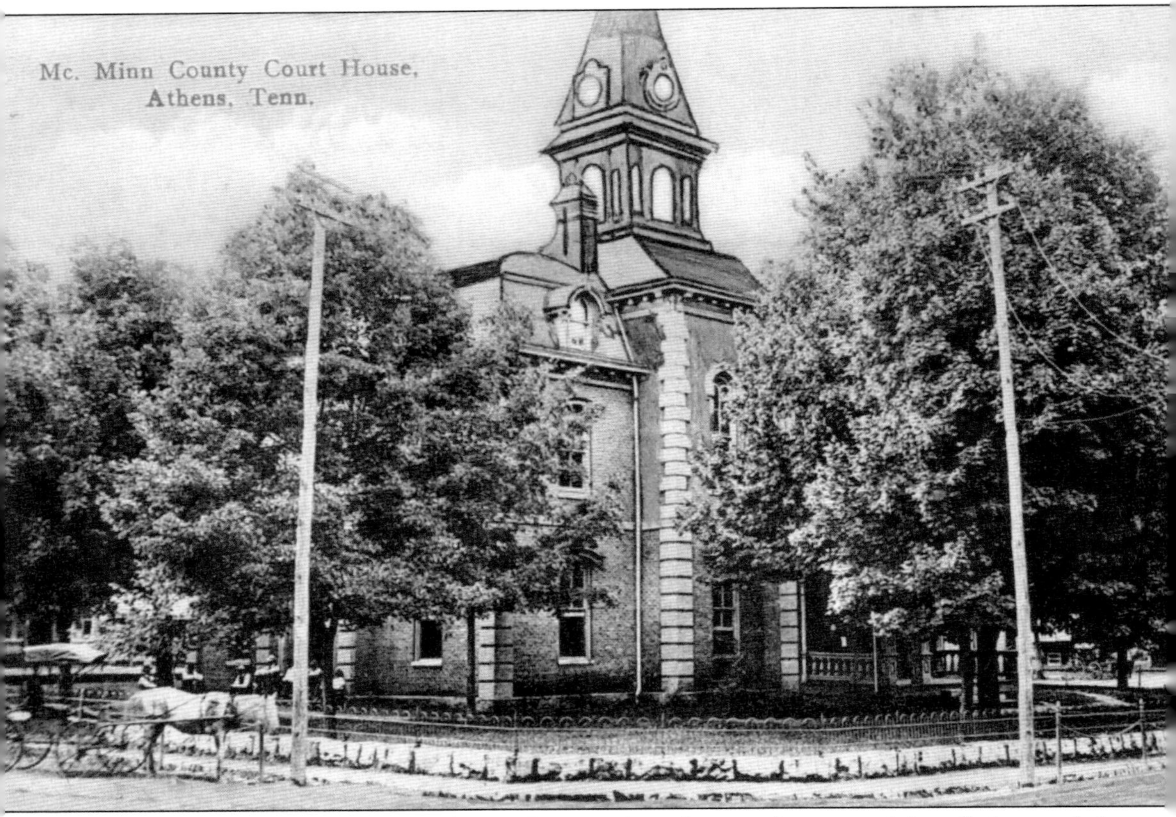


This 1908 view of the old courthouse shows an iron fence and stonework installed around the lawn. On court days, citizens came to town to watch trials, buy and sell goods, or simply sit under the courthouse trees to whittle and exchange news or tell tales. One of the issues dealt with in those days was the amount of animal waste left in the streets around the courthouse, making the square inhospitable on hot summer days.

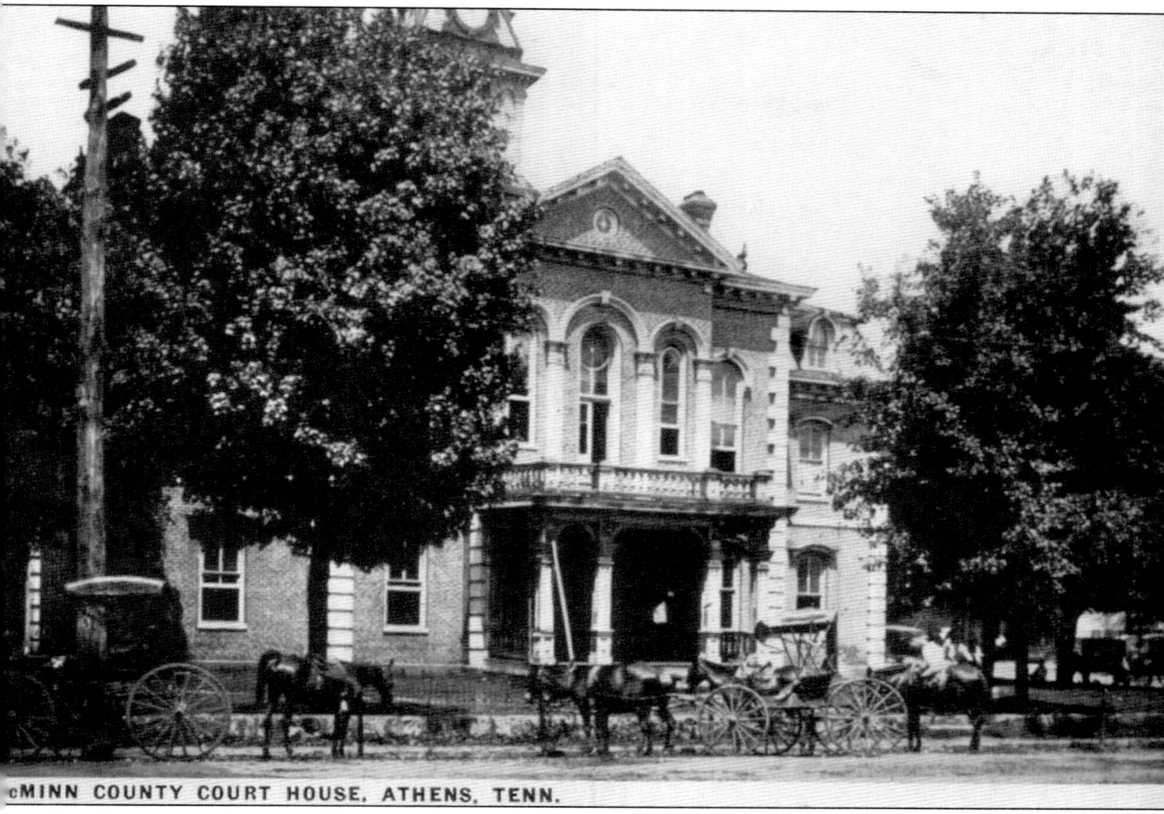


Another postcard view of the courthouse shows it bathed in sunlight on a summer day. Note the open windows on the top floor, where the main courtroom was located. In the days before air-conditioning, the upper floors and courtrooms were almost unbearable during July and August. Carriages and wagons remained the most common means of transportation in this photograph, taken around 1910.

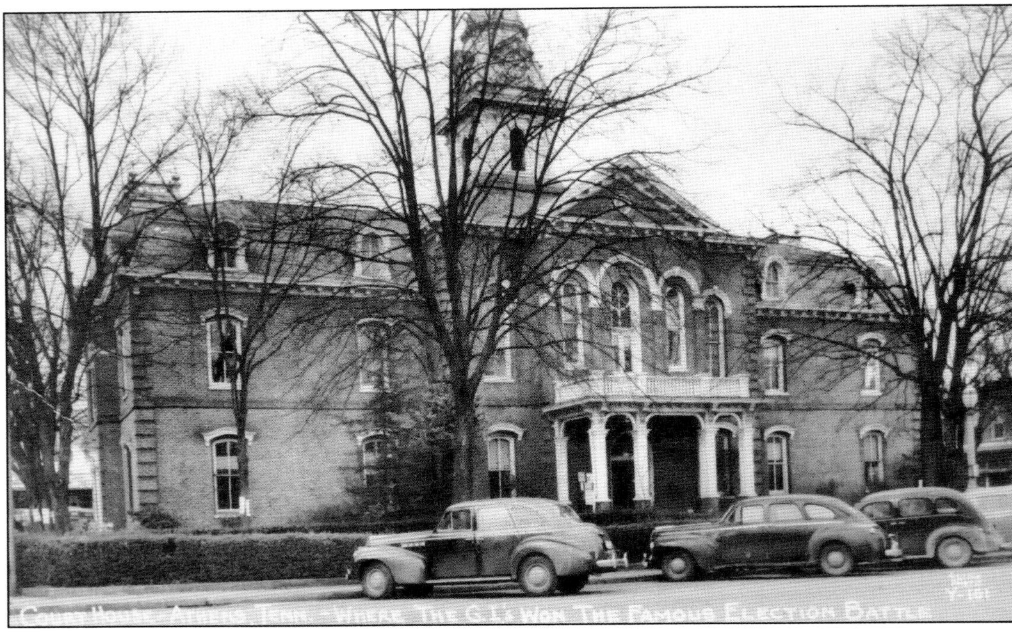


By the time this photograph was taken in the 1940s, the old courthouse had undergone substantial renovations, with the 1928 extensions of the wings on the east and west sides. A hedge has also replaced the iron fencing, and automobiles take the place of buggies and wagons. This was how the courthouse appeared during the Battle of Athens on August 1, 1946, when members of the GI party overthrew an established political machine after an election night shoot-out at the old jail a block away on White Street.

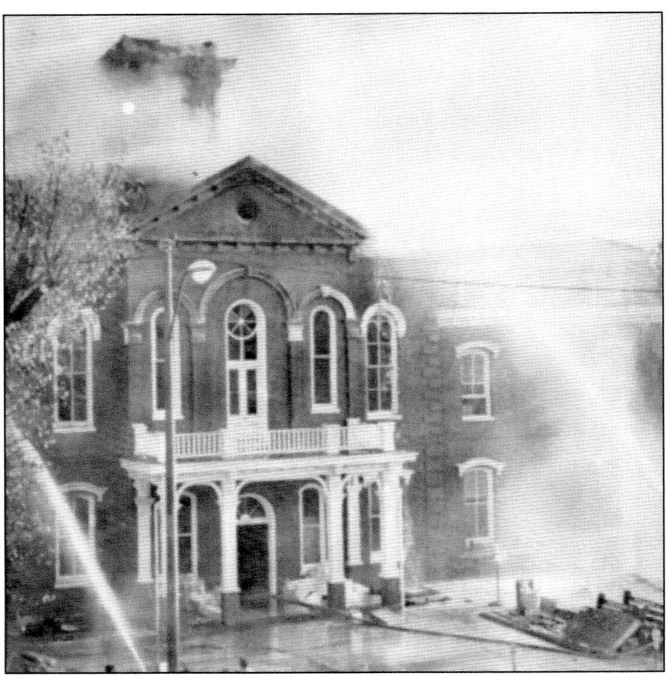

This picture shows the fire that devastated the McMinn County Courthouse on Election Day in November 1964. As the fire began in the cupola, employees and elected officials, along with Athens citizens, assisted in removing all records from the building. By the time of this picture, the roof had fallen in on the courtroom on the second floor, but no lives or records were lost. Even with severe damage, a group of affluent McMinn Countians lobbied to simply repair the stately old building rather than demolish it and build a new one, but the new project went forward, resulting in a new building in 1966. (Courtesy McMinn County Historical Society.)

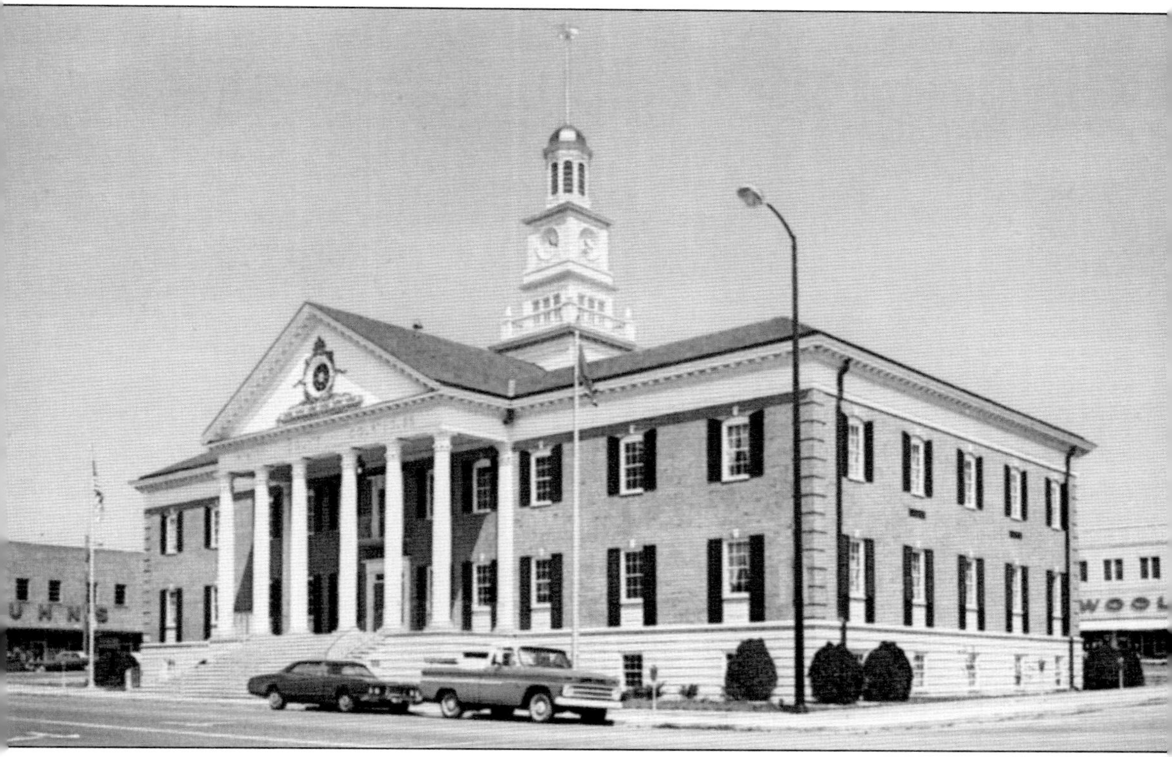


The present McMinn County Courthouse is pictured here not long after its 1966 construction. The new courthouse provided such amenities as air-conditioning, modern restrooms, an elevator, and substantial office space for all county officials. It remains the center of McMinn County government and is the centerpiece of the Athens downtown square. To the left, Khun's Department Store also bears signs of renovations, and to the right, Woolworth's sits on the former site of the Hotel Magill.

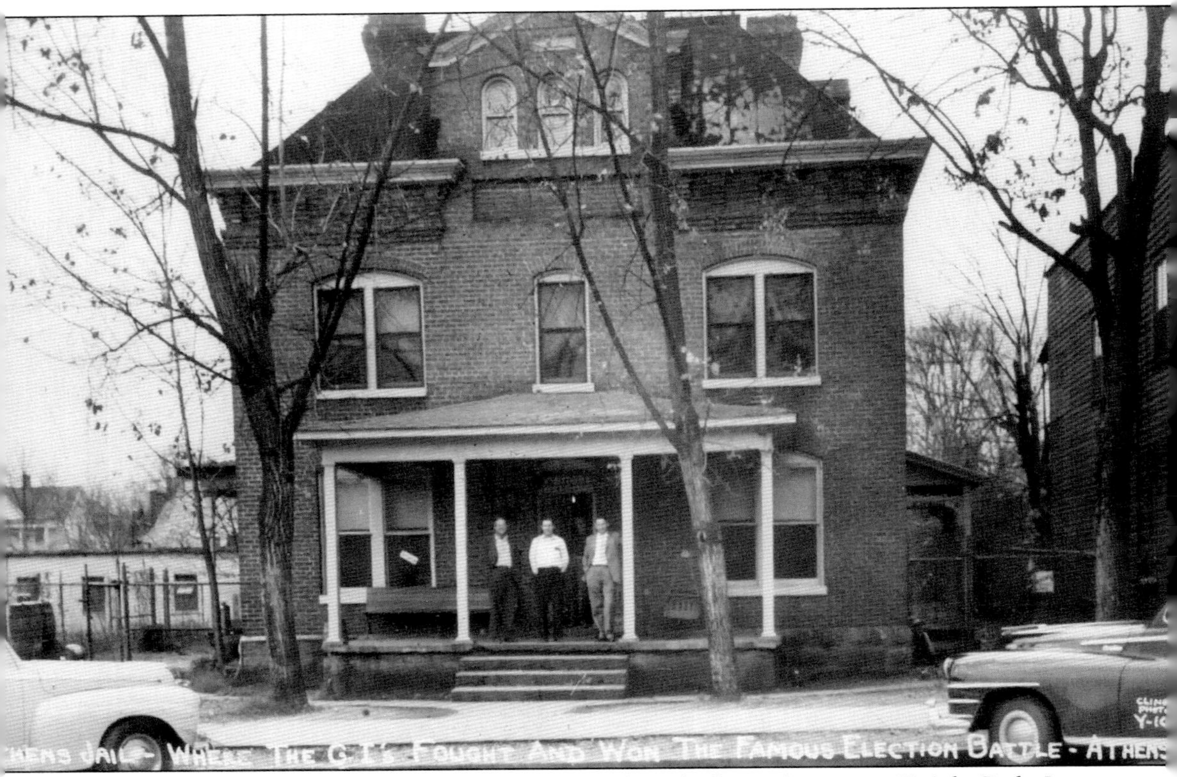


The first county jail in Athens stood on the north end of town in present Knight Park. It was a small brick building that was unsanitary and often filled with lice. The jail, pictured here, was built in 1878 with the jail cells and offices on the first floor and room upstairs for the sheriff's residence. To the left was the yard where public hangings were carried out, the last of which was Beulah McGee in 1908. In August 1946, this was the scene of the Battle of Athens. Members of the GI political party fired on the jail from the hillside across the street until the deputies inside agreed to surrender and relinquish ballot boxes they had taken the day before. This photograph, taken after the battle, shows newly elected Sheriff Knox Henry standing in the center on the porch. The building was razed when a new jail was built one block east in 1951.

# *Two*

# Athens Businesses, Churches, and Schools

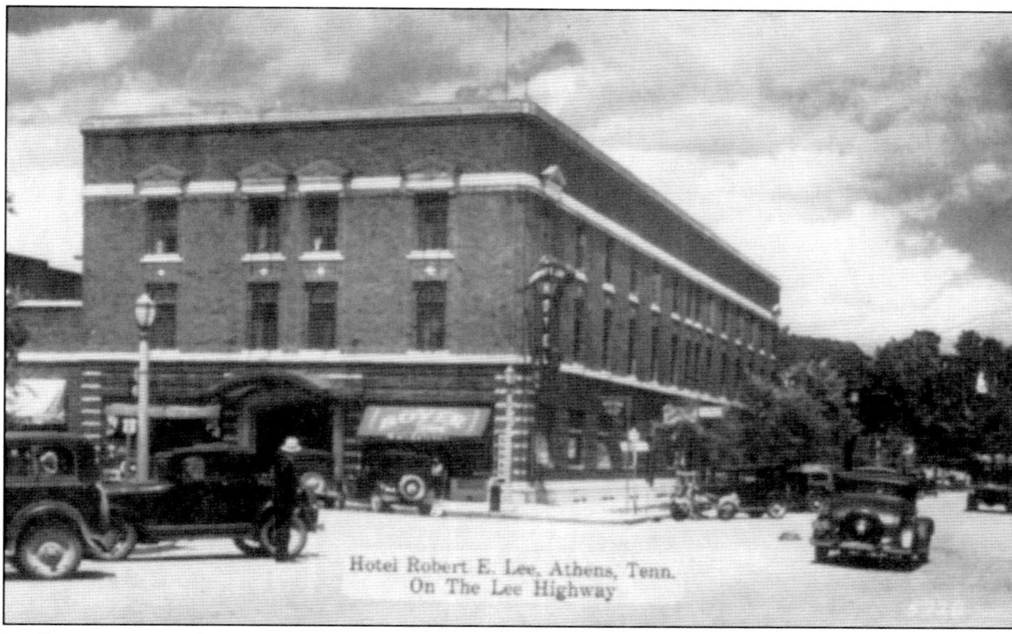


Built in 1926 on the site of the Athens Hotel, the Robert E. Lee was a convenient and upscale hotel located directly between Knoxville and Chattanooga. The hotel is pictured here not long after its opening. S. B. "Bullett" Boyer's drugstore is seen here in the hotel's right storefront. On July 30, 1932, "Bullett," along with employee Howard Bales, pulled one of the best-known practical jokes in the history of Athens. During a violent hailstorm, Boyer and Bales retrieved a 30-pound chunk of ice from their icebox and dropped it from the second floor window onto the street below. The subsequent public attention and news coverage of the "Giant Hailstone" reached as far as the newspapers in New York City, eventually bringing a sheepish confession from Boyer and Bales.

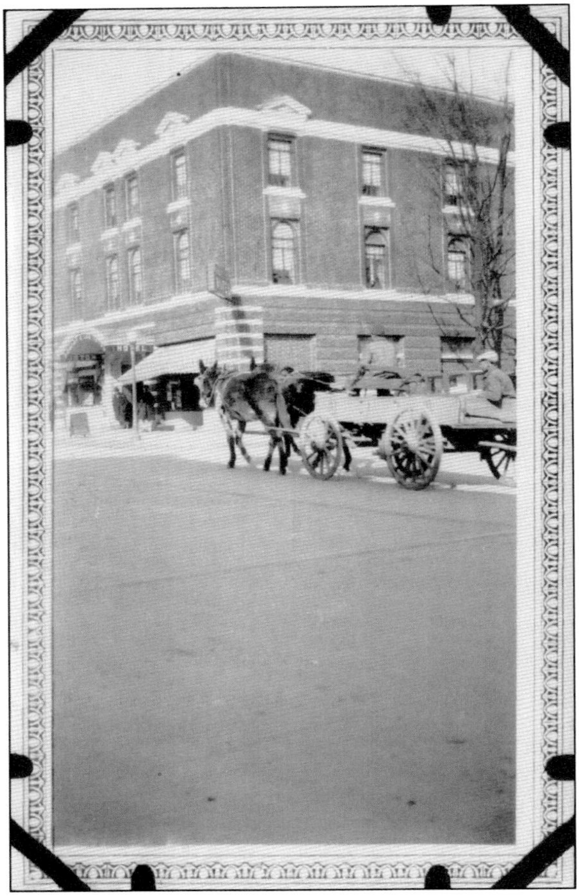

Another early view of the Robert E. Lee shows a wagon being driven over Athens's paved streets, evident of the changing times. While towns in McMinn County had concrete or asphalt streets by the 1940s, much of rural McMinn County's roads remained dirt or gravel well into the late 1970s.

The Robert E. Lee is pictured below in a postcard photograph taken in the 1940s. Snow's drugstore has replaced Boyer's, and more modern traffic lights help cars navigate Athens's busy streets. The old Buick dealership is visible on the far right down Madison Avenue.

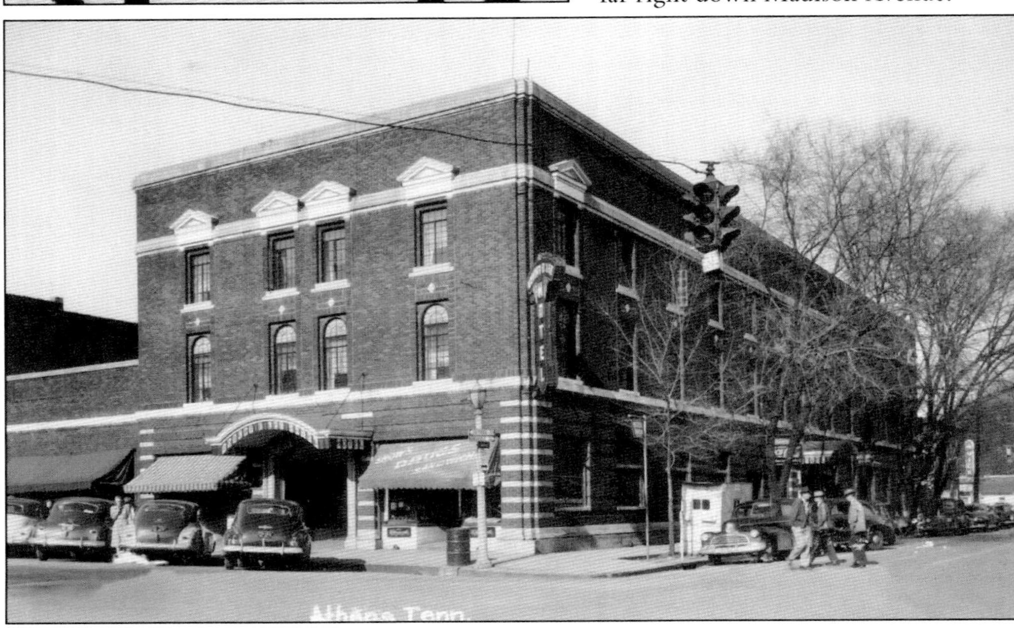

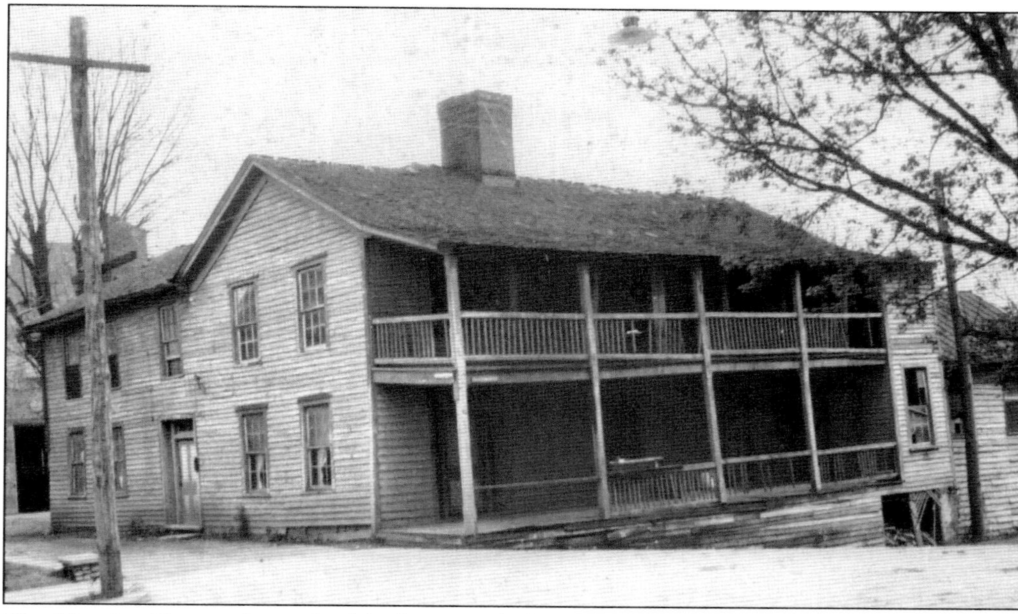

The Monday House, shown in this photograph from 1923, was also a popular hotel in Athens. Sitting near the bank of Eastanaulee Creek on White Street, it was also known as the Gibbs Hotel. A Mrs. Monday cooked the guests' food, and the fare was so tasty that the business was most often known as Monday House, rather than by any other name. It was demolished in 1935. (Courtesy McMinn County Historical Society.)

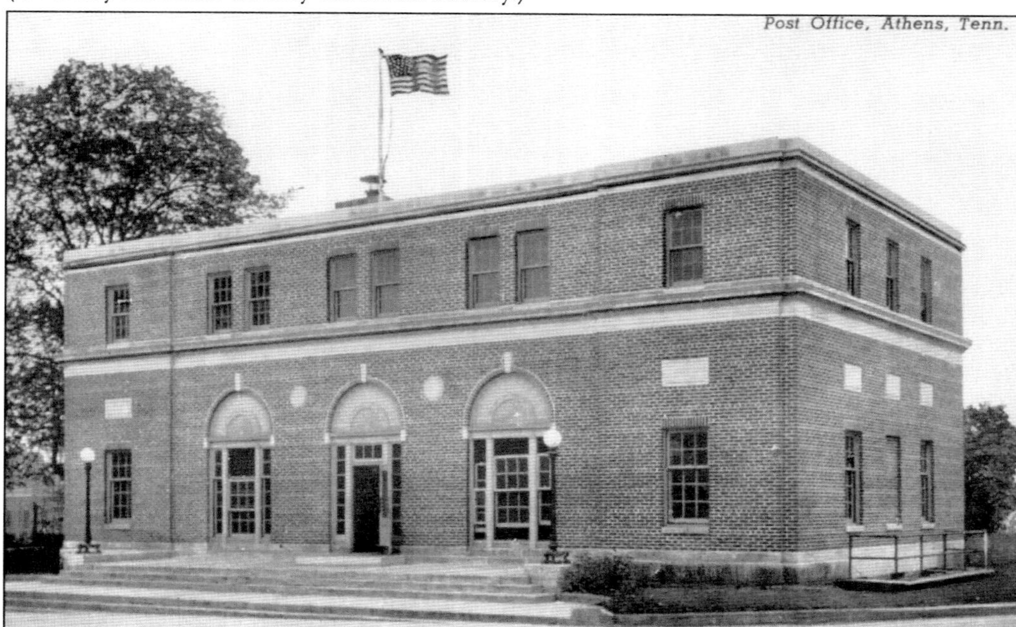


Athens post offices were in numerous stores around the square from 1822 until 1925, when the post office building was constructed on a vacant lot on Jackson Street. The post office operated here for some 40 years until it was relocated to the present site on South White Street. This building housed the post office and later many federal and state government offices.

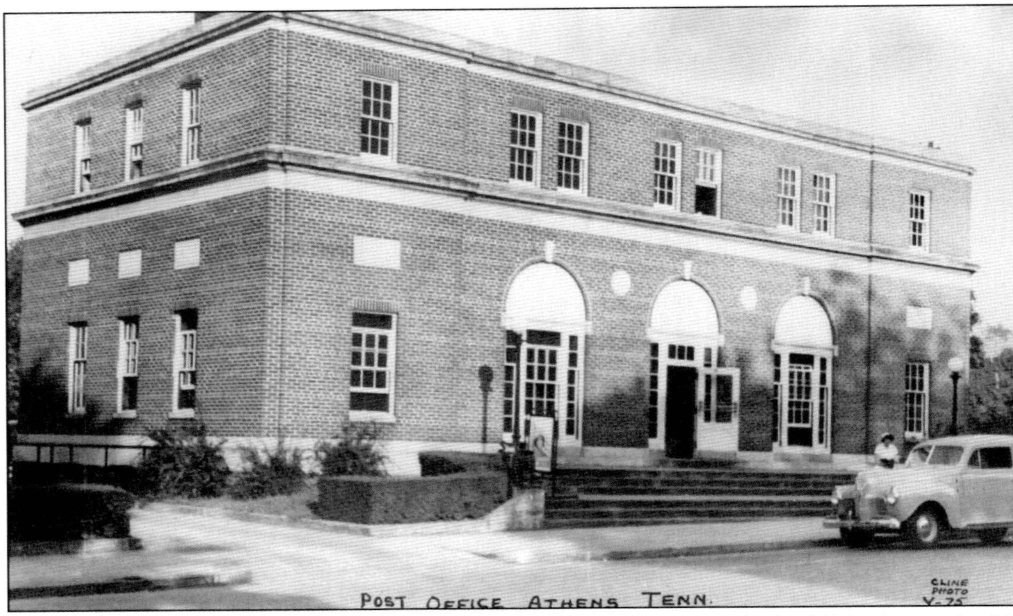


This is another postcard showing the old post office in the 1940s. The building sits on the hill used by GIs during the Battle of Athens shoot-out and narrowly escaped damage during the political melee.

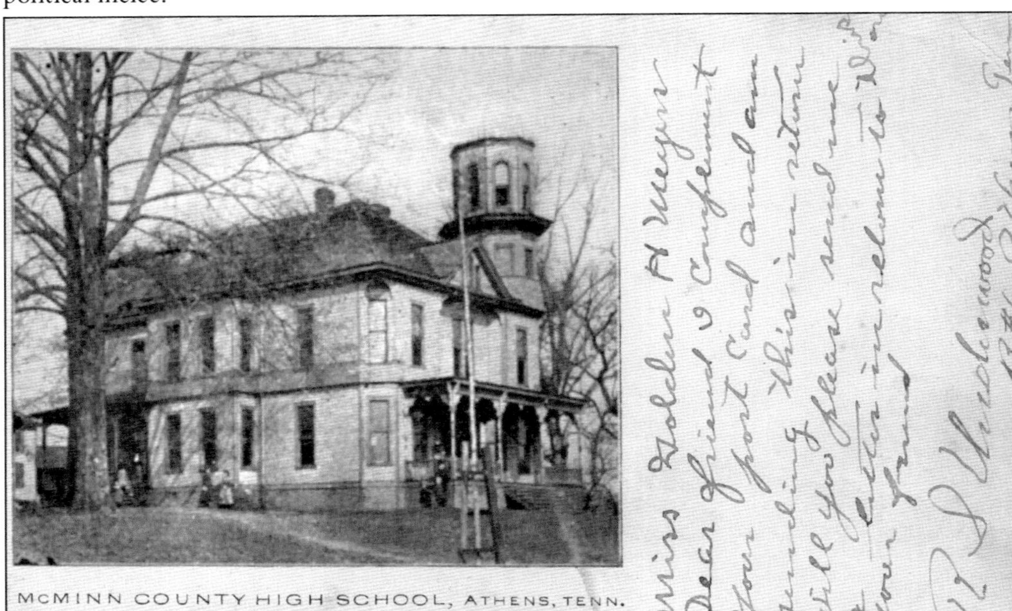


Founded in 1903, McMinn County High School is the second-oldest high school in the state of Tennessee. Surprisingly, its establishment by the county court was met with strong opposition. The school had a three-year course of study, and the education of area teachers was one of the more important aspects of the curriculum. This postcard from 1906 features the high school's first building, which stood on the site of the building now occupied by the McMinn County Living Heritage Museum on West Madison Avenue.

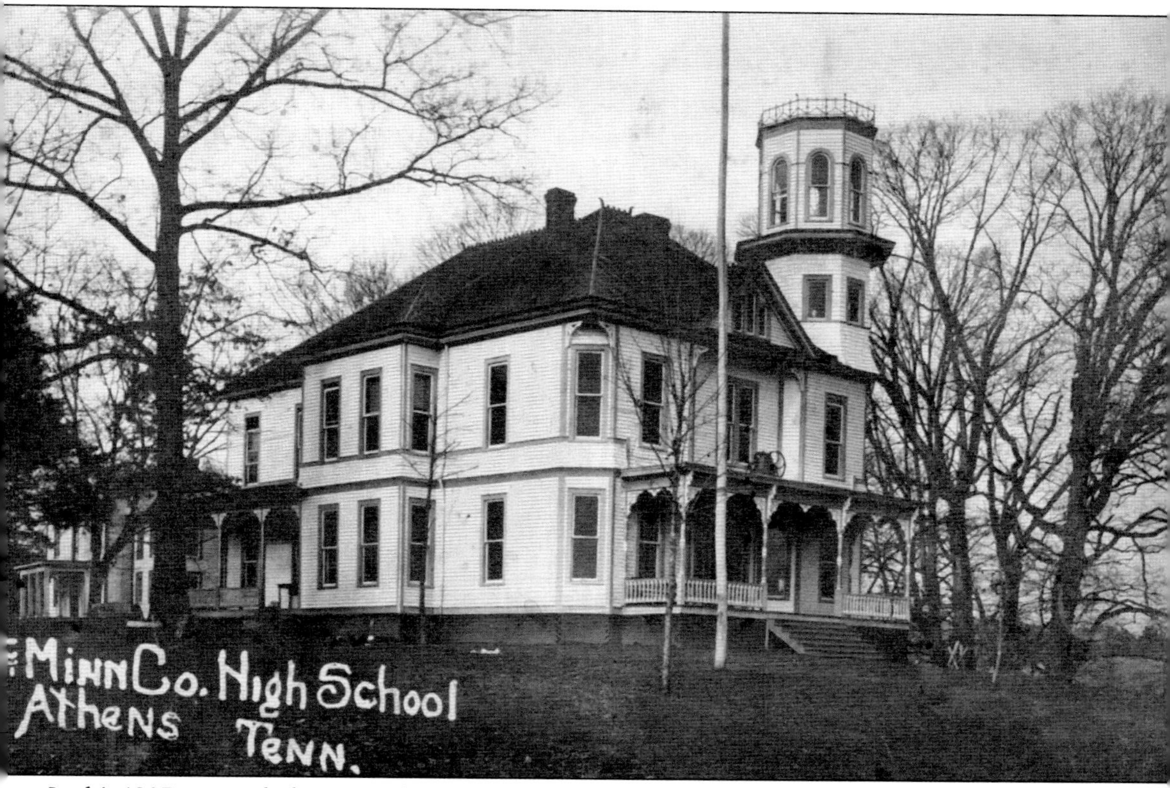


In this 1907 postcard, the original high school building appears to have had some improvements and fresh paint. Fewer students had either the means or the time to attend high school in those days, as McMinn County's largely agrarian economy demanded that many students leave school by the sixth grade in order to help out on the farm.

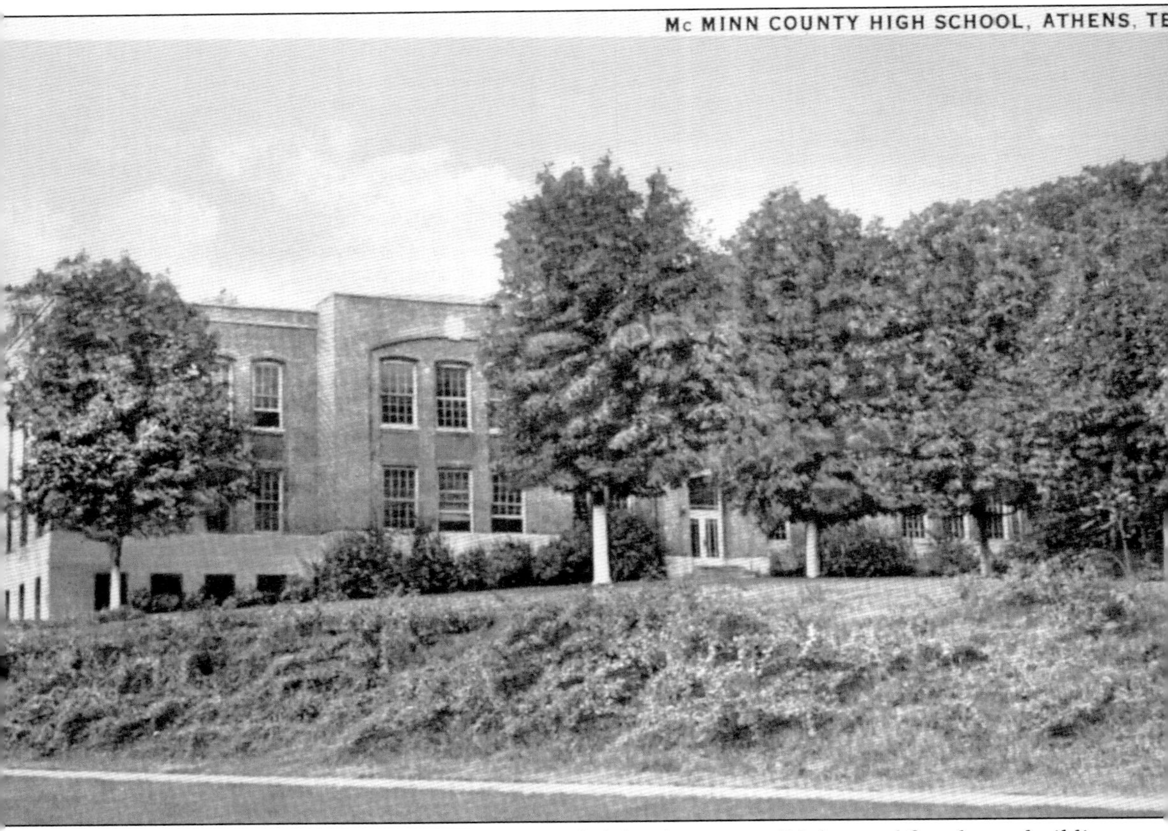


As the student body at McMinn County High School grew, so did the need for a larger building. This was the high school's second building, constructed of brick. A wing was added on the left for a cafeteria and library. Later a gymnasium was added to the left of the building. Football was played on a field two blocks south. This site was used until the present building was constructed in 1980 and now houses the county history museum.

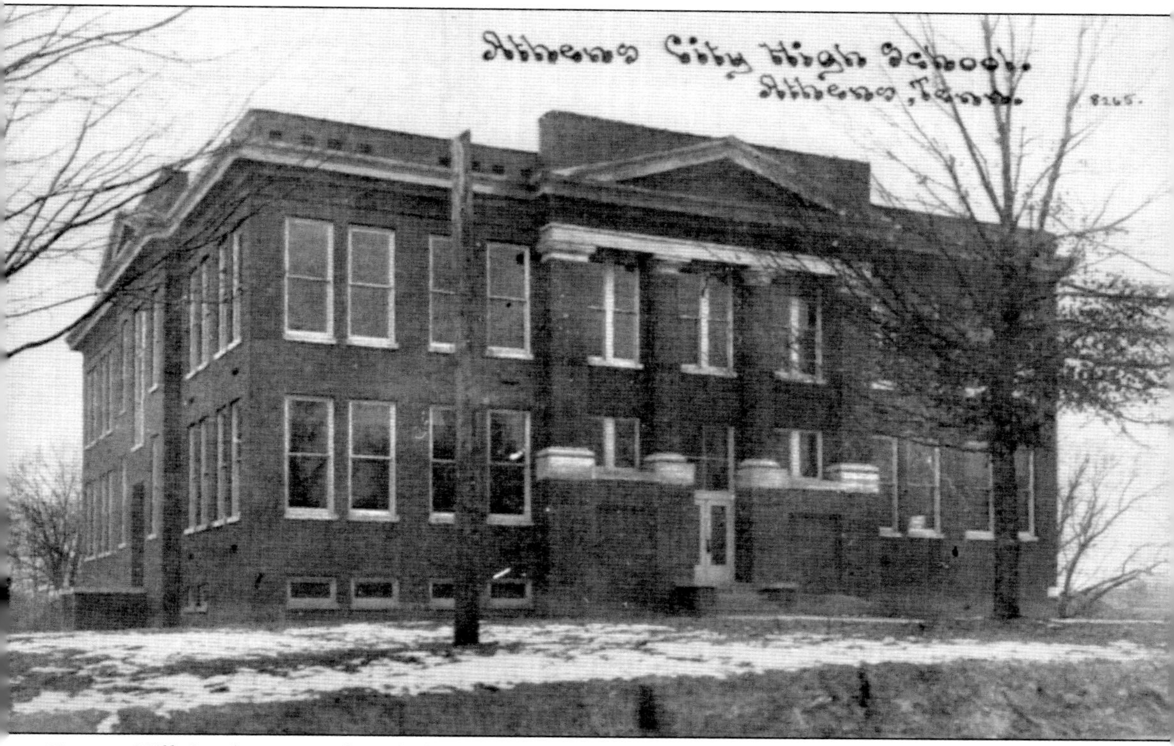


Forrest Hill Academy was founded in 1830 near a large spring 2 miles east of Athens. After a destructive fire in 1850, the school was moved to a new brick building on College Street closer to downtown. After being taken over by the City of Athens, a larger building was constructed two blocks farther north and, for a while, was operated as Athens High School. Here it is pictured with a fresh dusting of snow on a 1913 postcard.

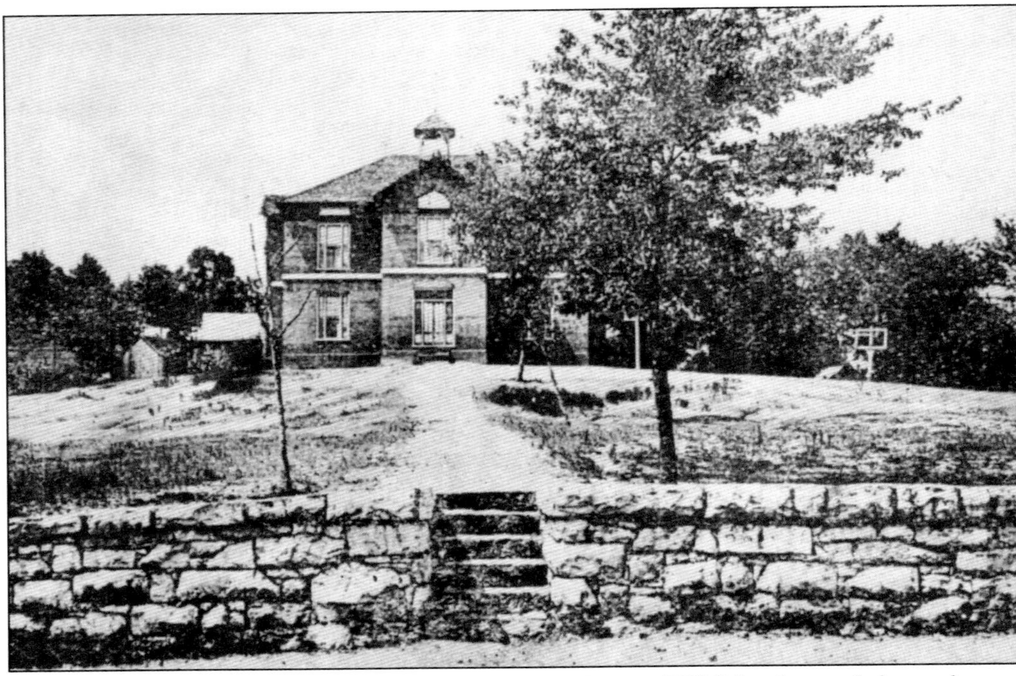

Relocated to this hilltop on College Street in 1850, Forrest Hill School served the students of Athens until well into the 20th century, when it was taken over by the City of Athens. During the Civil War, Forrest Hill, like nearby Old College, was used to house sick and injured soldiers. (Courtesy McMinn County Historical Society.)

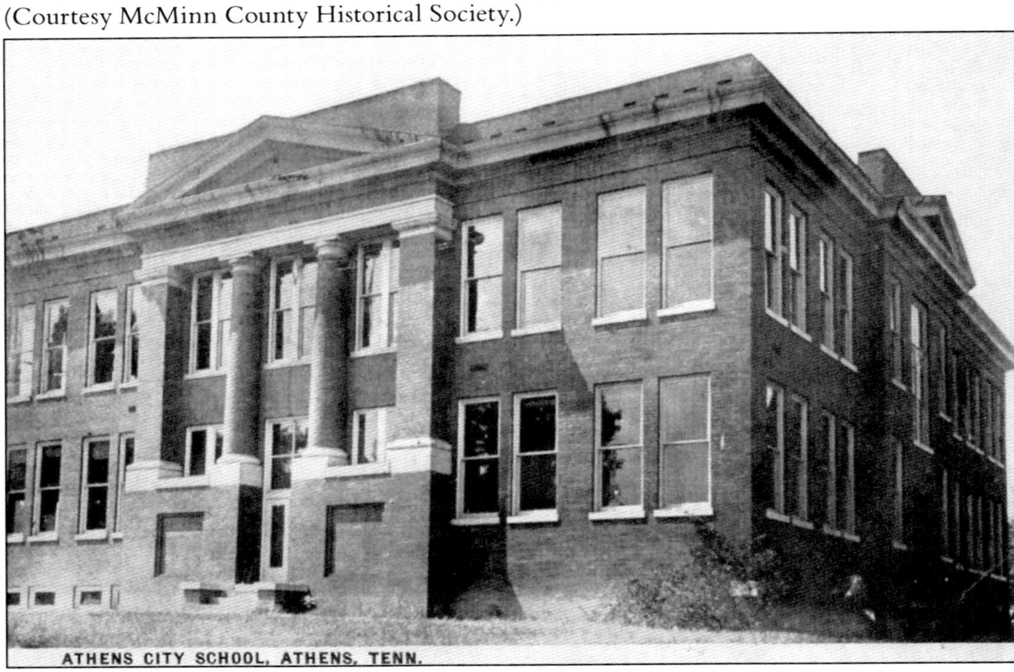


Another view of Athens City School is depicted on this postcard from 1922. Likely sent from a visiting athlete, the card's message, addressed to Bulls Gap, Tennessee, reads, "We are here for two days got beat yesterday but had some game. Will see you Sun. KRQ."

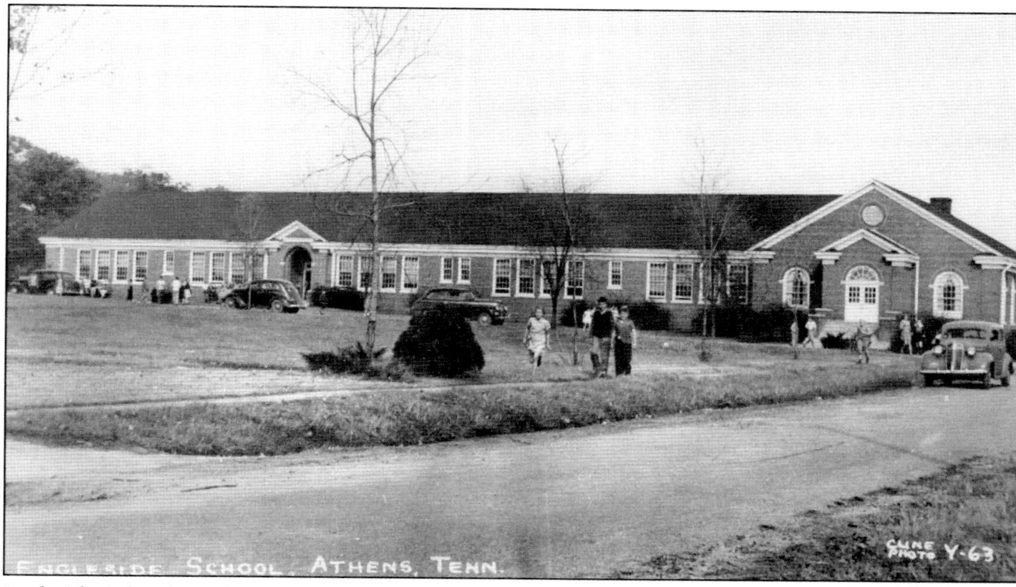

Ingleside School was built off of Forrest Avenue in 1937 on land that was formerly part of Ingleside Dairy. As Athens's flagship elementary school, its location was made even more visible when Lee Highway was re-routed to a straighter course into Athens, giving visitors an indication of Athens's progress in education.

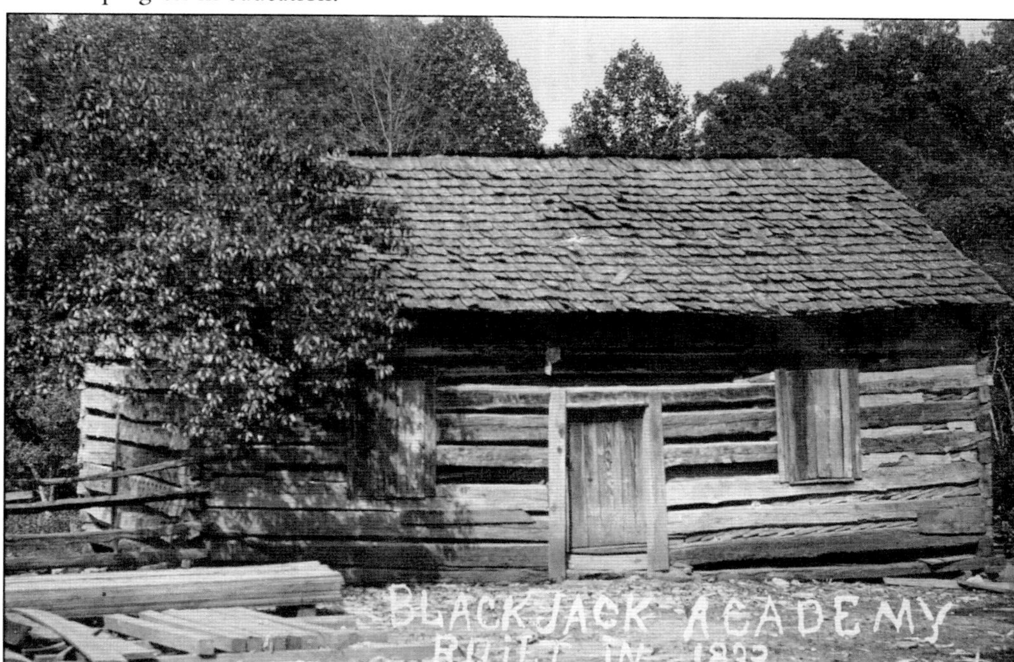

Blackjack Academy was typical of the early schools in McMinn County. Built and founded by members of the surrounding community, teachers were paid by the parents of the students who attended. This one-room log building was founded around 1833 and was located on the Crabtree farm at the head of Lick Creek near present-day County Road 781. (Courtesy McMinn County Historical Society.)

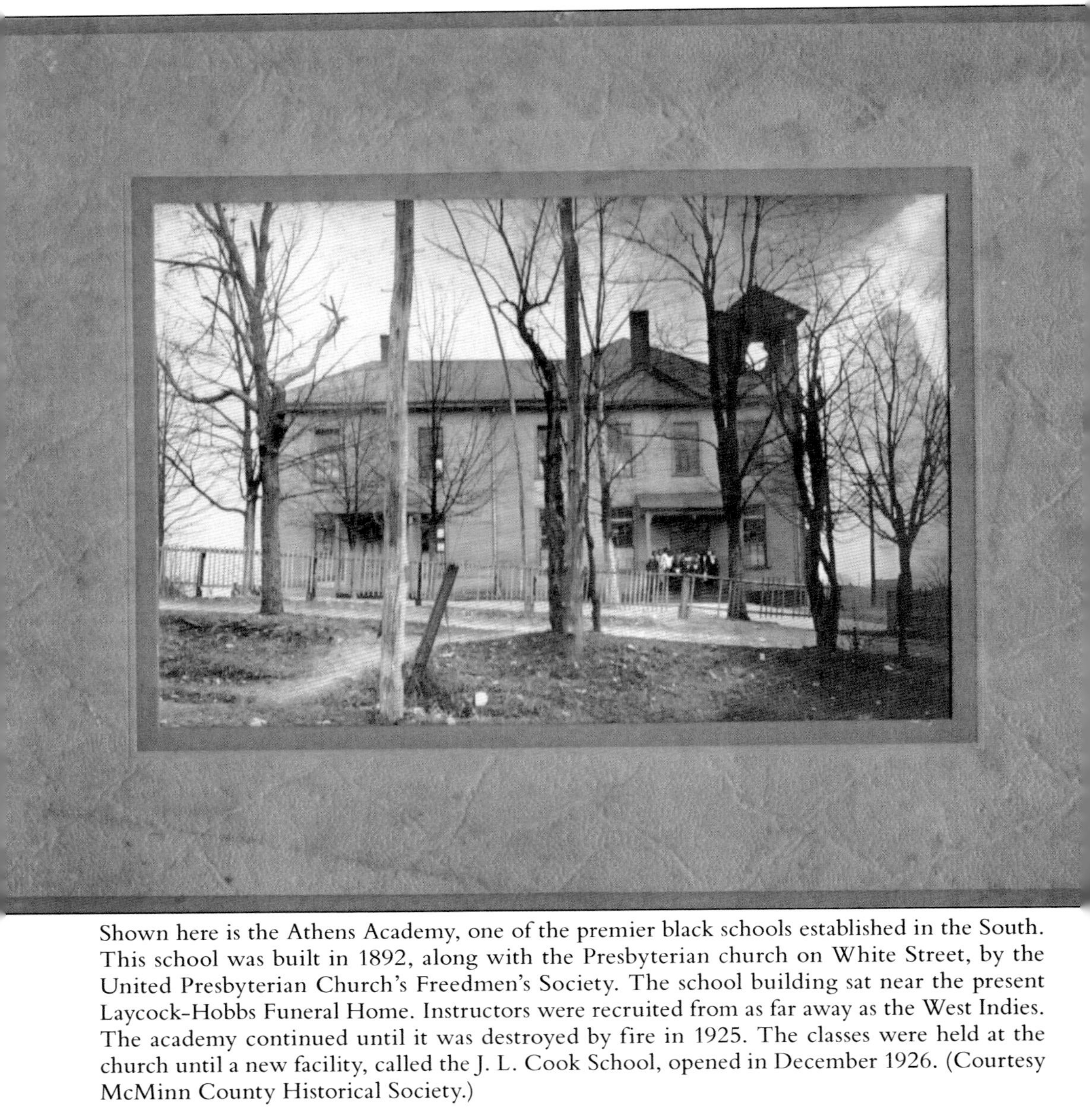

Shown here is the Athens Academy, one of the premier black schools established in the South. This school was built in 1892, along with the Presbyterian church on White Street, by the United Presbyterian Church's Freedmen's Society. The school building sat near the present Laycock-Hobbs Funeral Home. Instructors were recruited from as far away as the West Indies. The academy continued until it was destroyed by fire in 1925. The classes were held at the church until a new facility, called the J. L. Cook School, opened in December 1926. (Courtesy McMinn County Historical Society.)

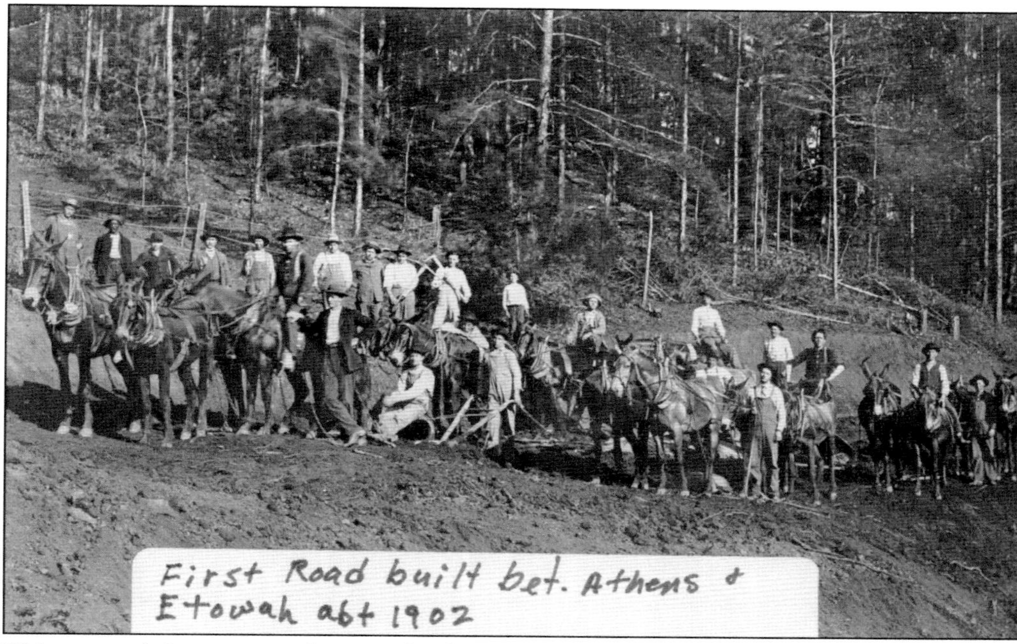


This postcard shows a rare photograph of the road between Athens and the new railroad town (to become known as Etowah) being built around 1902. This location is just south of the present Jenkins Restaurant. Plows, dredgers, and hand tools were used to build this modern road.

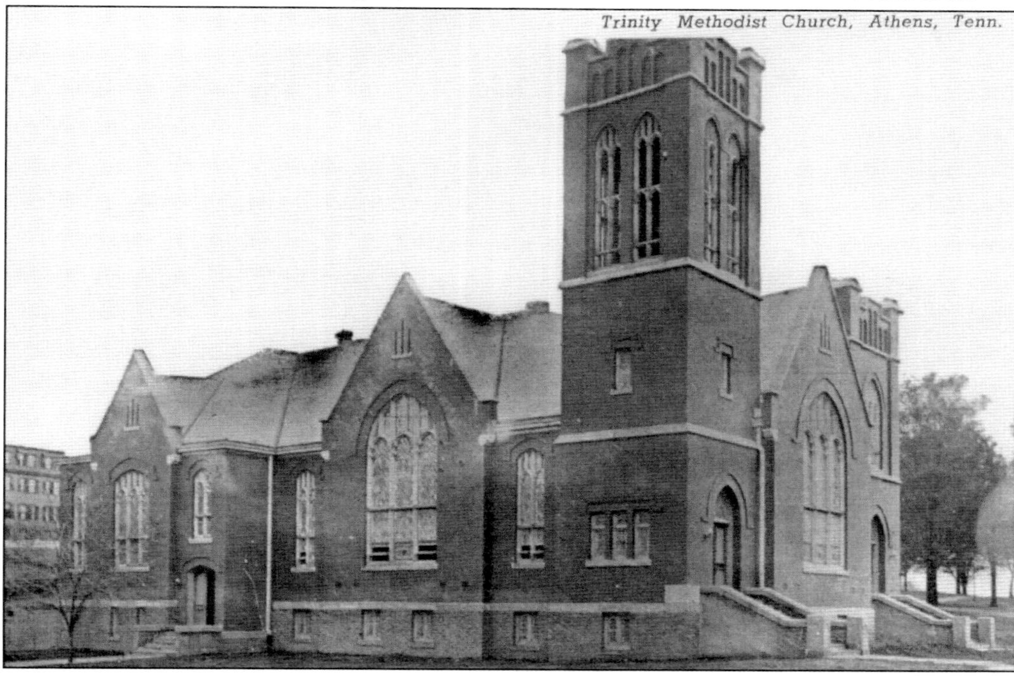


Trinity Methodist Church was built in 1909 on the site of Foster's Livery Stable. The congregation aligned itself with the Methodist Episcopal Church South. This view from College Street also shows Ritter Hall on the far left, which was a residence hall on the campus of Grant University, later Tennessee Wesleyan College.

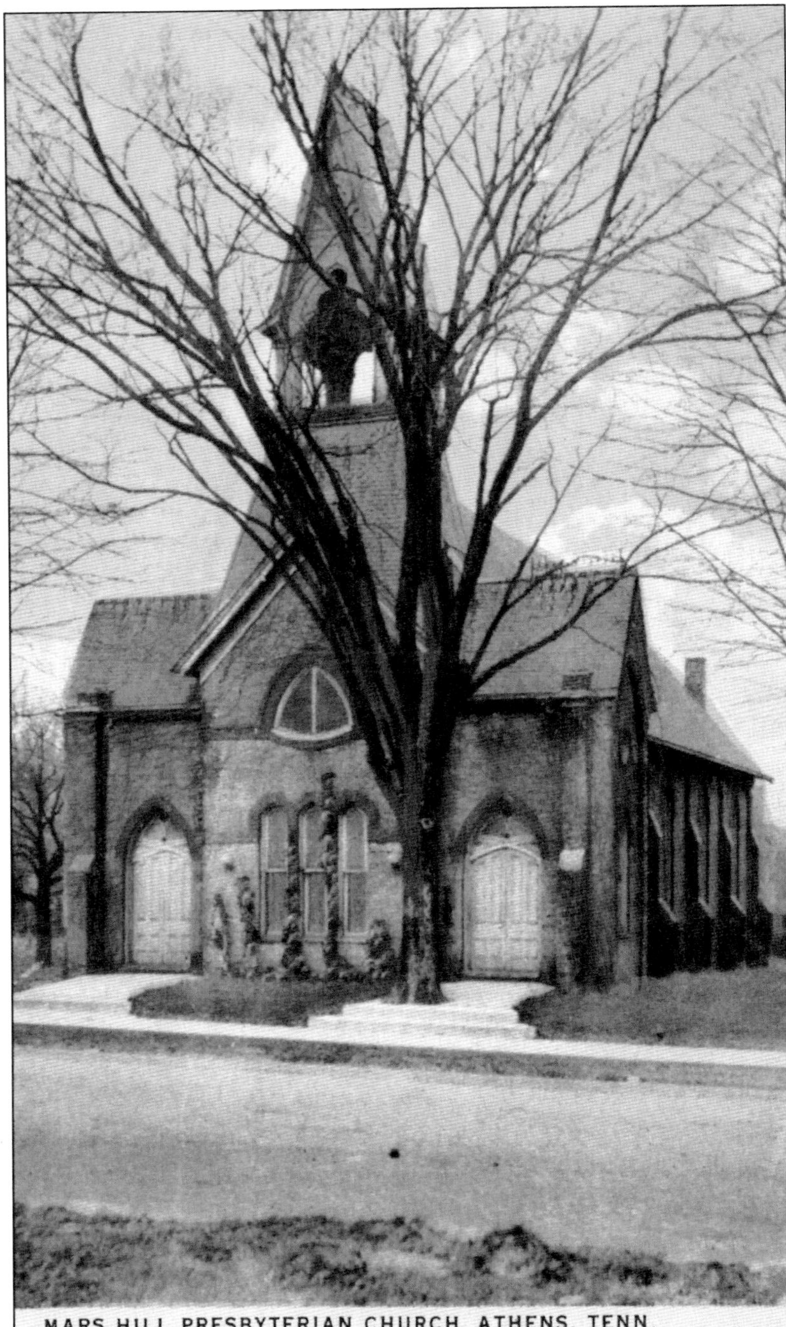


Athens's first Presbyterian congregation shared a building with the town's first Baptist congregation in the present Cedar Grove Cemetery. As the town grew, the Presbyterians built Mars Hill Church in 1834 on Jackson Street, one block from the public square. The builder was Samuel Cleage, and its bricks were made by hand by Cleage's slaves. When the first building was torn down in 1888, the bricks made by Cleage's slaves were of such high quality that they were used again in rebuilding the structure shown in this postcard.

A later postcard shows Mars Hill Presbyterian Church with the trees removed from the front of the building, likely in the mid-1940s. The building remains today.

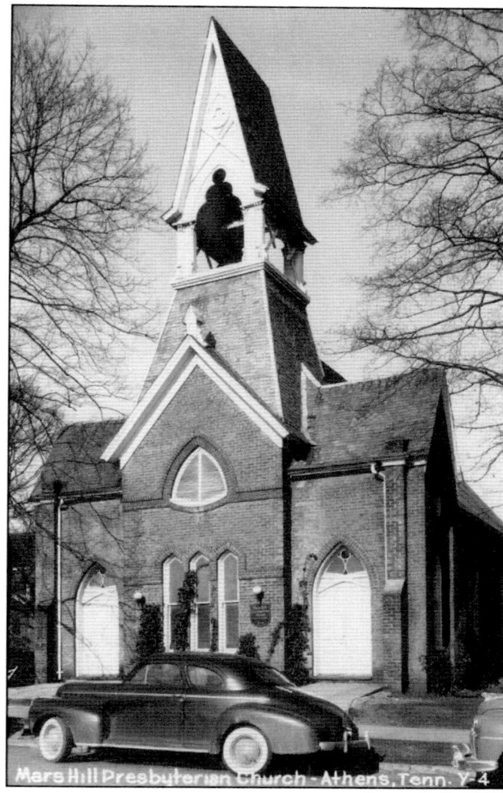


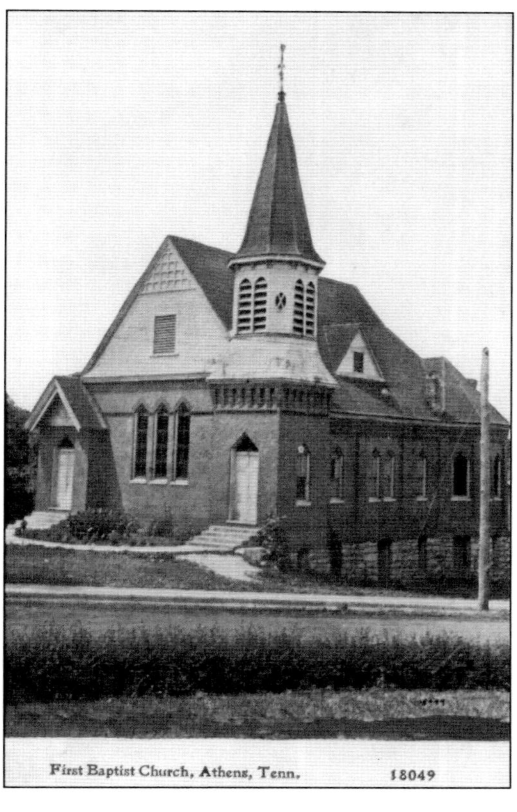


Athens's First Baptist Church worshipped in this brick building that sat on a triangle of land at the intersections of Madison Avenue, Green Street, and Eastanaulee Avenue. This 1917 card shows Athens's First Baptist Church's east-facing entrances with messages that read, "We are among hills and negroes" and "This is a pretty place."

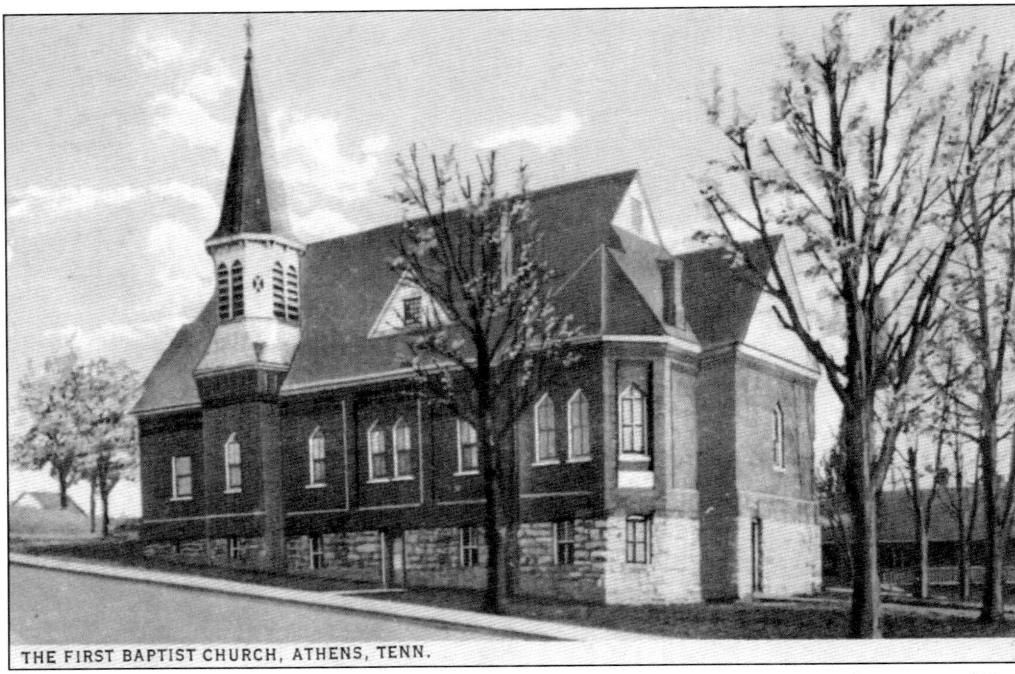


Perhaps it was a good Baptist traveler who sent this 1928 card that featured another view of First Baptist Church to Puryear, Tennessee, with the message, "Dear mama, I dreamed of you last. We camped near Cleveland last night. Leaving here for Etowah Tenn. With love, Lacy."

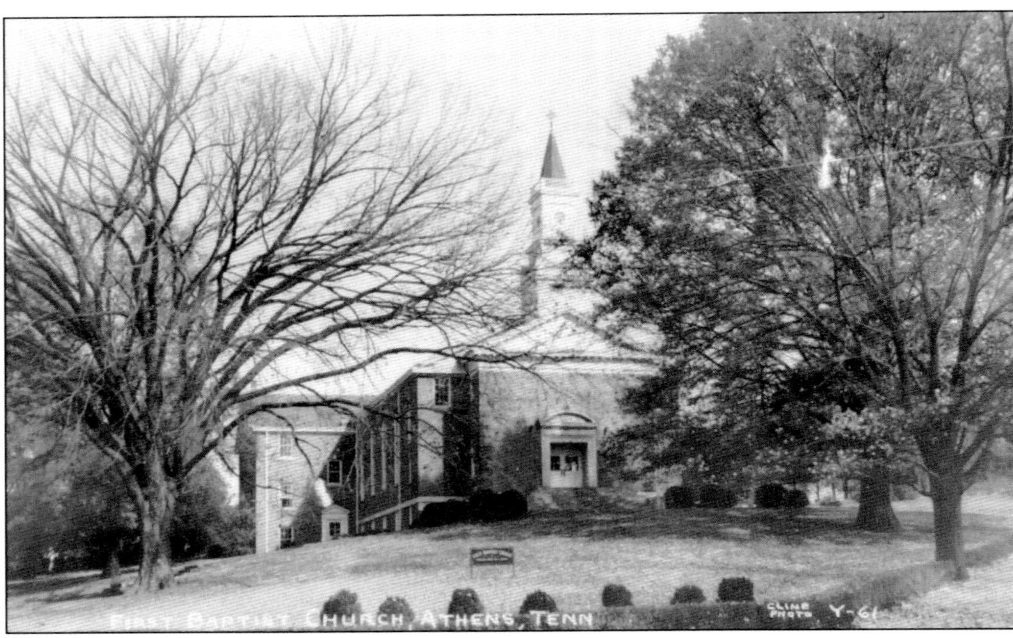


The First Baptist Church grew throughout the first half of the 20th century until a new building was deemed necessary. The congregation purchased the beautiful R. J. Fisher mansion next door, had it demolished, and constructed this large building on the top of the hill.

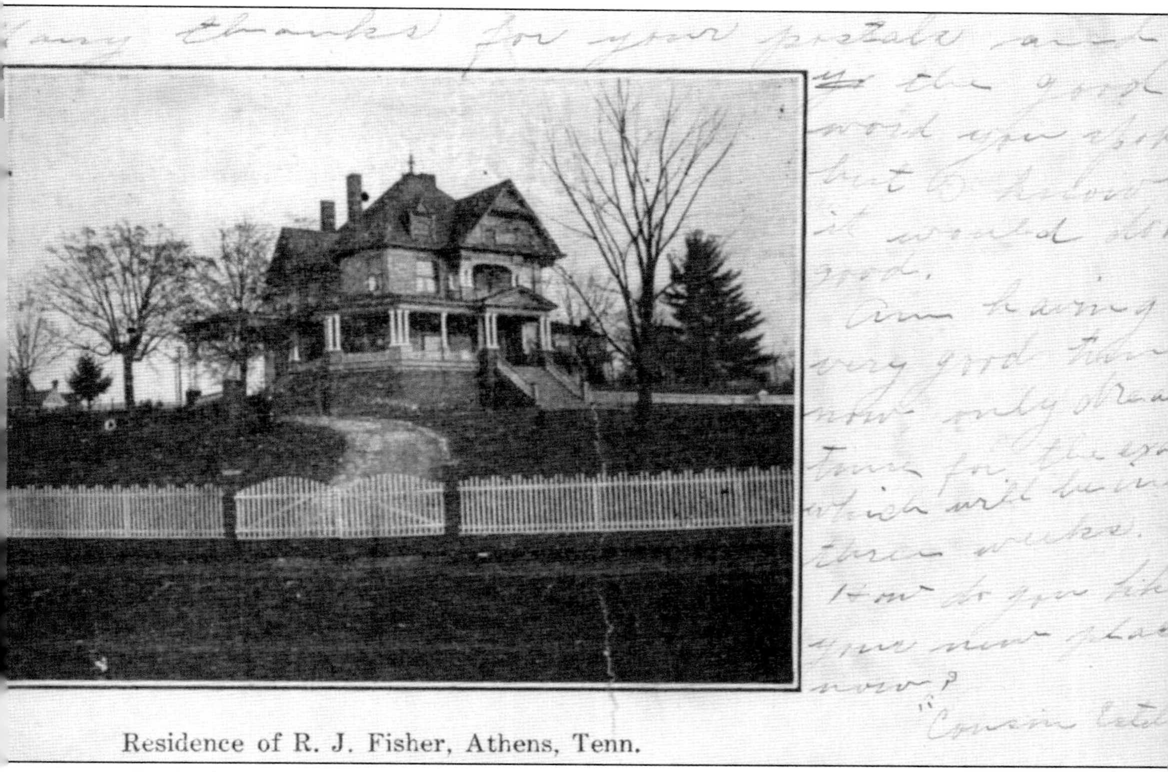


R. J. Fisher built the fine home shown in this 1906 postcard on a hill overlooking Green Street in Athens with an attached greenhouse. Fisher, a local businessman, started many area enterprises, including the First National Bank in 1883, Athens Woolen Mills in 1885, and North Athens Land Company in 1887 as part of the Athens Mining and Manufacturing Company. Fisher invented a typewriter that typed on ledger books and became quite famous for it.

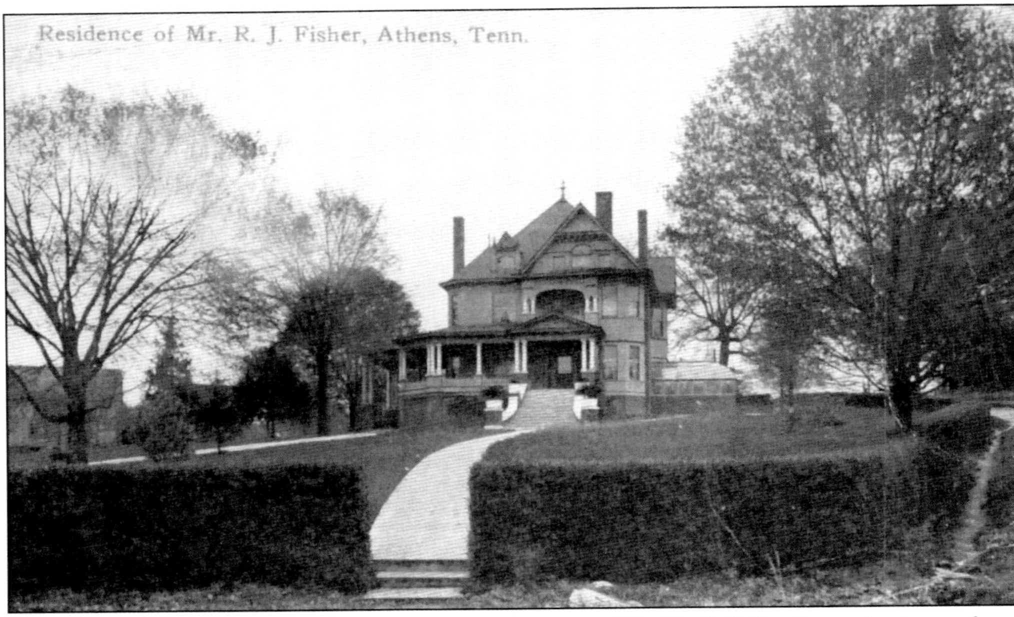


The R. J. Fisher house is pictured above in the summer of 1912 on its hill overlooking Athens. The picket fence has been replaced by a hedge that fronted the lawn along Green Street. Fisher was also the director of the Bank of Athens and was president of Athens Stove Works. He was involved in starting the Athens Hosiery Mill, gaining rail line extensions to industrial sites, and organizing the Athens Water Works. His influence is still felt today.

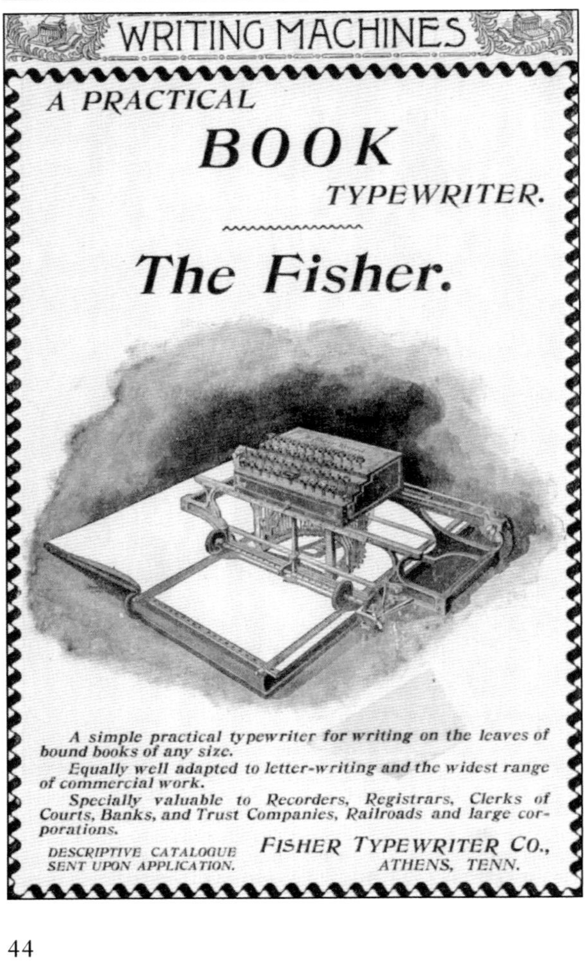


This advertisement for R. J. Fisher's "Practical Book Typewriter" appeared in an unknown magazine and refers to Fisher's Typewriter Company in Athens.

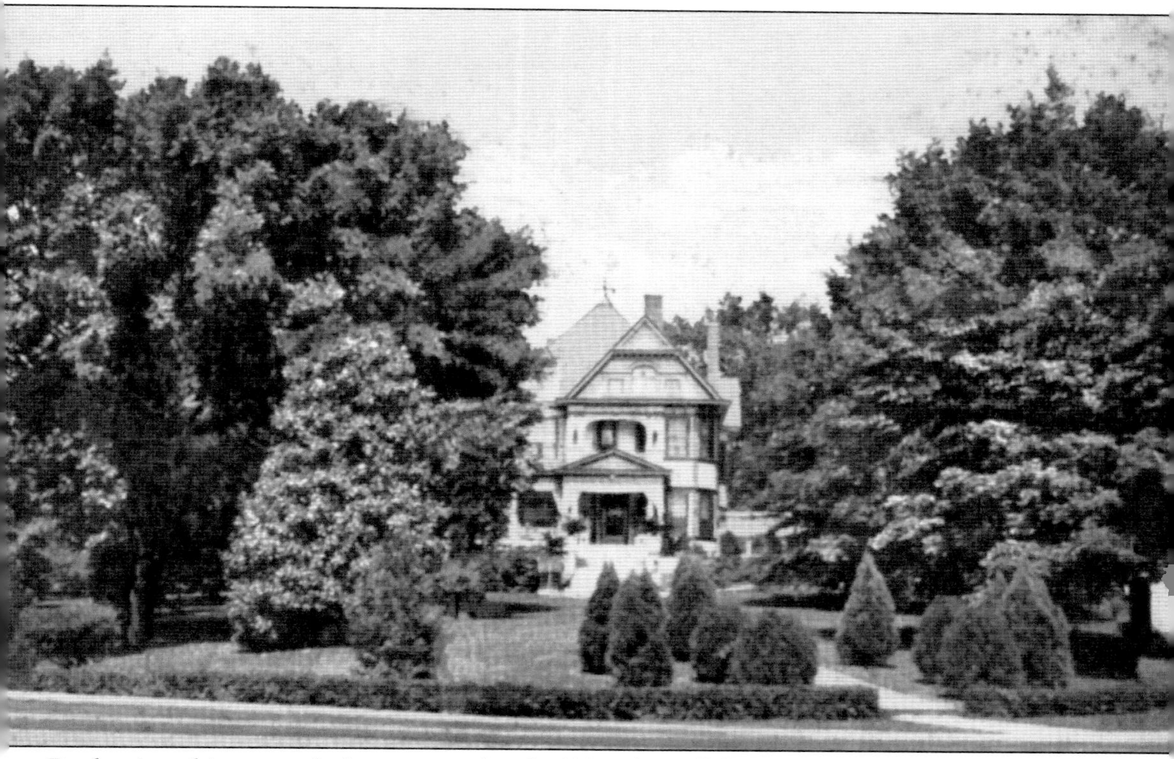

By the time this postcard picture was taken in 1926, the well-kept lawn and grounds featured many varieties of trees and plants. The house and property was visible to all visitors in Athens and indicated Fisher's wealth and influence in the community. After his death in 1932, the house was leased by Quisenberry Funeral Home. It was sold and demolished in 1940 to make way for the new First Baptist Church building.

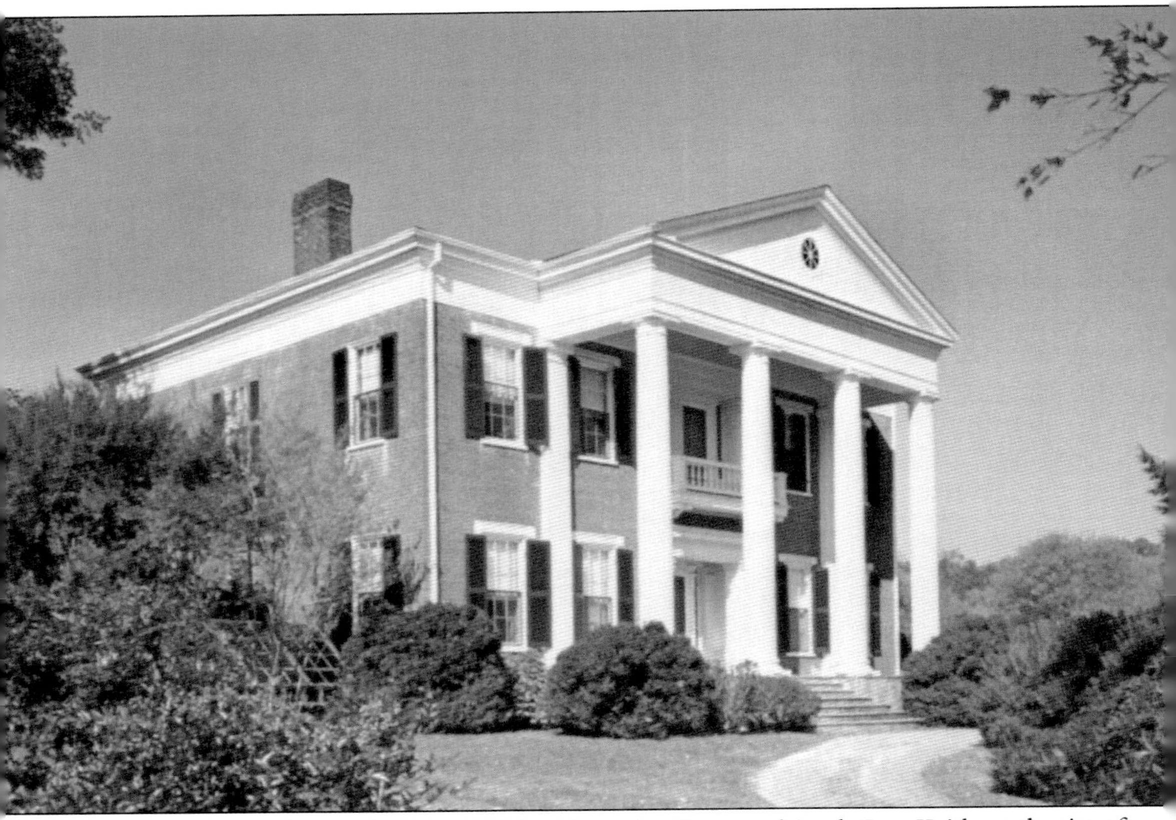

The Keith Mansion was built in 1858 by Alexander Hume and Sarah Fore Keith on the site of the former mansion of Sarah's father that burned in 1856. The house is solidly built with 32-inch exterior walls and 13-inch interior walls, all of solid brick. Initially called Elmwood, the home featured a smaller portico that was torn away by Union troops camped around the home in 1864. Later the columned portico was added, and the house remained in the Keith family until 1986. Since that time, the house has served as a private residence as well as a bed-and-breakfast. Its picturesque location is often the scene of weddings and civic club meetings. On a darker note, the house is reportedly haunted, with doors that lock by themselves and stains in the floor that cannot be removed.

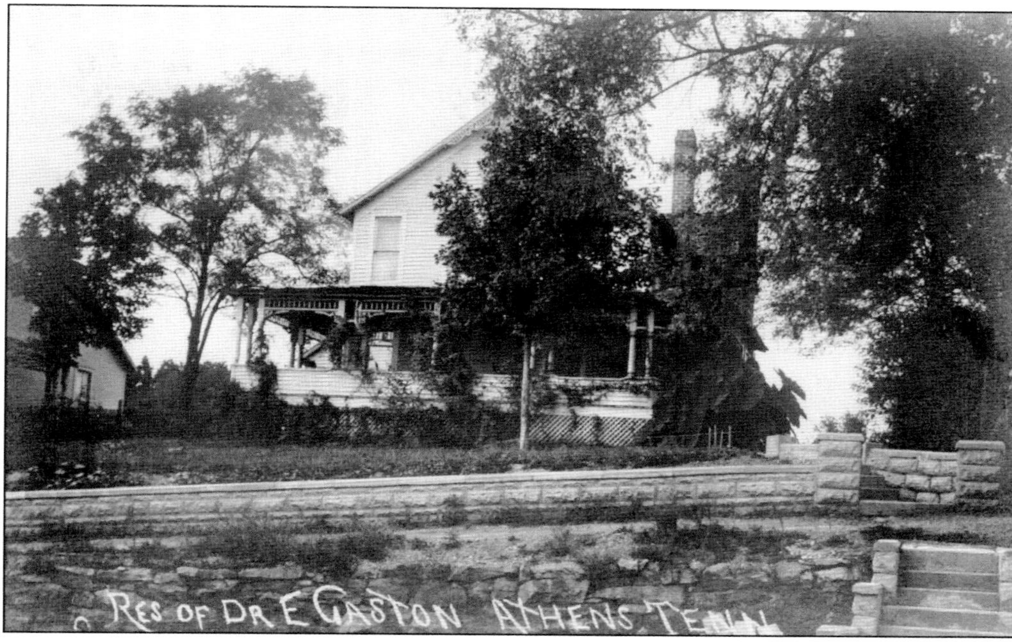


This postcard from 1906 features the home of Dr. E. Gaston on College Street. The card is addressed to "Rev. Wm Gaston DD" in Cleveland, Ohio, with the short, scribbled message, "Come and see us," likely sent from Dr. E. Gaston to his father.

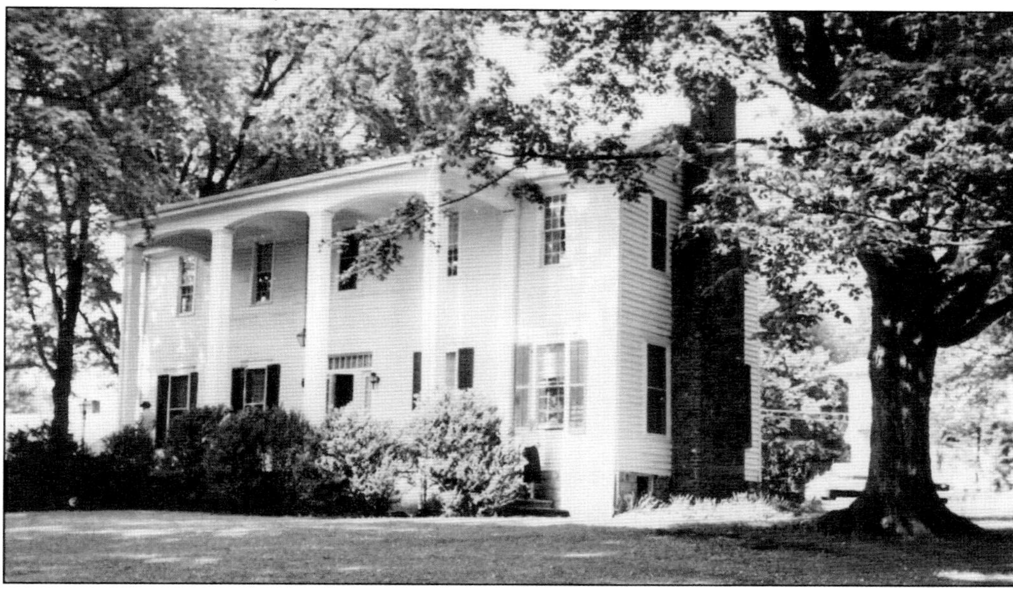

This house was built in 1820 by William Lowery, who bought the land that would soon become Athens. When Lowery arrived at his property, he found a squatter, an Irishman named William Gardenhire, already living there. Lowery paid Gardenhire for his improvements, which included a small cabin. While doing renovations some 10 years ago, what is believed to be Gardenhire's original cabin was found within the walls of the kitchen that attaches to the back of the frame house. Lowery sold acreage to the commissioners of the Town of Athens for the new county seat in 1822. (Courtesy McMinn County Historical Society.)

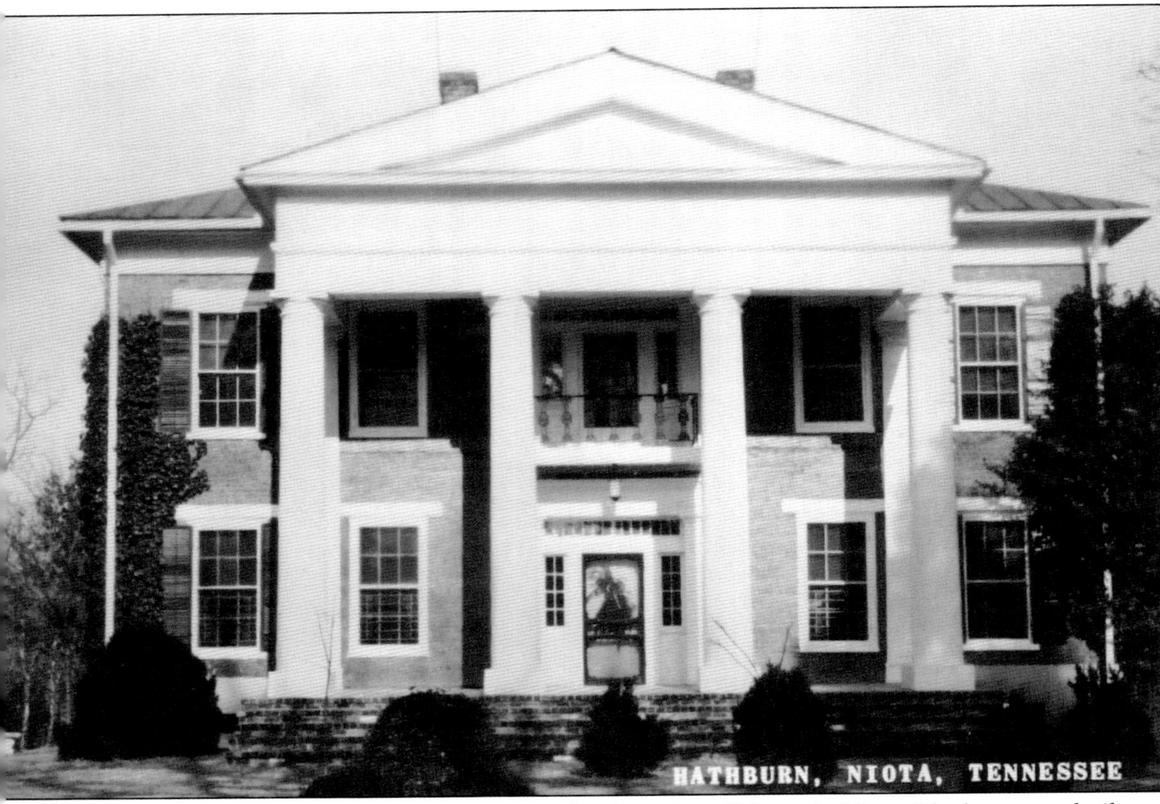


Hathburn was the family home of the Burn family on Farrell Street in Niota. The house was built prior to the Civil War by the Shearman family, who sold it after grieving for a child killed on the railroad tracks at the rear of the house. The porticos came from the Col. Archibald Blizzard home that once stood on White Street in Athens. (Courtesy McMinn County Historical Society.)

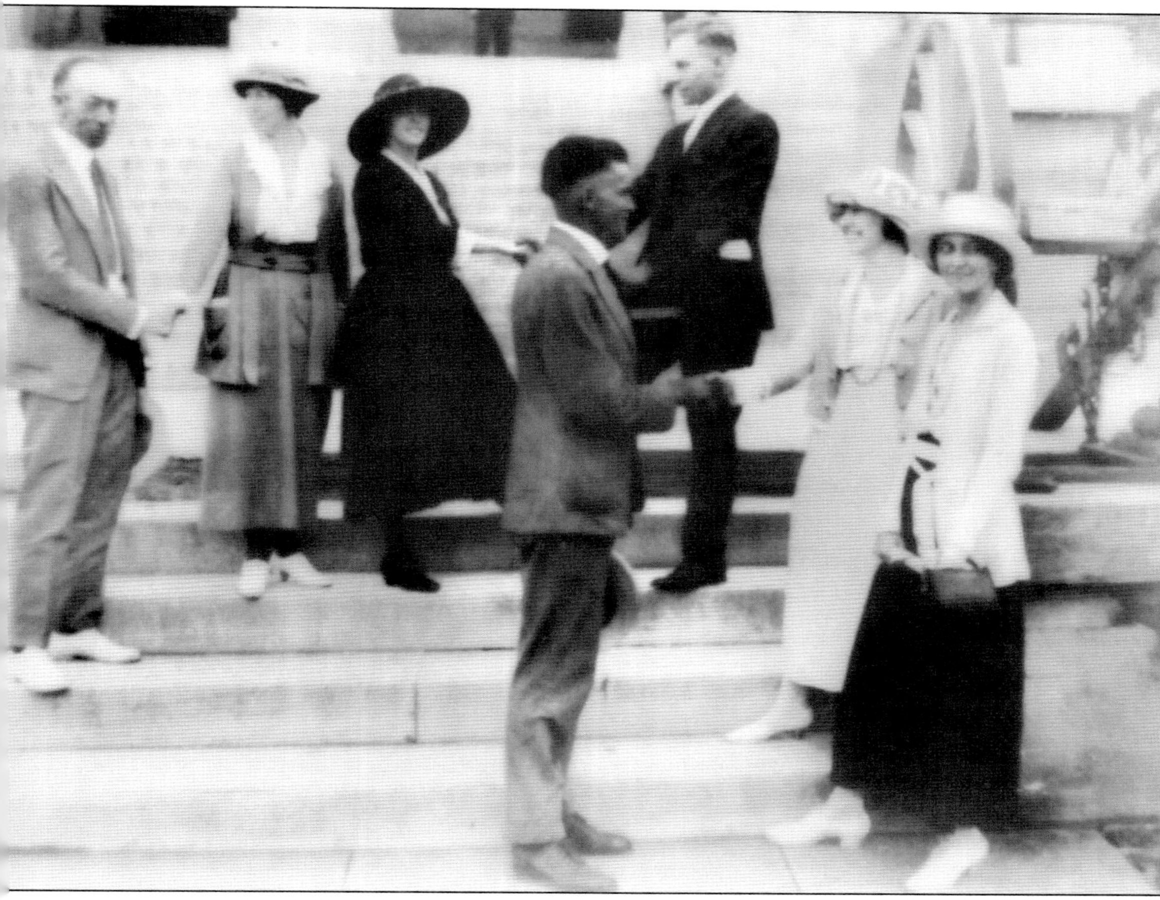

One of McMinn County's most famous citizens, Harry T. Burn, a young state representative from Niota, cast the deciding vote to ratify the 19th Amendment to the U.S. Constitution on August 19, 1920. This picture, popular at the time on postcards and in newspapers, shows Burn at front center receiving congratulations from suffrage leaders on the steps of the Tennessee State Capitol. (Courtesy McMinn County Historical Society.)

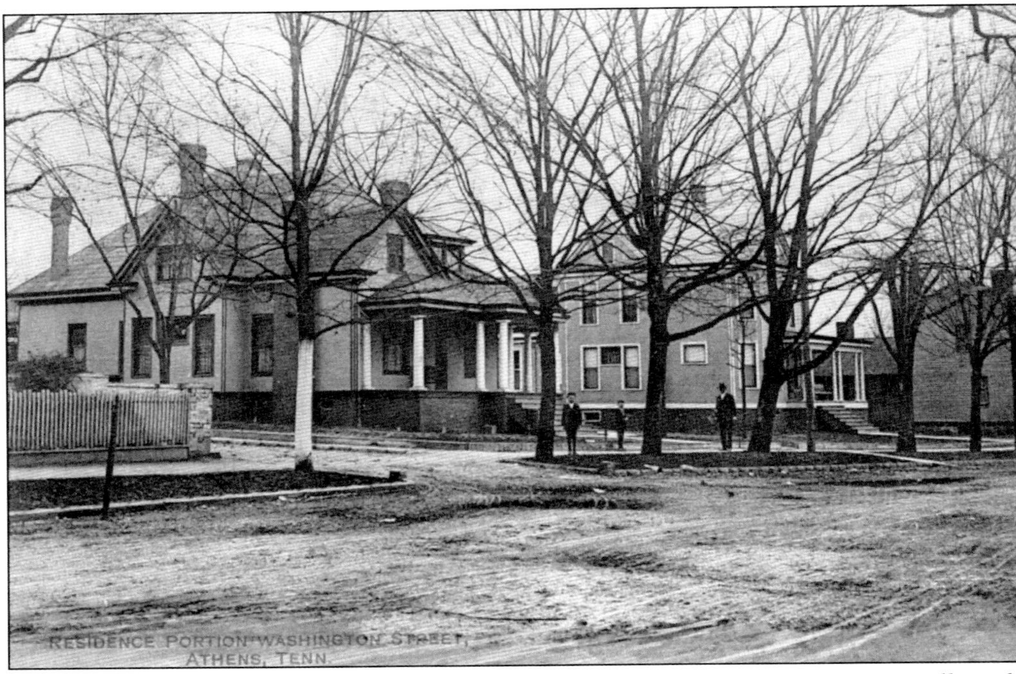


Residences along Washington Street are pictured in this postcard from 1900. Many well-to-do Athenians built along this street, one of the first subdivisions in town.

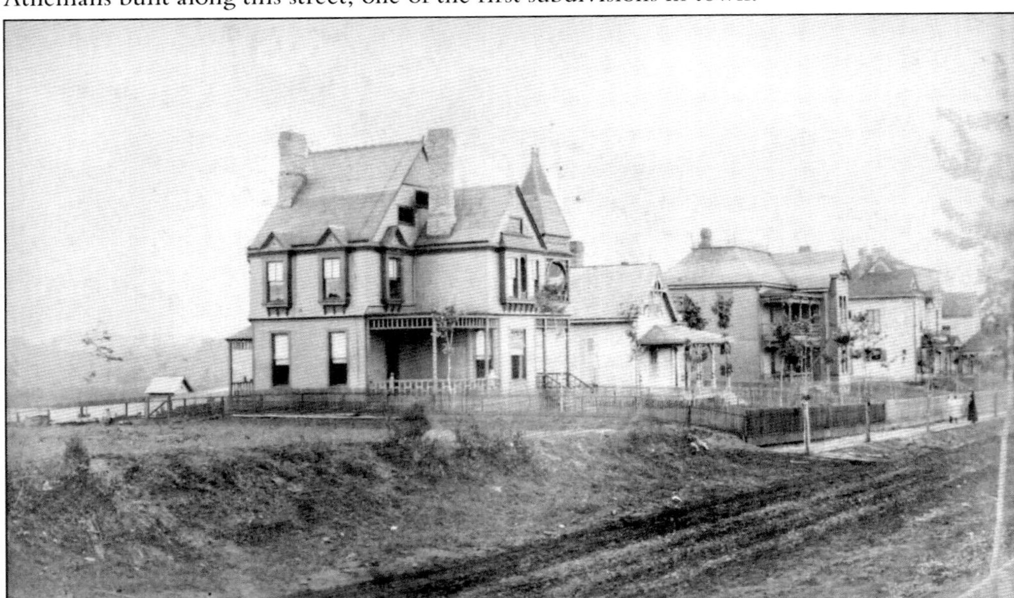

Shown here around 1890 are houses on Madison Avenue. From left to right are the Candler house, the Moody house, and the J. A. Turley house. Originally from the Cog Hill community, Capt. John A. Turley and his wife, Mary Ann Scarbrough Turley, were prominent Athens citizens. Turley served on the committee that oversaw the building of the second courthouse in 1878 and was a lawyer, railroad commissioner, and Athens postmaster. Later the house was home to Charles and Katherine Keith. (Courtesy McMinn County Historical Society.)

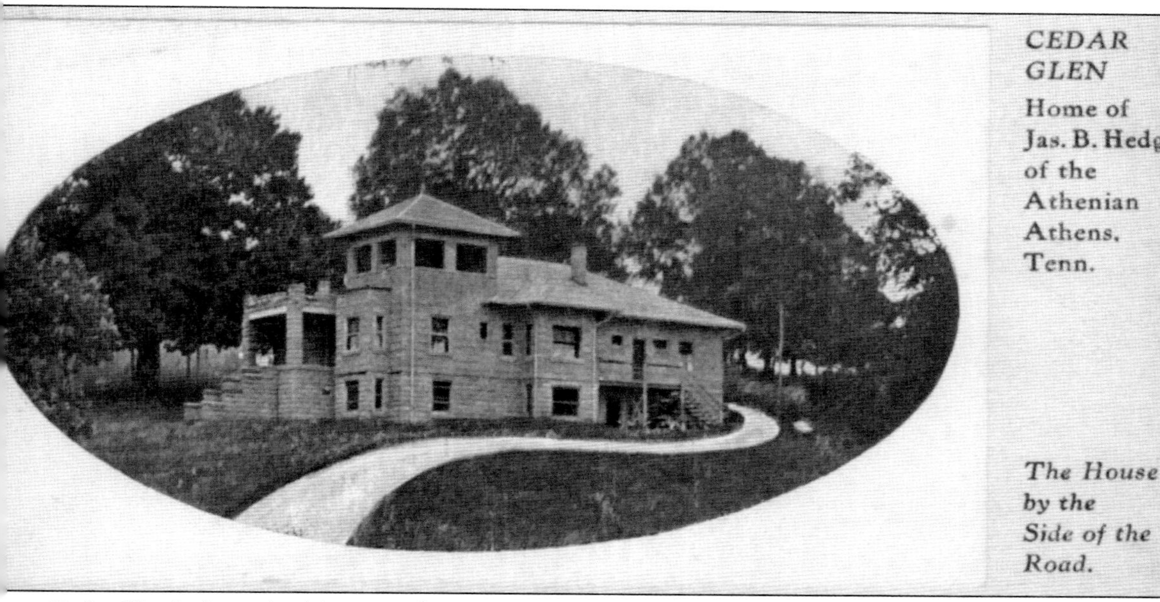


Cedar Glen is shown in this postcard. It was the home of James B. Hedge, publisher of the *Athenian* newspaper. The imposing brick structure still stands on Forrest Avenue and Gettys Lane.

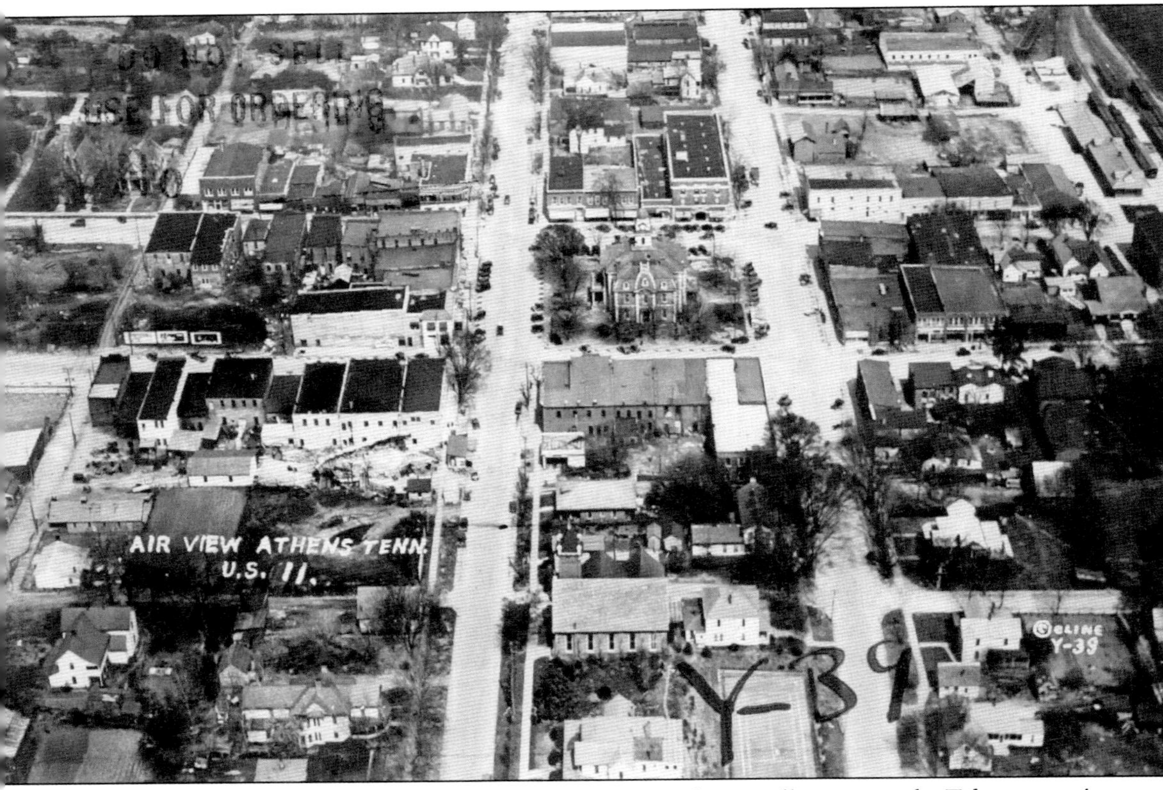


This aerial view of Athens appears in many photographs as well as postcards. Taken sometime in the 1940s, many sites in the downtown area are captured here. This view to the east shows the courthouse at center, with Madison Avenue at right center and Washington Avenue at left center. The Robert E. Lee Hotel is seen on the corner of Jackson Street and Madison Avenue, with the Ivens House just across the street to the right and the Rice House just above. The Louisville and Nashville (L&N) Depot and rail yard are clearly visible on the upper right and Athens Plow Factory at the top right. The old First Baptist Church and the Fisher house are at top center.

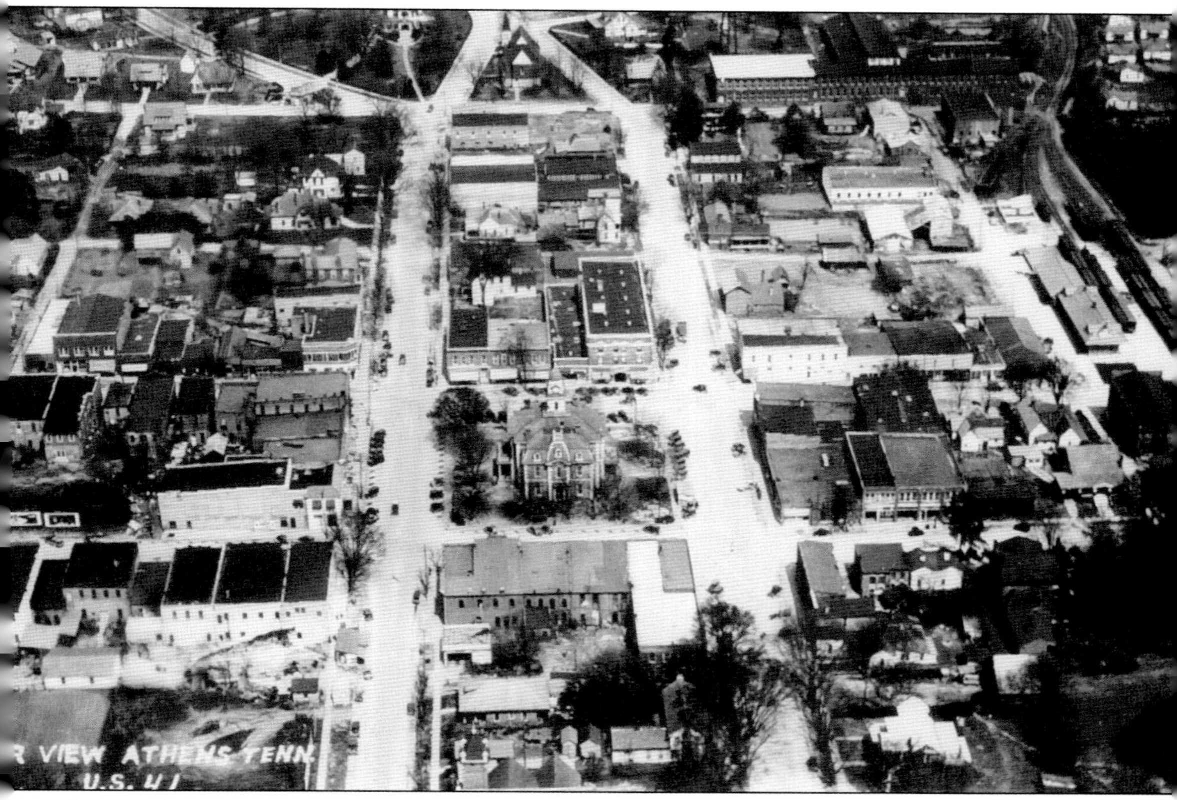


This aerial photograph was likely taken at the same time, facing east but showing more of the west side of town. At bottom center is the Methodist Church on Washington Avenue. Note the tennis court behind it. At the upper left, on the edge of the picture, is Kyker and Quisenberry Funeral Home. When a gypsy queen died in the 1920s at a campsite near Riceville, her funeral was held here. The gypsies, as was their custom, camped out around the funeral home and continued the wake for several days after the burial. It was with only with the threat of force that the funeral home staff were able to persuade the troupe to move on.

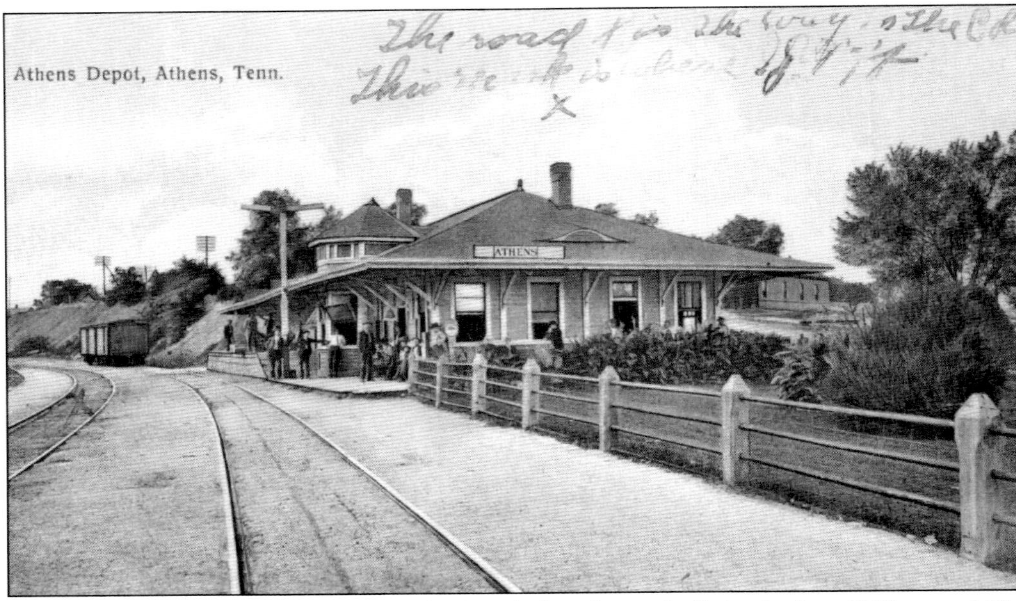


The Southern Depot sat on the site of Athens's first depot, built in the late 1850s on a hill a few blocks to the north of downtown. Here trains first passed through Athens on the Hiwassee Railroad and later the East Tennessee and Georgia Railroad and later still the Southern Railroad. With passenger service coming to an end in the mid-1960s, the depot fell into disuse, and it was torn down in the late 1970s. This area of town is still known as Depot Hill.

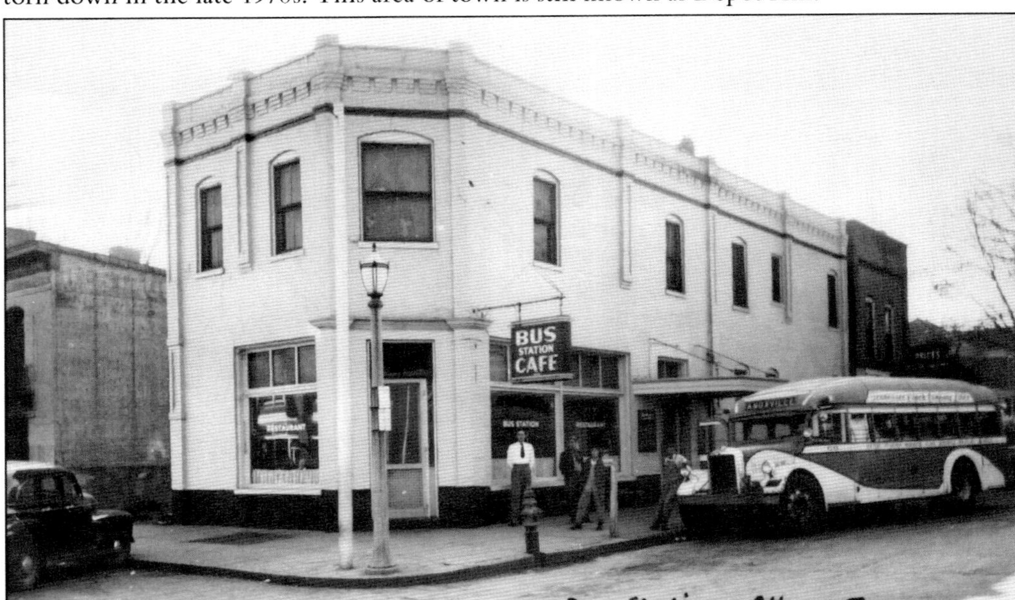


Showing the old bus station, on Dewitt Corner at Madison and White Streets, this September 1946 postcard was mailed only a month after the Battle of Athens. Here a Tennessee Coach Company bus pauses for passenger exchange on a northbound run up Lee Highway to Knoxville. Passengers waited and ate at the diner. Just behind the bus is the old Tuell Store, one of Athens's oldest buildings. Both structures still stand.

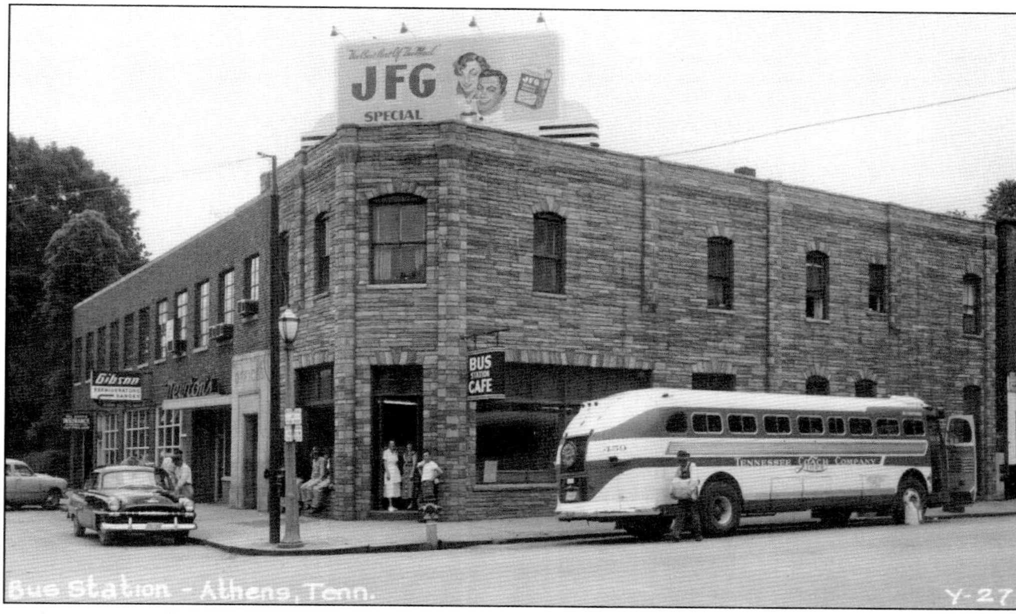


In this picture from the mid-1960s, the bus station had acquired its new stonework that remains to this day. Next door, on the right, the Hammer Supply Store has been added, along with Newton's Store. Tennessee Coach Line bus 459 waits to resume its southbound route.

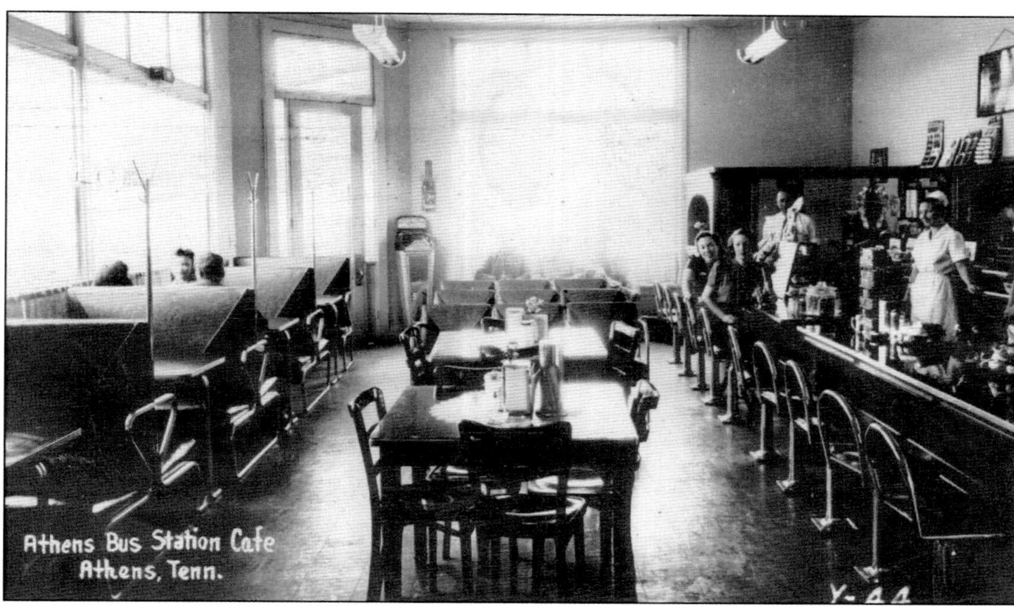


This is a 1946 postcard showing the interior of the Bus Station Café. Patrons sat in booths, at tables, or at the bar to get a hot meal, wait on the next bus, or to simply catch up on the latest news and see who was coming into town. During the Battle of Athens that August, it was told that a sleepy bus driver pulled up and opened the bus door just as a burst of gunfire erupted two blocks away at the besieged county jail. The story goes that the bus driver, now fully awake, quickly closed the door and pulled off, saying, "It ain't safe to get off here!"

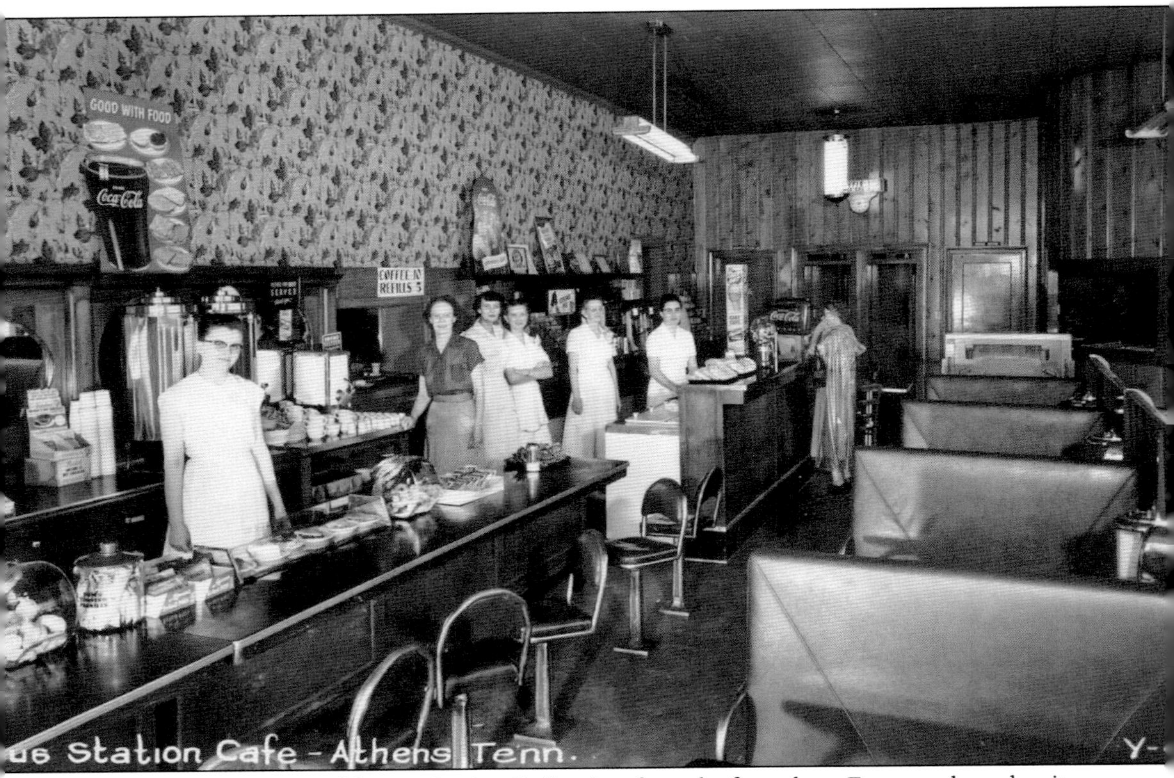


This is another view of the Bus Station Café, taken from the front door. Eager cooks and waitresses wait on new customers. Burkette Witt was a young black cook who worked here, although Jim Crow laws prohibited him from ever coming from behind the counter when white customers were present. The entire time he was employed, Witt entered the café through a narrow back alley, never through the front door. Years later, Witt served a long tenure as an Athens City councilman and mayor.

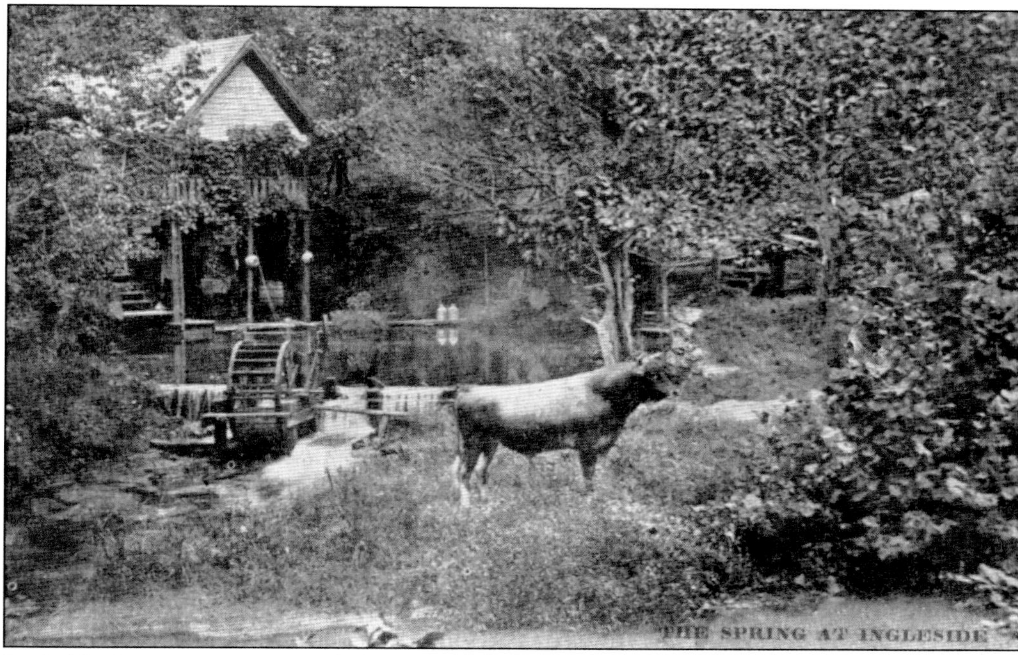


Ingleside Dairy once occupied the area of Ingleside Avenue, Mayfields Dairy, and Ingleside School. The free-flowing spring is listed as a landmark in many historical references, some of the earliest of which refer to its use as the water source for Forrest Hill School, established on the hill above in 1825. This postcard is dated 1912.

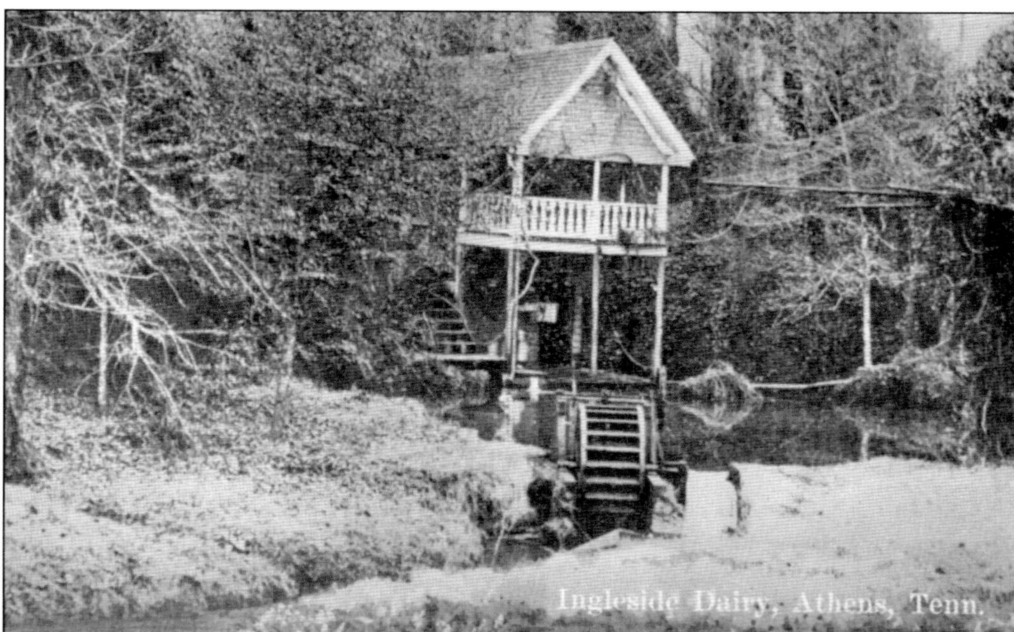


The springhouse at Ingleside Dairy was a popular gathering place for locals at the beginning of the 19th century. Its elevated deck overlooked the half-acre spring pool that flowed into Eastanaulee Creek. The spring pool remains today and was, for many years, the water source for Athens.

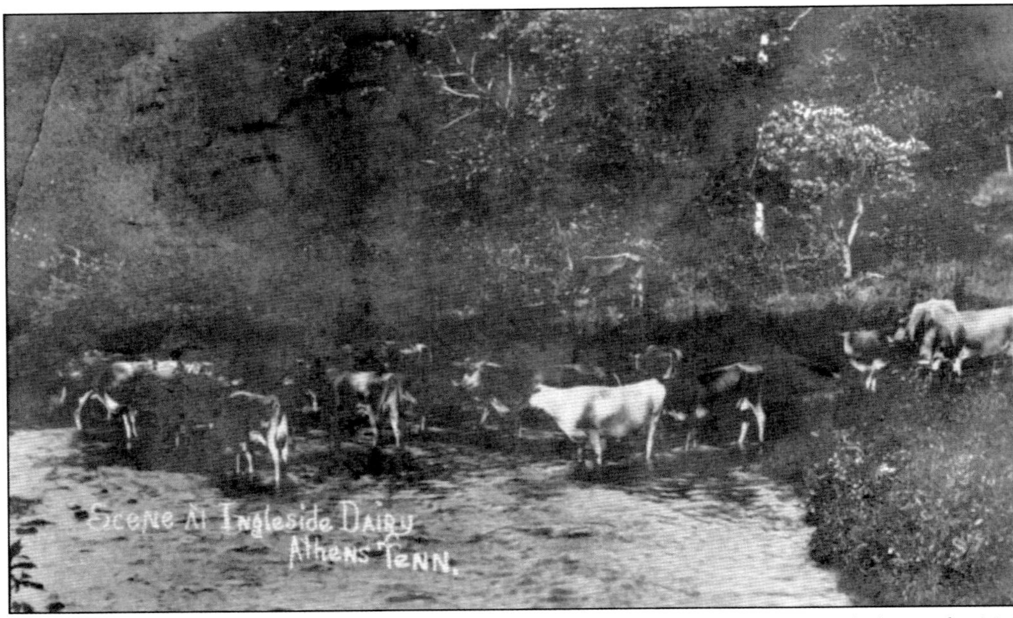


Ingleside Dairy was owned by Wilberforce Gettys and was operated until the early 20th century. Part of the registered Jersey herd is shown wading in the spring pool in this postcard from 1907.

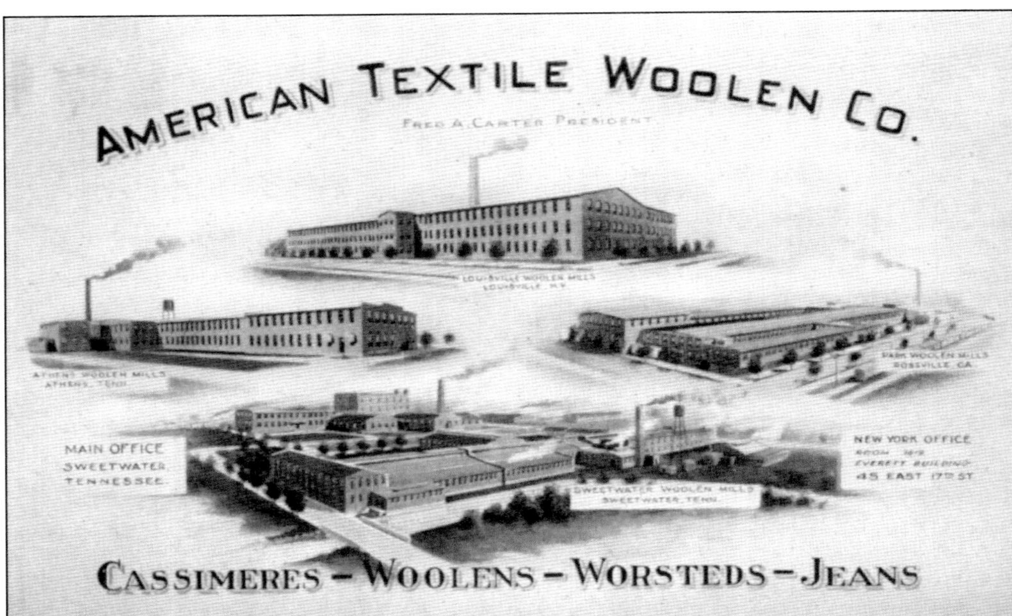


With so many swift-flowing creeks in McMinn County, the mill industry has been a part of the Athens area since the county was founded. The milling of grains, along with textile production, was first powered with water and later with electricity. The Athens Woolen Mills were organized by R. J. Fisher in 1885, one of many industrial ventures by the successful inventor and businessman.

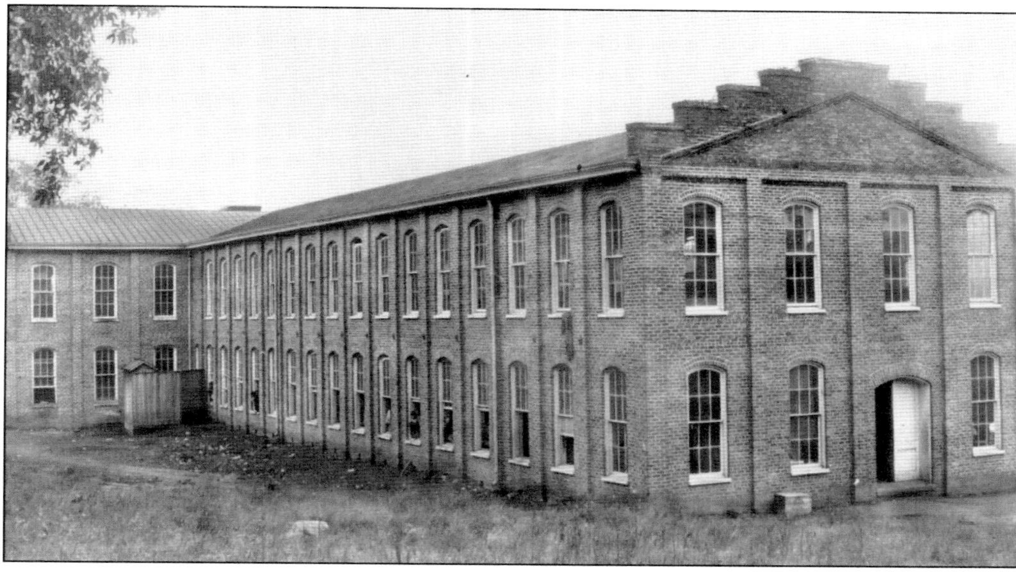

Athens Woolen Mills is seen in this photograph. The building sat on Tellico Avenue, with the railroad just behind it. It was part of the Athens Mineral and Mining Corporation but survived the failure of the greater corporation. (Courtesy McMinn County Historical Society.)

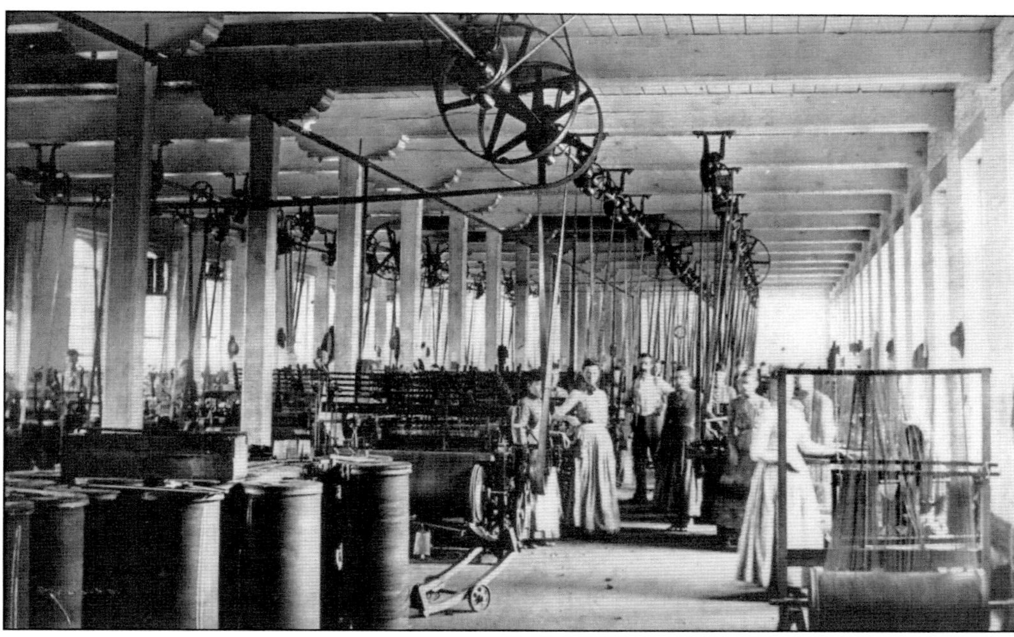

This view of the interior of the Athens Woolen Mills shows the cramped conditions for workers. Safety was of no concern in those days. Young employees, who were deemed old enough if they could reach the machines, walked barefoot around uncovered pulleys and spinning machinery. (Courtesy McMinn County Historical Society.)

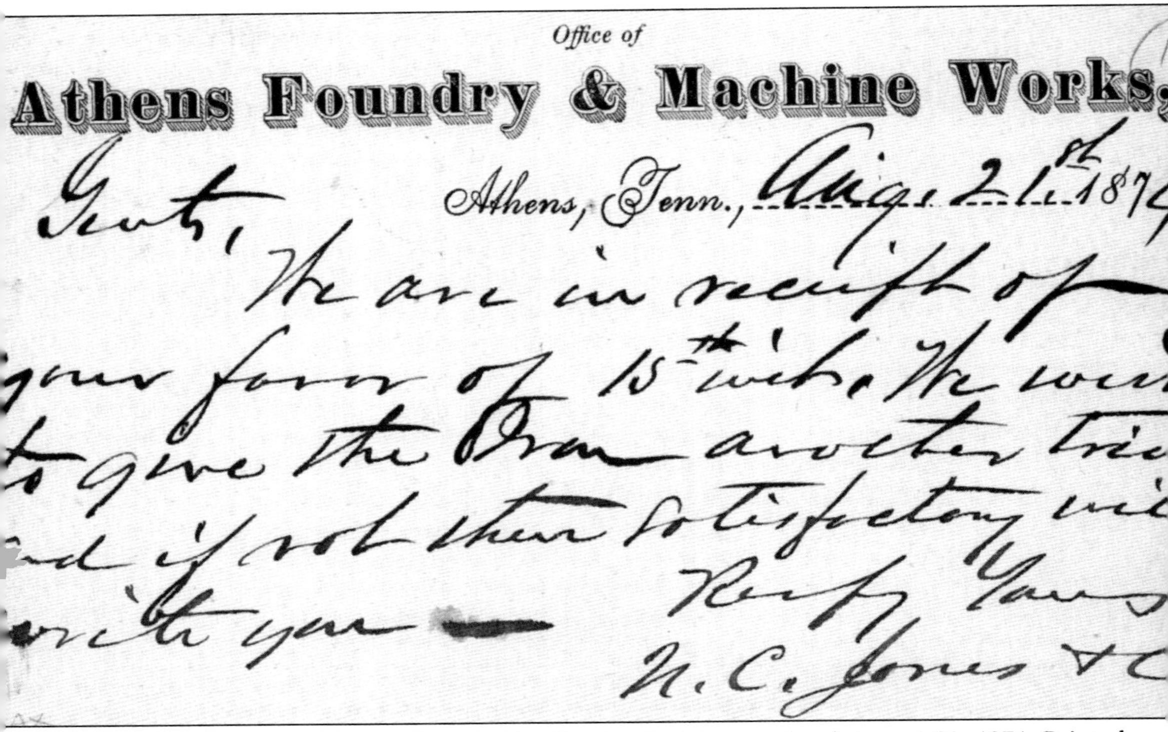

*Office of*

**Athens Foundry & Machine Works,**

Athens, Tenn., Aug. 21st 1874

Gents,

We are in receipt of your favor of 15th inst. We will give the Bran another trial and if not then satisfactory will ... with you —

Resp'y Yours

N. C. Jones & Co

The oldest postcard in the Don Reid collection is this one, dated August 21, 1874. Printed specifically for the office of Athens Foundry and Machine Works, the card appears to be for correspondence between the mill and its vendors and customers. Athens Foundry was another of the town's longtime industrial sites. The Athens Foundry was owned by John Thomas until 1856, when it was purchased by Cyrus Zimmerman. It was later sold to George Wheeland, who later moved the entire operation to Chattanooga, where it grew into the huge Wheeland Foundry on the bank of the Tennessee River below Lookout Mountain.

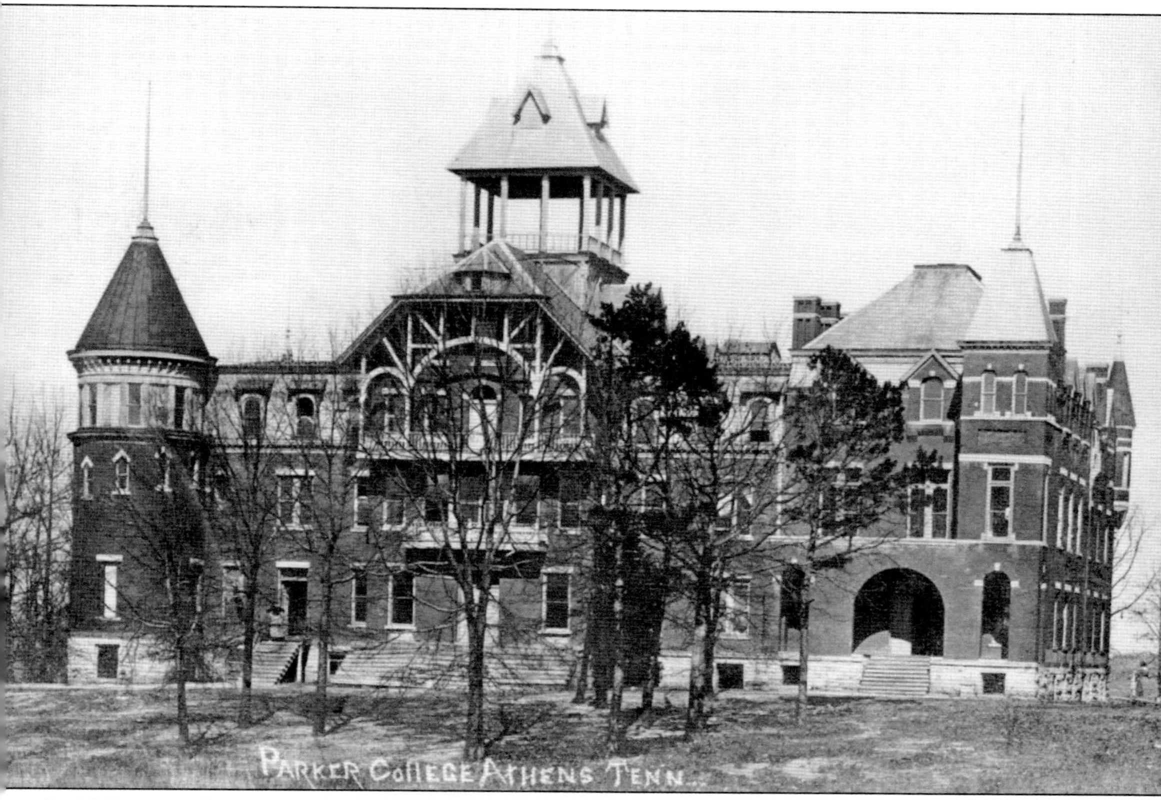

In 1887, an ambitious investment scheme was hatched by a group of prominent Athenians, led by R. J. Fisher, to develop land just north of the downtown area. The project, called the Athens Mineral and Mining Corporation, sought to construct a new town, complete with a railroad depot, a school, housing, mills, stores, and other necessities. The centerpiece was the Grand View Hotel, built of red brick on the hill overlooking the development on Woodward Avenue between present-day Clayton and Royal Streets. Nicknamed the "Red Elephant," the hotel construction stalled as the entire project became mired in lack of investments and management problems in the mid-1890s. Sold to Grant University (now Tennessee Wesleyan College) in 1890, the building was finally finished in 1907 as Parker College.

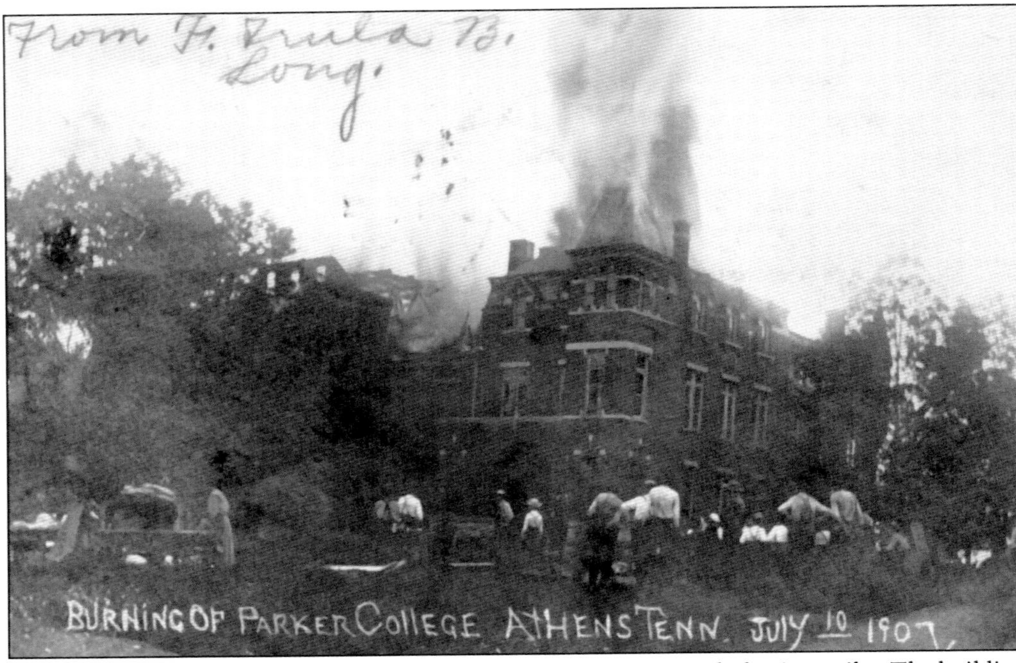


But on July 10, 1907, the Red Elephant caught fire, possibly due to a lightning strike. The building was a total loss and was torn down without ever being used as a hotel and only graduating one class as a college. Captured in this postcard photograph is the actual fire from that date. Somewhat humorous are the men seated on pews and tables around the building, watching it burn. Postcard photographs such as this are rare.

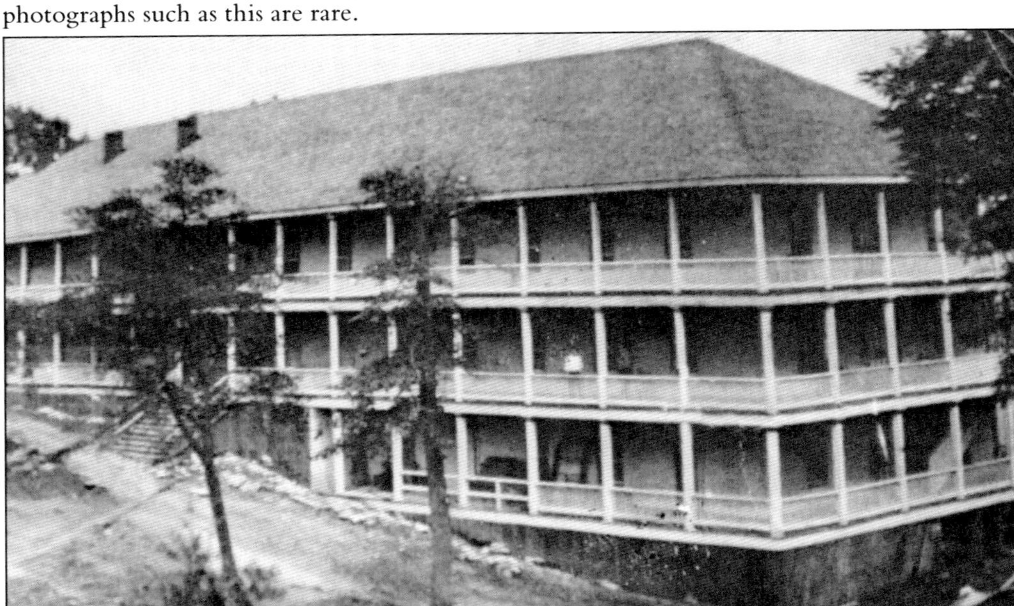

White Cliff Hotel, on the western summit of Starr Mountain on the McMinn-Monroe county line, was built and operated by J. Harvey Magill, who also owned the Hotel Magill in Athens. The three-story "Saratoga of the South" was a thriving resort during the last half of the 19th century, attracting guests from all over the country. (Courtesy McMinn County Historical Society.)

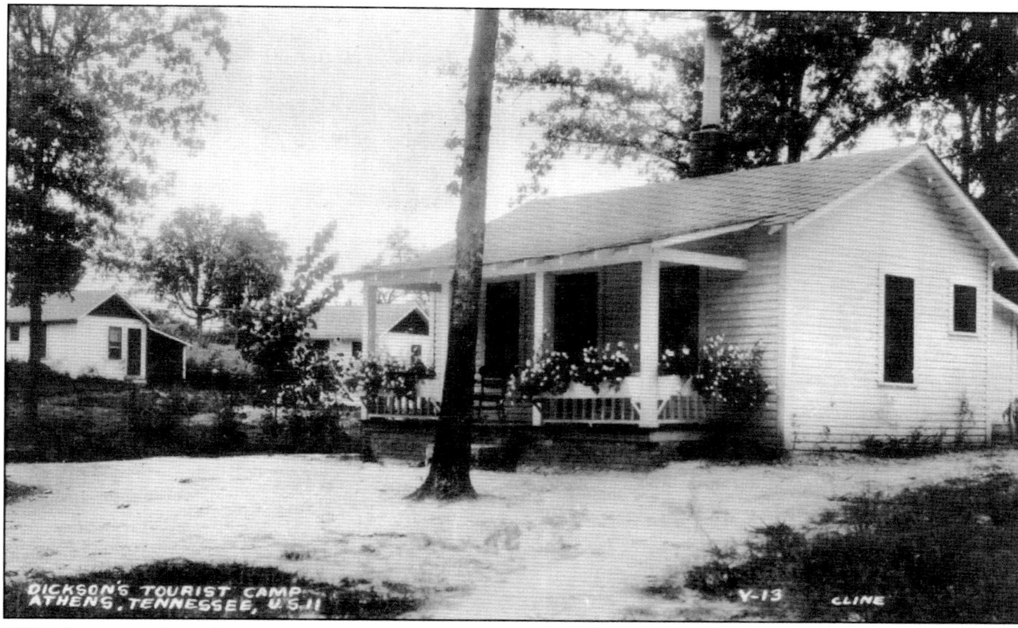


With improved roads in East Tennessee came more automobile travelers in the 1920s, 1930s, and 1940s. "Tourist Courts" sprang up in towns like Athens, providing guests with private cabins for overnight stays. This 1934 postcard shows Dickson's Tourist Camp, located on Highway 11, with the main office at center.

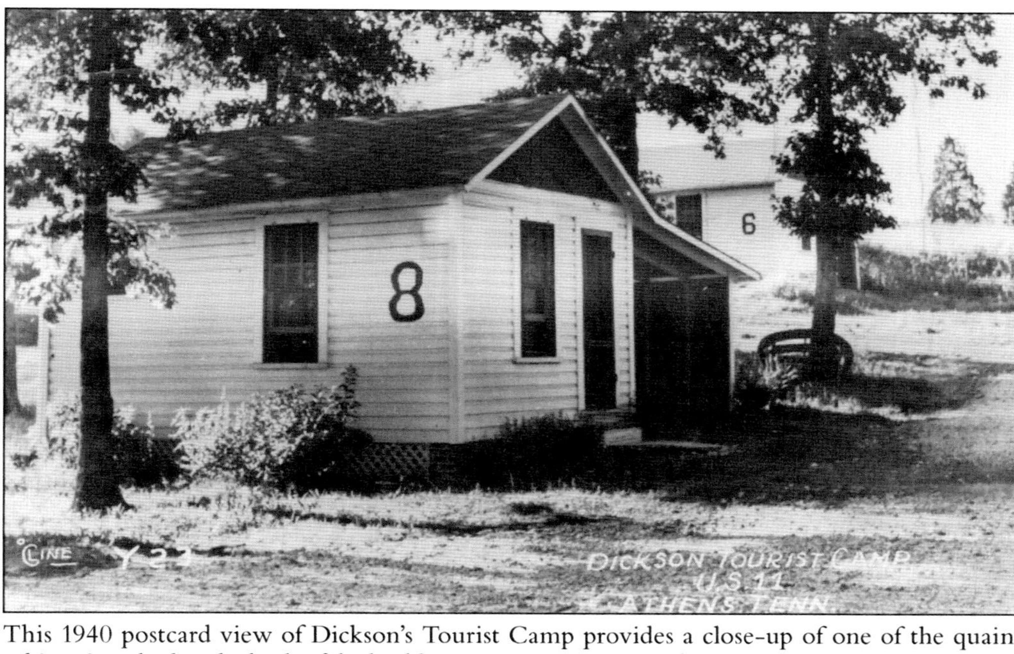


This 1940 postcard view of Dickson's Tourist Camp provides a close-up of one of the quaint cabins. Attached to the back of the building is a covered carport for customers' vehicles. The back message reads, "Here's the cabin we stayed in tonight at Athens. Some country. Saw Lookout Mountain today. To Knoxville Tuesday. Have driven 846 tonight. Tell Mother I'm OK."

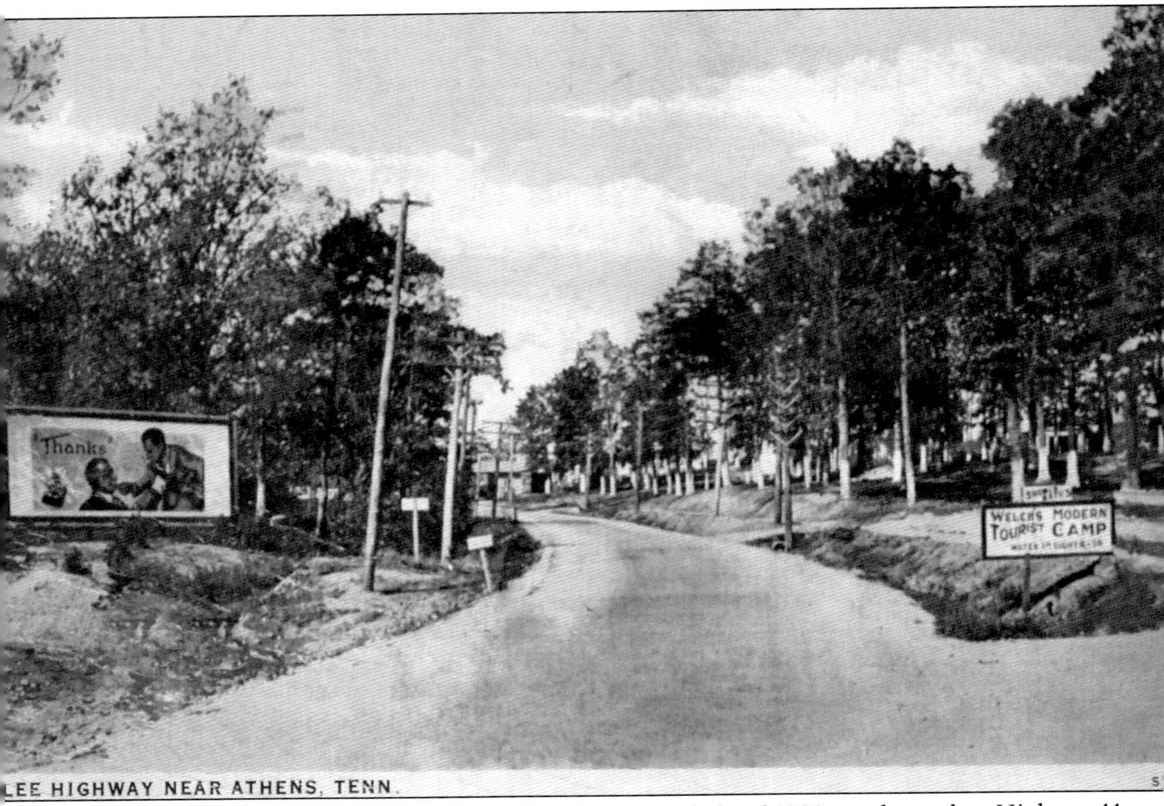


Welch's Modern Tourist Camp, featured in this postcard, dated 1929, was located on Highway 11 south of Athens. Its whitewashed trees were an immediate attention-getter for passing travelers. The postcard's message reads, "We came on the Lee Highway today. Staying in Athens tonight. Sun shown all day, getting warm now. Dad."

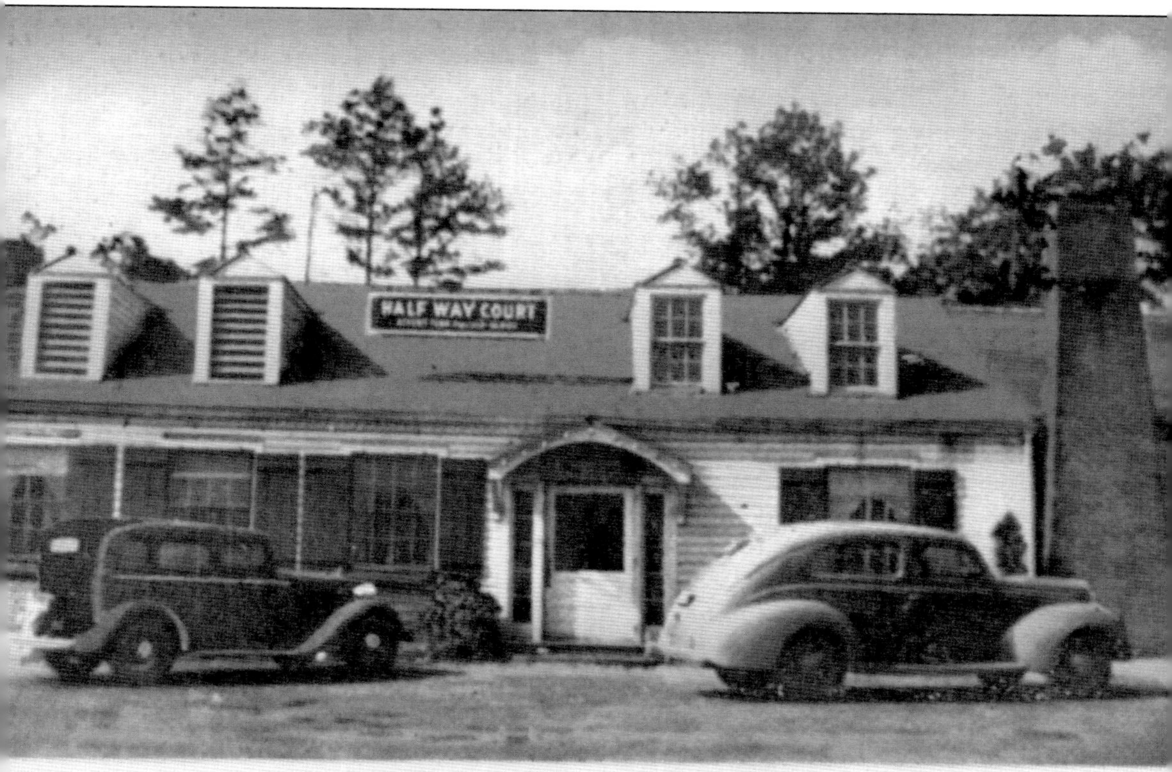


HALF WAY COURT, U. S. NO. 11, ATHENS, TENNESSEE

One of the better-known tourist camps in Athens was the Half Way Court. Located on Highway 11(Lee Highway) just north of Athens, a 1940s newspaper advertisement read, "Half Way Court is a modern tourist camp located just outside the city limits of Athens on the Lee Highway leading to Knoxville. This modern tourist court along with its roomy modern cabins is situated in a beautiful grove of trees and is a real beauty spot, this tourist camp, which is very popular, is patronized by tourists from far and near. It was formerly known as Irby's Park. This tourist camp is half-way between Knoxville and Chattanooga, and half-way between Miami and New York. It is owned by CL Williams and Edwin Foree." A portion of the main office still stands on Ingleside Avenue near Hiwassee Mental Health.

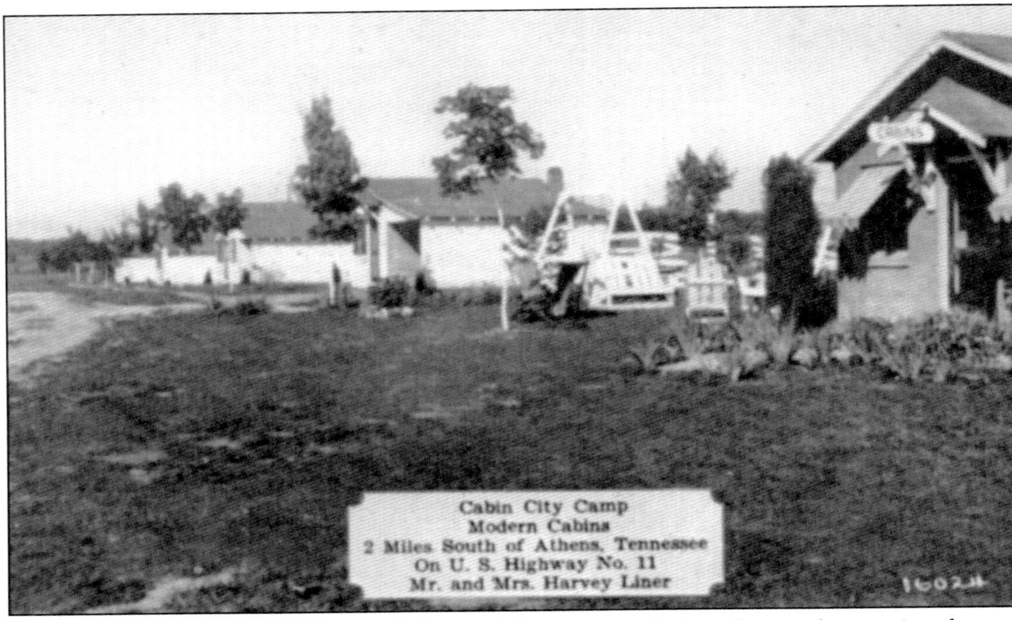


Cabin City Tourist Camp also provided overnight accommodations for travelers passing through McMinn County. Owned by Mr. and Mrs. Harvey Liner, Cabin City was 2 miles south of Athens on Highway 11. Harvey also owned the Dixie Café in downtown Athens, just down White Street from the jail.

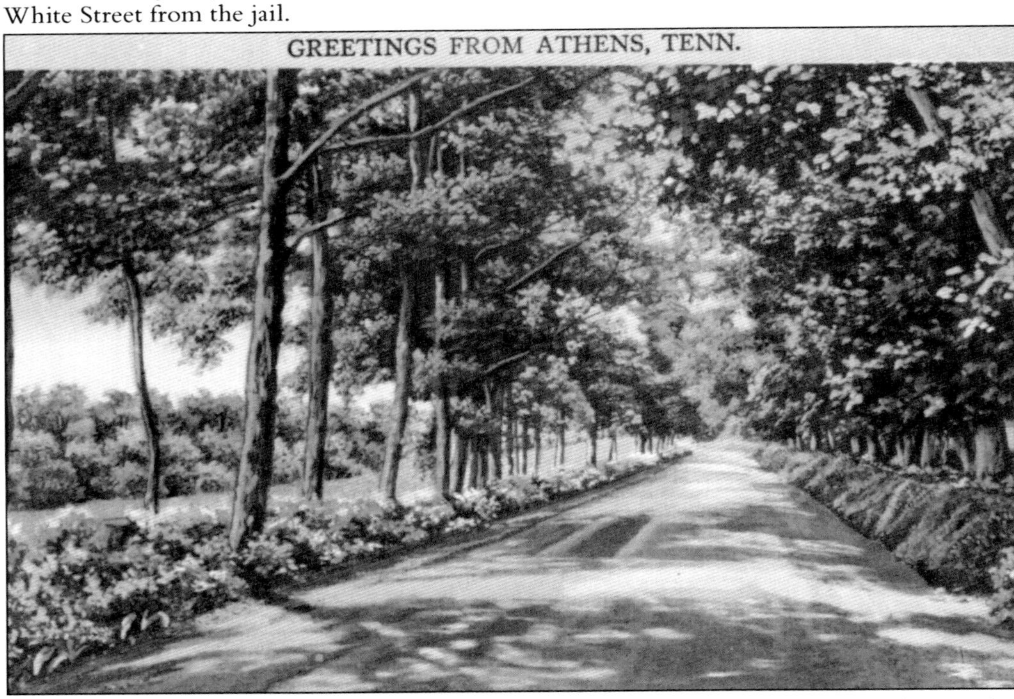


Athens has long promoted its image as the "Friendly City" and, along with that, has tried to maintain its identity as a growing city with rural, small-town values. Postcards such as this artwork may or may not have represented an actual scene in the Athens area but certainly promoted the ideal setting of a rural country lane. This card is dated 1953.

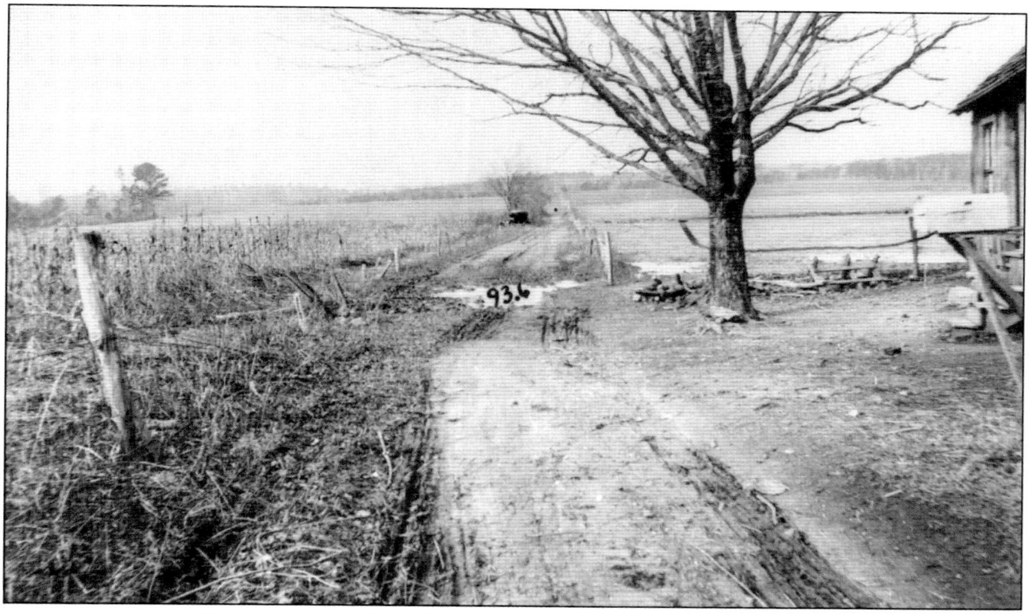


Actual county roads were more like what is shown in this old photograph. In the 1950s, only the main highways and city streets were paved, and few county roads had gravel. Some were simple dirt roads, like the one shown here, that turned into muddy lanes during the rainy winter months. On these roads, a horse and wagon were more reliable transportation than automobiles. (Courtesy McMinn County Historical Society.)

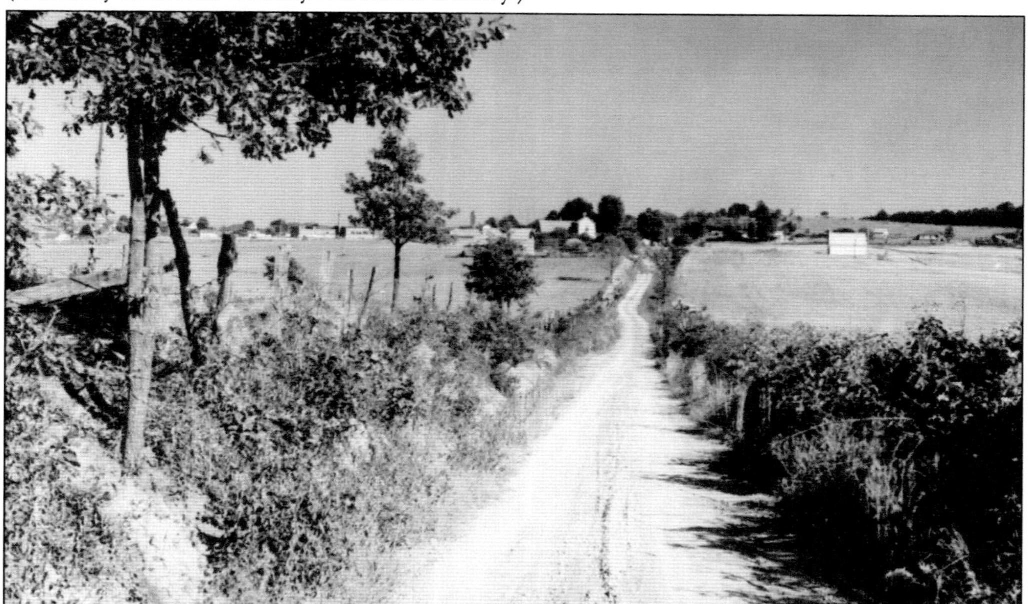

This photograph shows the Tom Edgmond farm on Lower Decatur Road around 1900, looking west. Today the road is Decatur Pike–State Highway 30 and in the distance is where four lanes of U.S. Highway 11 cross. The entire area began to be developed upon Highway 11's construction in the late 1940s and is today covered in fast food restaurants, shopping centers, and traffic. (Courtesy McMinn County Historical Society.)

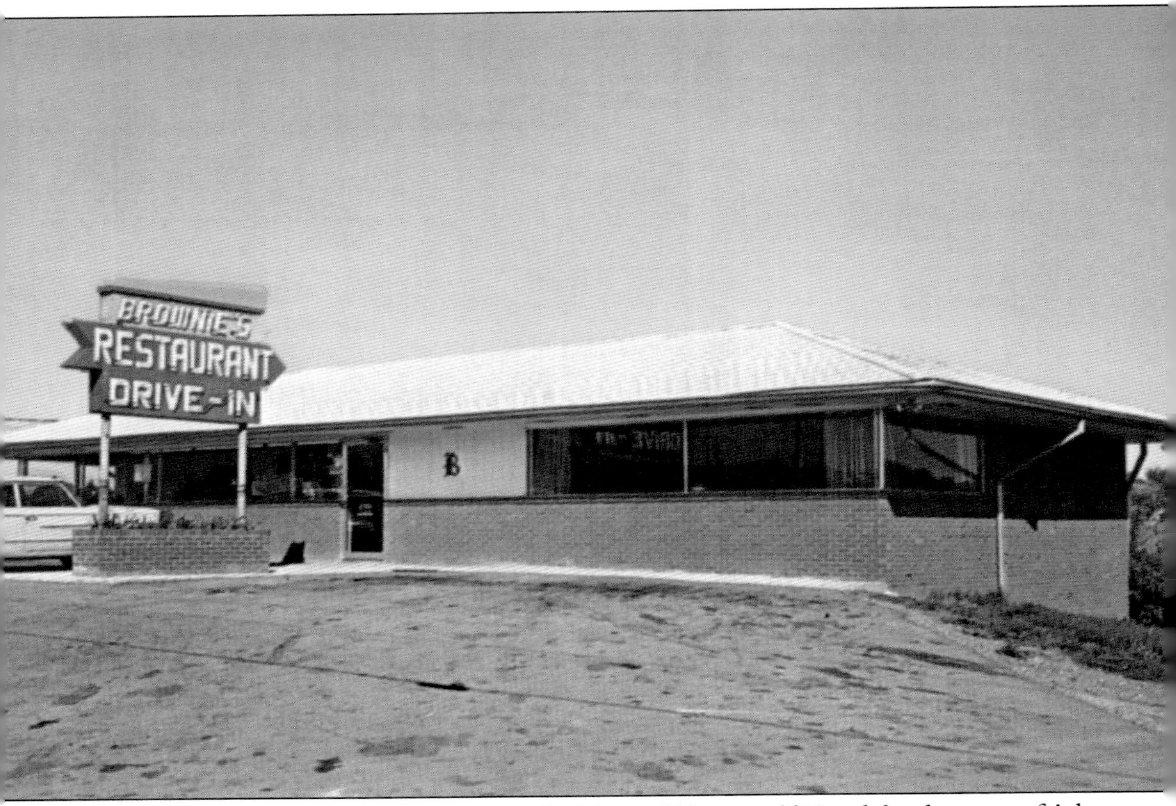


The construction of the Athens bypass of Highway 11 began additional development of Athens to the west. Many new businesses sprang up on the new road, and others relocated from the old downtown. One of the businesses to relocate in 1961 was Brownie's Restaurant, established downtown in 1947, and shown in this postcard from the mid-1960s. Brownie's continues to serve burgers, hotdogs, and plate lunches today in the same location.

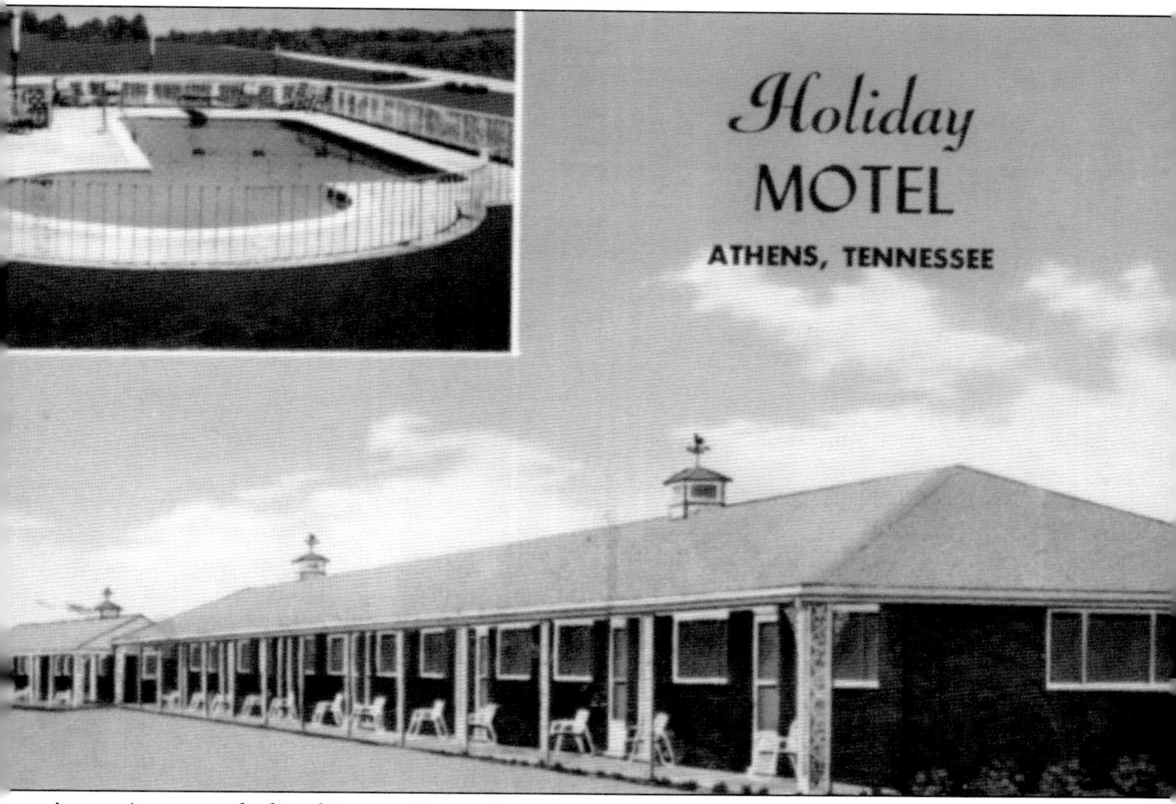

As tourist camps declined in use, the modern motel began developing along the Athens bypass. This 1963 postcard shows the Holiday Motel, located on a hill overlooking the highway near the intersection with Velma Road. This motel offered connecting rooms for larger families, as well as a refreshing swimming pool.

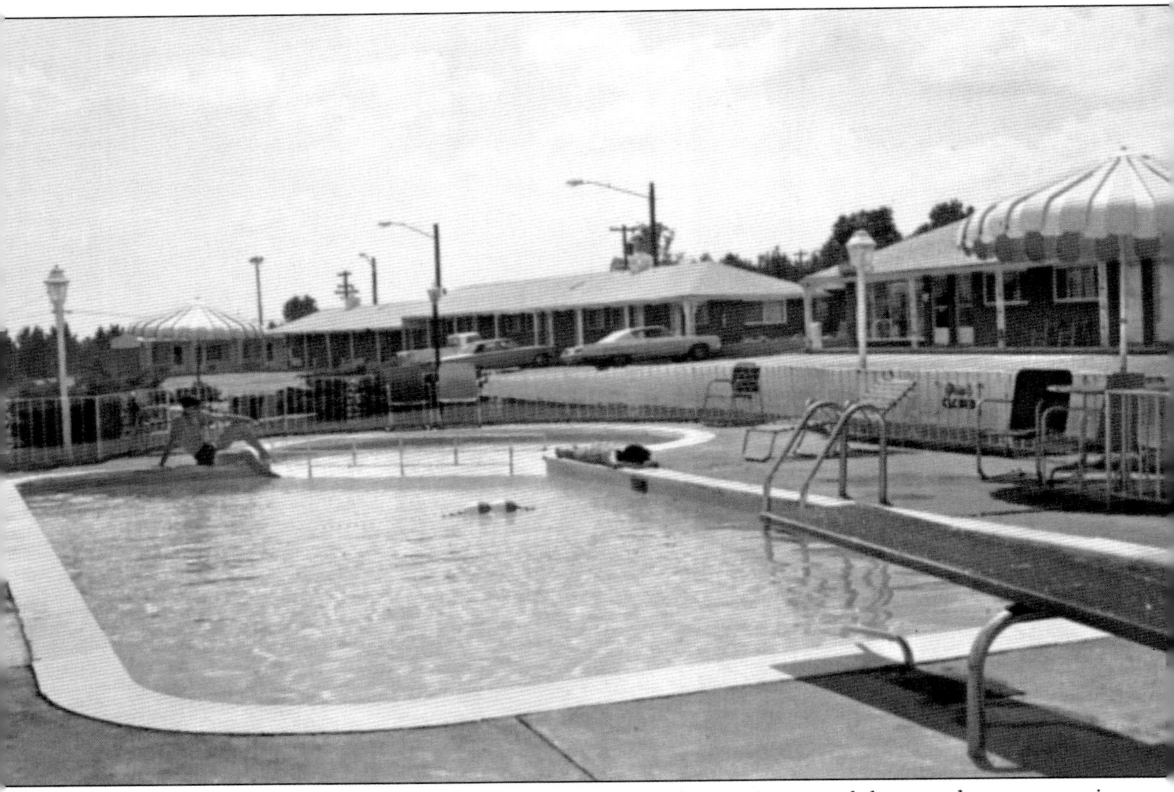

The close-up of the Holiday Motel swimming pool in this 1972 postcard shows only two attractive sunbathers lounging around the pool, seemingly enjoying the pool as if it were their own. Actually, the motel pool would often be filled with splashing children and less-than-attractive bathers. This advertising technique of implied "privacy" is still in use today.

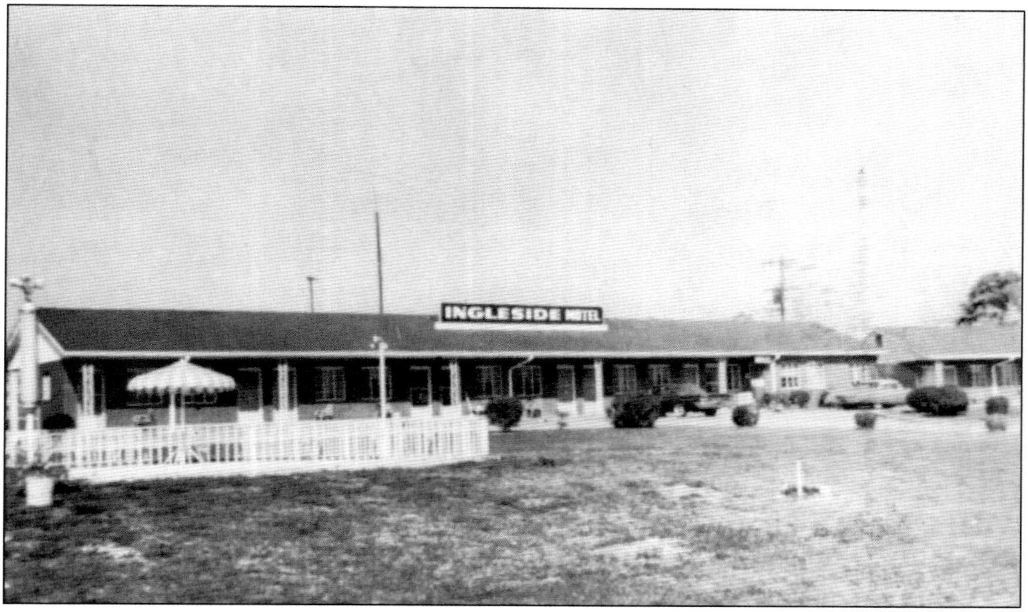


Ingleside Motel, featured in this postcard photograph from around 1960, is located on the Athens bypass north of the Highway 30 intersection. Similar to the Holiday Motel, Ingleside provided single-level rooms with parking outside, as well as a gated swimming pool. Later a second-story addition was added on one of the wings. The motel now serves as low-rent apartments.

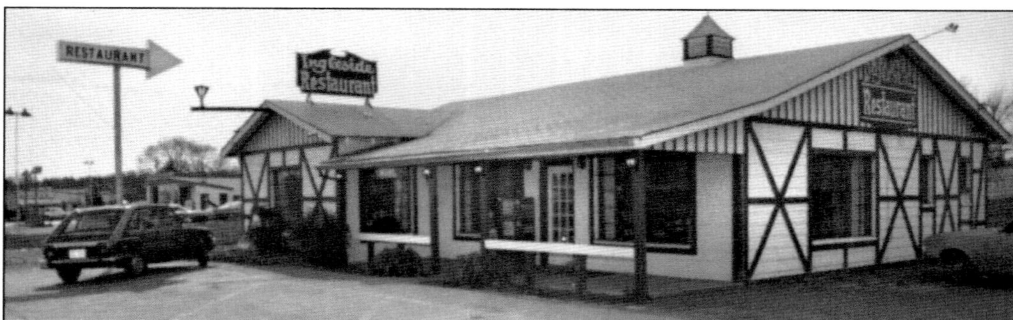


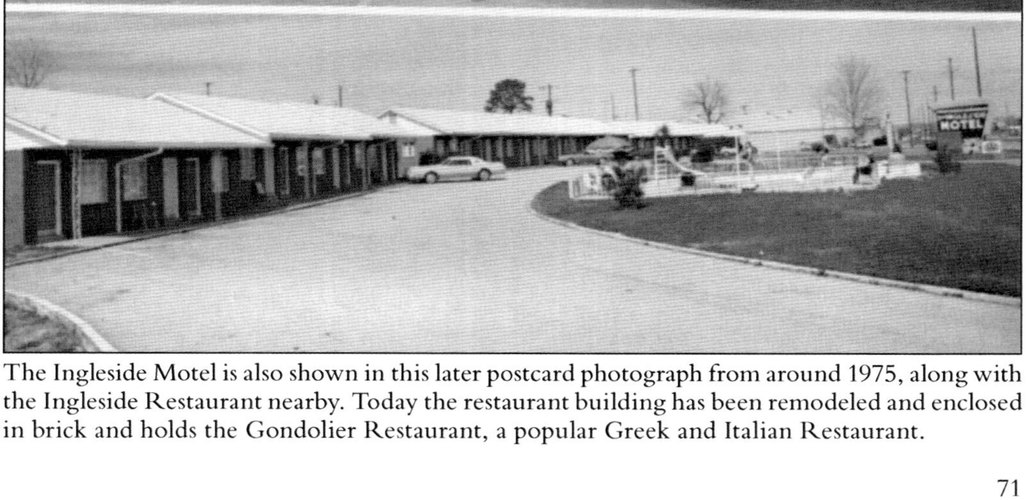


The Ingleside Motel is also shown in this later postcard photograph from around 1975, along with the Ingleside Restaurant nearby. Today the restaurant building has been remodeled and enclosed in brick and holds the Gondolier Restaurant, a popular Greek and Italian Restaurant.

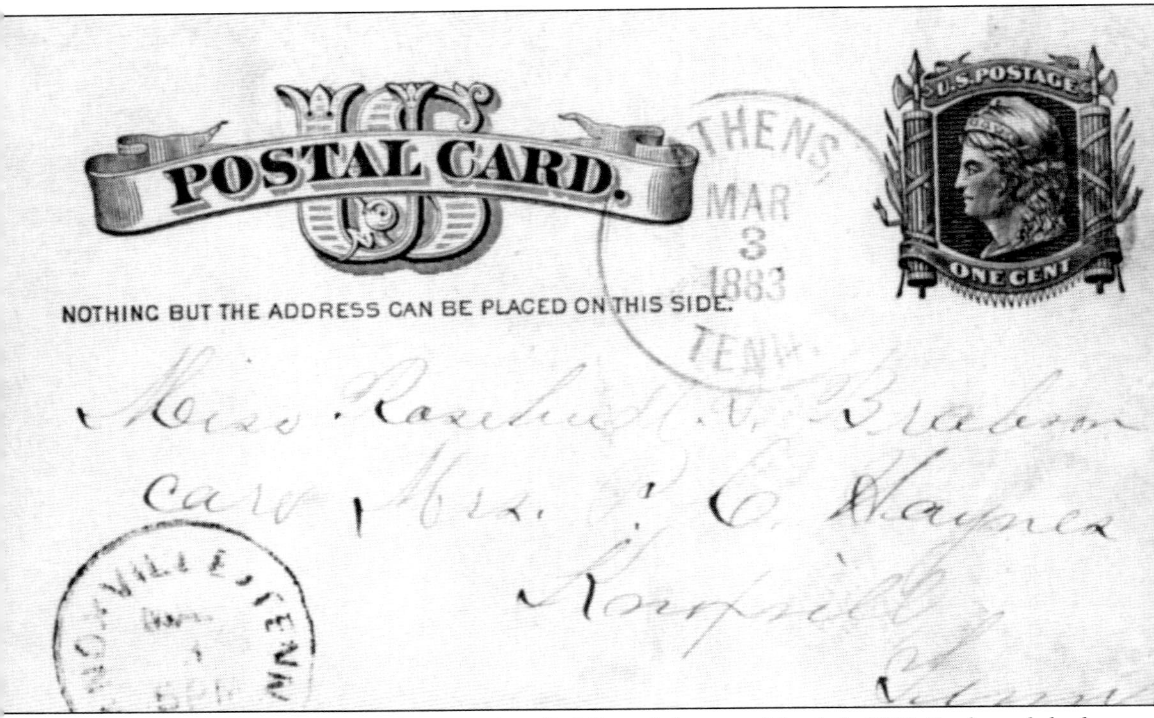


Here is an example of an old postcard mailed from Athens on March 3, 1883. Such cards had no photograph and were simply for the purpose of correspondence. This card was sent to Rosebud Brabson in Knoxville, and the message, though written in small script, takes up the entire side of the card, with the writer even scribbling in the margins. The hurried message refers to sickness sweeping through a family and states, "The hands have all gone to the woods to fight the fire that is almost near our kitchen." It is part of the Don Reid collection.

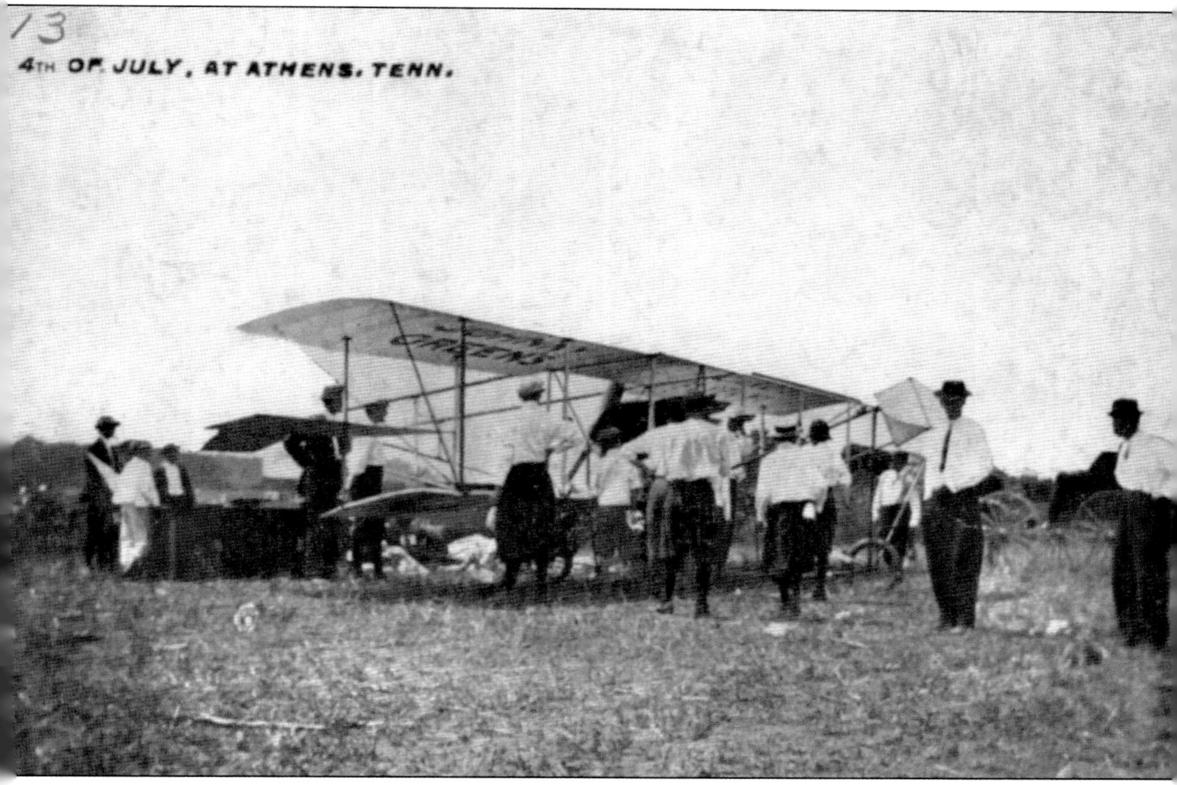


A crowd takes a closer look at Johnny Green's stunt bi-plane at the old grass-covered McMinn County Airfield in this postcard dated 1913. Green was possibly performing as part of the county's Fourth of July celebration that year. The aircraft appears similar to the Wright Brothers airplane that flew at Kitty Hawk less than a decade before. McMinn County has had a long involvement in aviation since the operation of this first airfield.

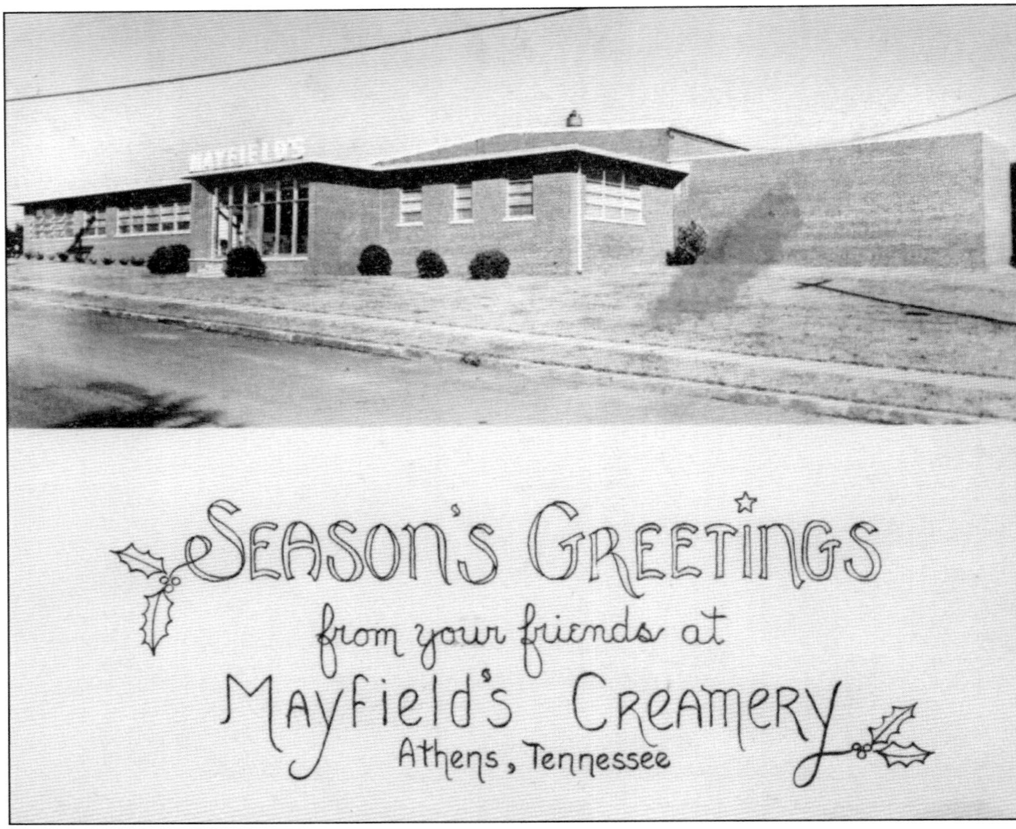


One cannot record the history of McMinn County and Athens without a mention of Mayfield Dairy. What began as a small, family-owned dairy operation in 1910 is now a multimillion dollar operation and division of Dean Foods Corporation. In this Christmas card from the late 1950s, the Mayfield plant is pictured at its Madison Avenue location, which went into operation in 1954. The original Mayfield's Farm is located a few miles north, and the first milk and ice-cream production plants were located near downtown on Green Street.

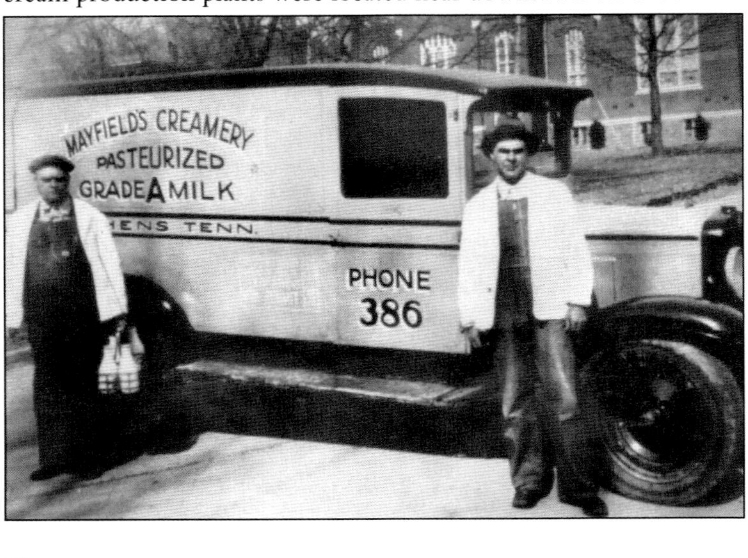


Mayfield's revolutionized the dairy industry in the South by being the first to use refrigerated delivery to homes and businesses. These two milkmen are shown during route delivery on White Street in Athens around 1939. Trinity Methodist Church is in the background. (Courtesy McMinn County Historical Society.)

## *Three*

# Tennessee Wesleyan College

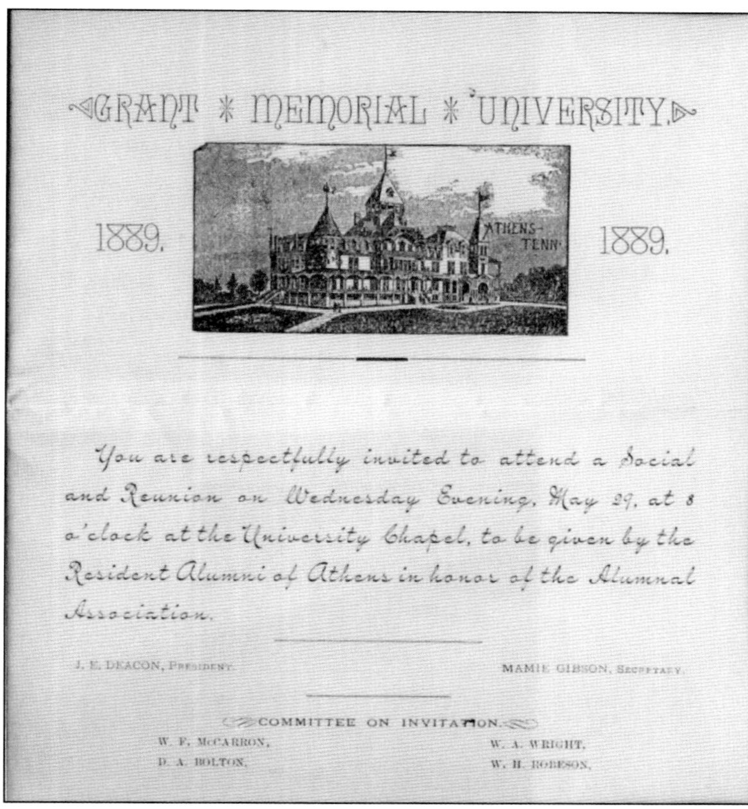

GRANT * MEMORIAL * UNIVERSITY.

1889. ATHENS-TENN. 1889.

You are respectfully invited to attend a Social and Reunion on Wednesday Evening, May 29, at 8 o'clock at the University Chapel, to be given by the Resident Alumni of Athens in honor of the Alumnal Association.

J. E. DEACON, President. MAMIE GIBSON, Secretary.

COMMITTEE ON INVITATION.

W. F. McCARRON, W. A. WRIGHT,
D. A. BOLTON, W. H. ROBESON,

Known throughout the years as Athens Female College, Athens School, East Tennessee Wesleyan University, Grant University, Athens Department of the University of Chattanooga, and now Tennessee Wesleyan College, this invitational card invites the recipient to attend the 1889 School Alumni Social and Reunion at the chapel of Grant University. The card bears dark edges with the appearance of having survived a fire.

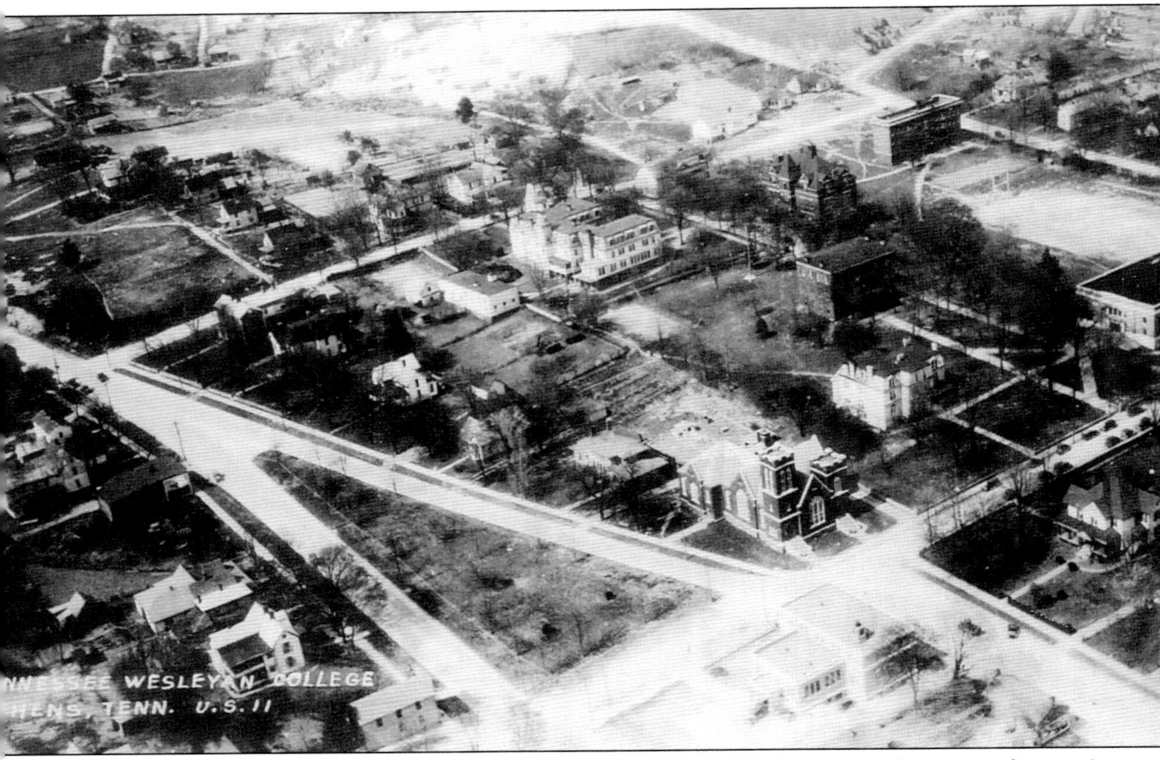


Here is an aerial view of Tennessee Wesleyan College from around 1940. The triangular portion of grounds is present-day Knight Park, where the town's first jail once stood. On the near corner of the campus is Trinity Methodist Church, with Ritter Residence Hall and the auditorium/gymnasium across the quad. Behind the gym, the goal posts of the old football field are visible on Green Street. At the back of the quad, at right center, is Old College, the original campus building constructed in 1857. In the center is Fowler Residence Hall, and just to the right is the distinctive spire of Banfield Hall.

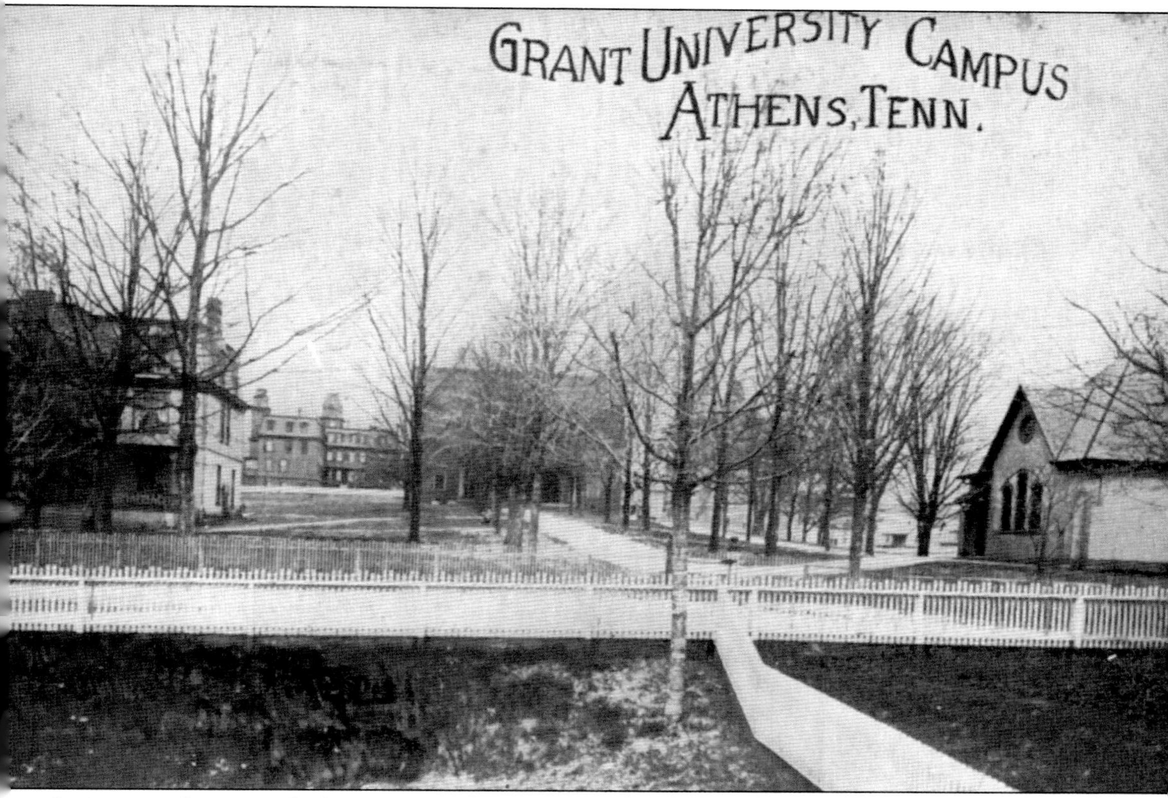


A photograph postcard of Grant University from the beginning of the 20th century shows the main campus area, with Old College at center behind the trees, Frazier Hall to the left, and the old chapel to the right. The picket fence runs along College Street.

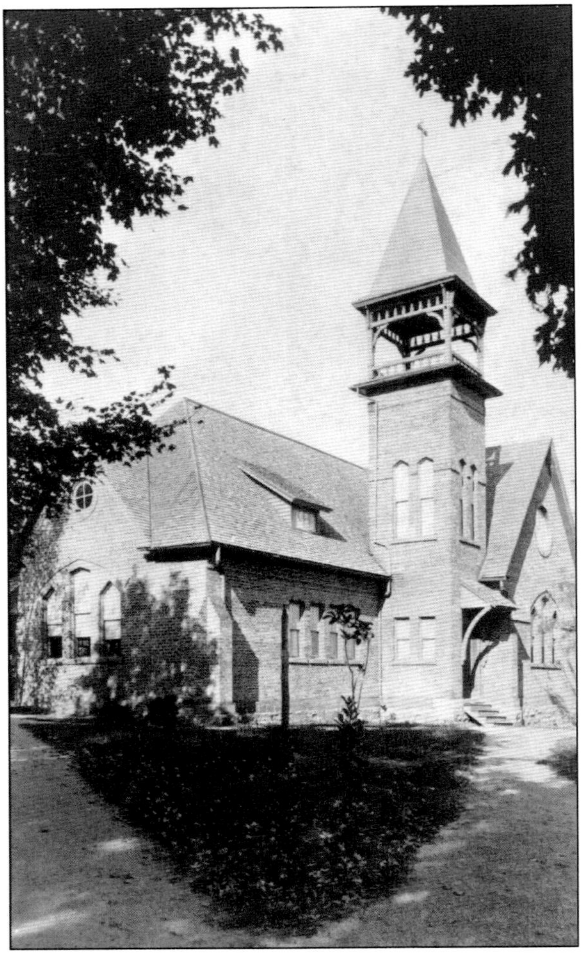

The college chapel is shown here prior to its removal and the construction of the new gymnasium. (Courtesy McMinn County Historical Society.)

Below, in this view of the college in 1921, the campus is covered in a winter snowfall. Ritter Hall is at left, and the chapel is at right, just a few years before its removal for the new auditorium/gymnasium in 1924. (Courtesy McMinn County Historical Society.)

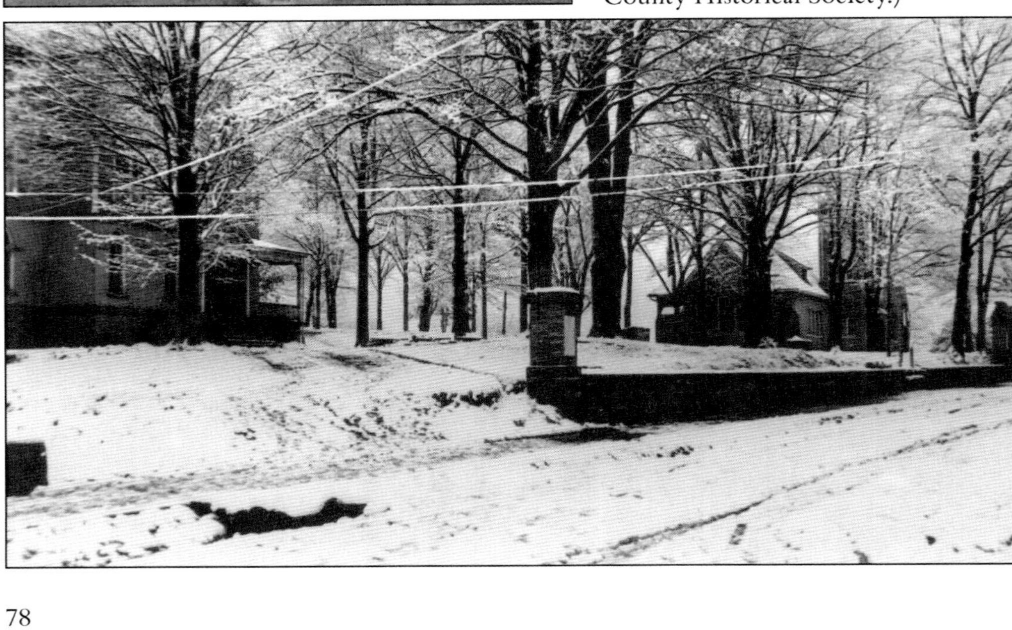

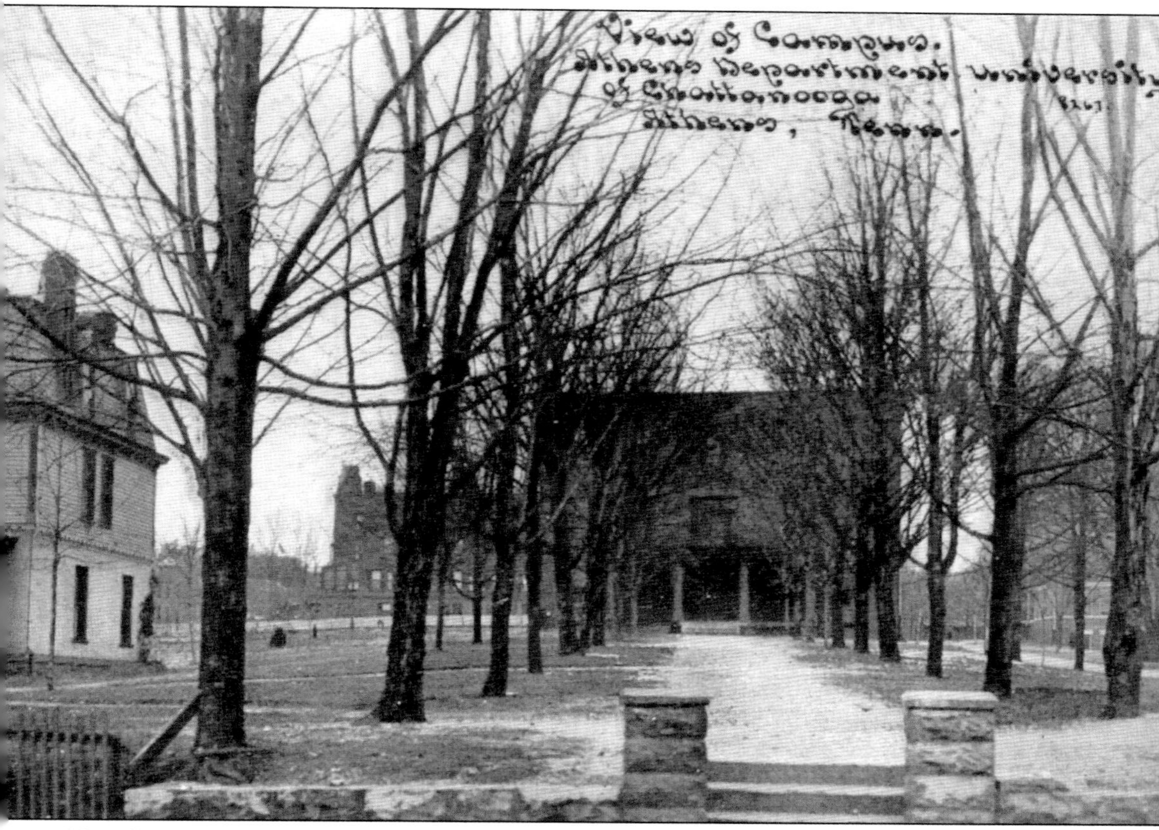


Old College sits in the center of this 1912 postcard of the Athens Department of the University of Chattanooga, with Frazier Hall to the left. Ritter Hall is seen in the distant rear, and Banfield Hall is barely visible behind the trees to the right. The stone columns marked the main campus entrance.

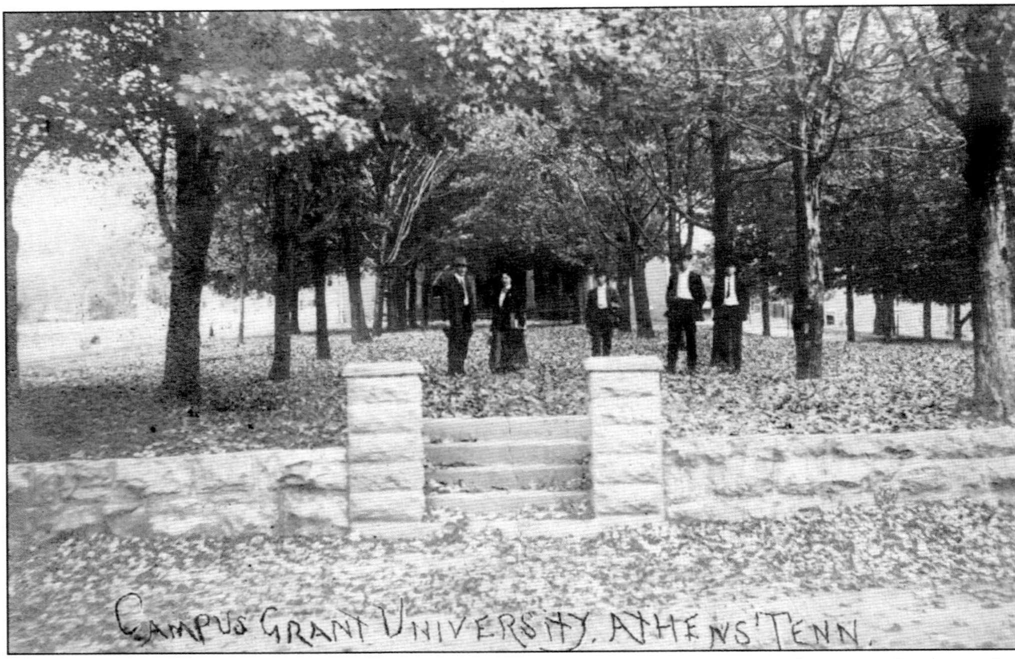


This 1927 postcard shows the main entrance to the Grant University Campus during what appears to be the fall term. A group of students poses on the quad.

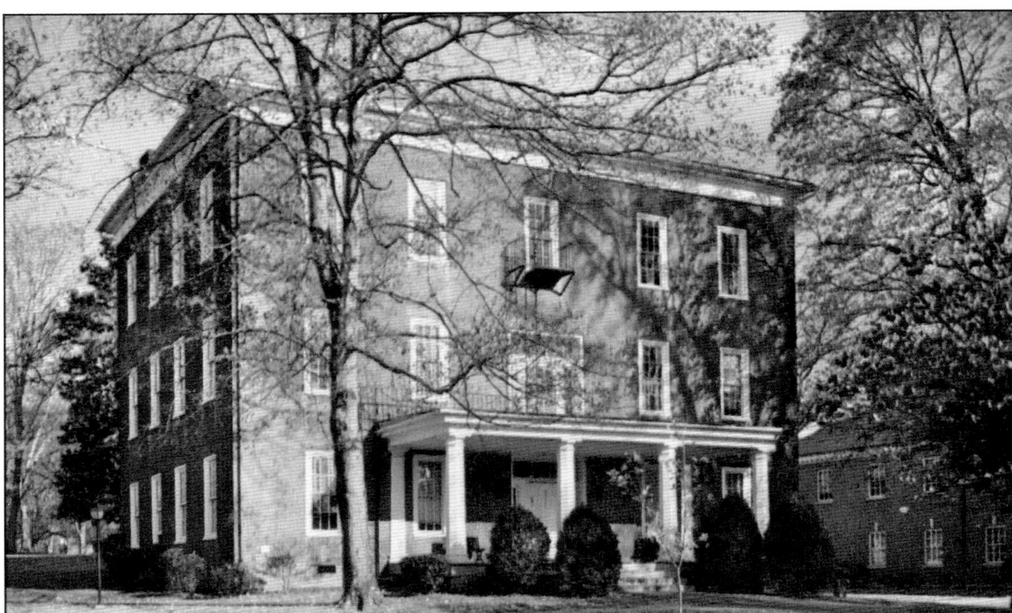

A more contemporary view of Old College is shown in this postcard. The building remains virtually unchanged since its construction in 1857. It once held administrative offices as well as classrooms and the library. During the Civil War, it was one of several locations in Athens used as a hospital for sick and invalid soldiers, both Union and Confederate. Today the picturesque building houses administrative offices.

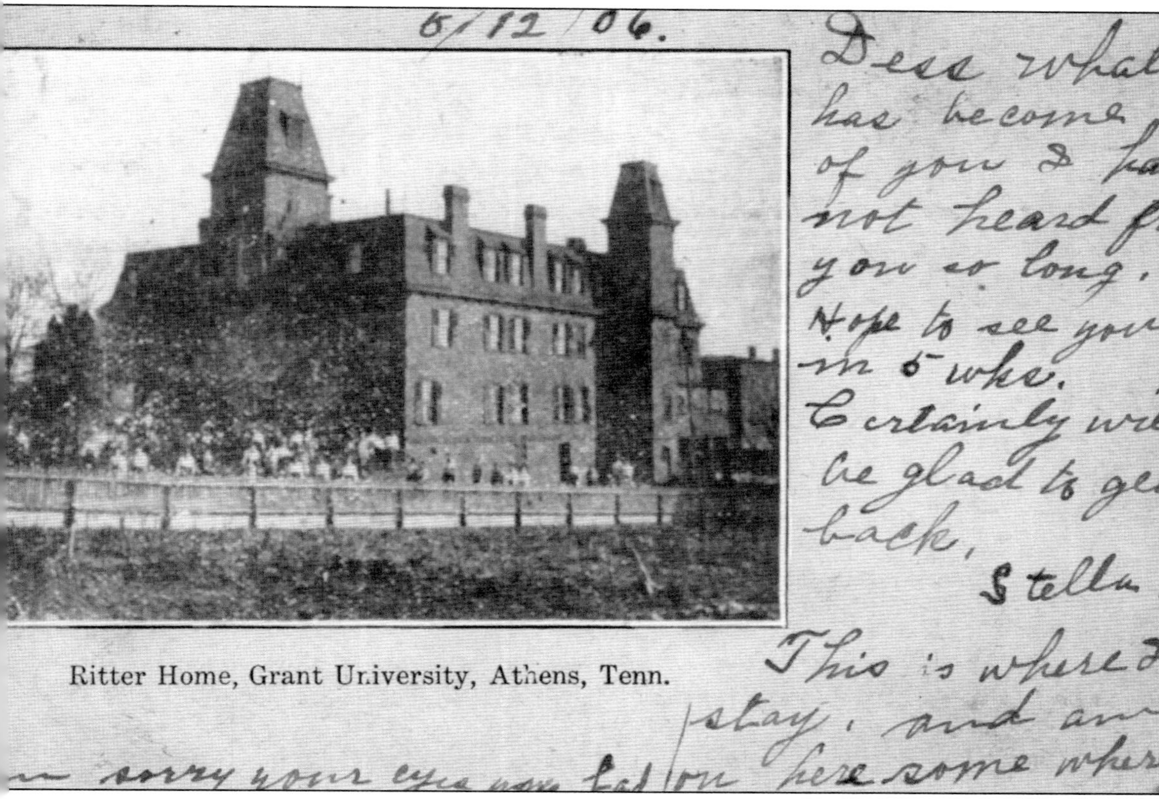


Ritter Home at Grant University provided dormitory housing for female students attending the school. The student who sent this May 1906 postcard near the end of the school term indicates she is in the picture. The message reads, "Dess, what has become of you I have not heard from you so long. Hope to see you in 5 wks. Certainly will be glad to get back. Stella. This is where I stay. And am on here somewhere."

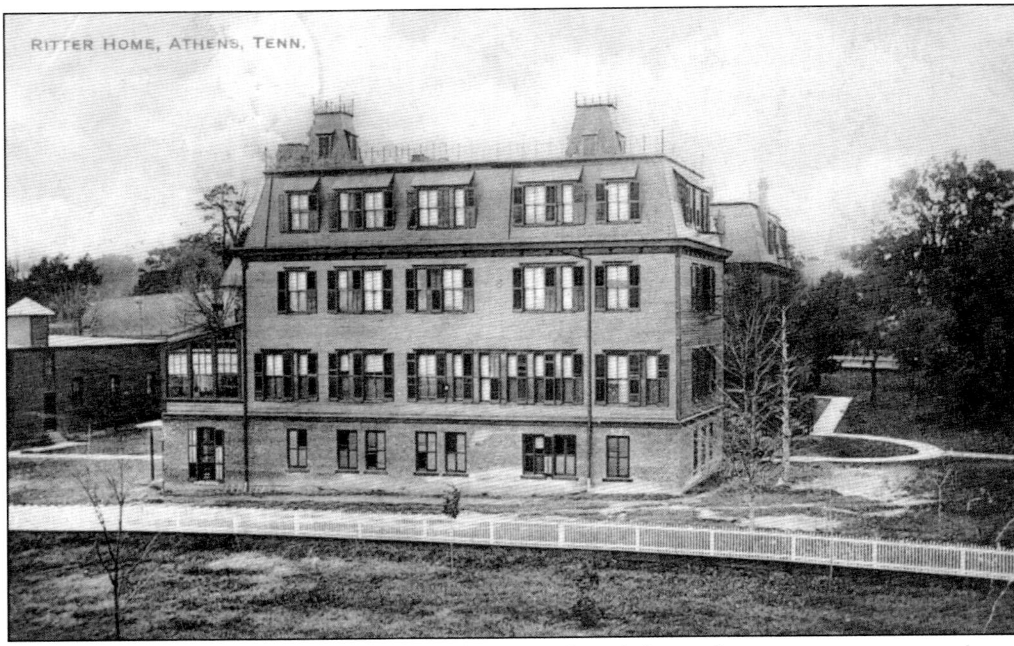


This 1909 postcard shows Ritter Hall looking north and shows the neat campus grounds and sidewalks. Ritter had its own dining hall, which was another benefit to its female residents.

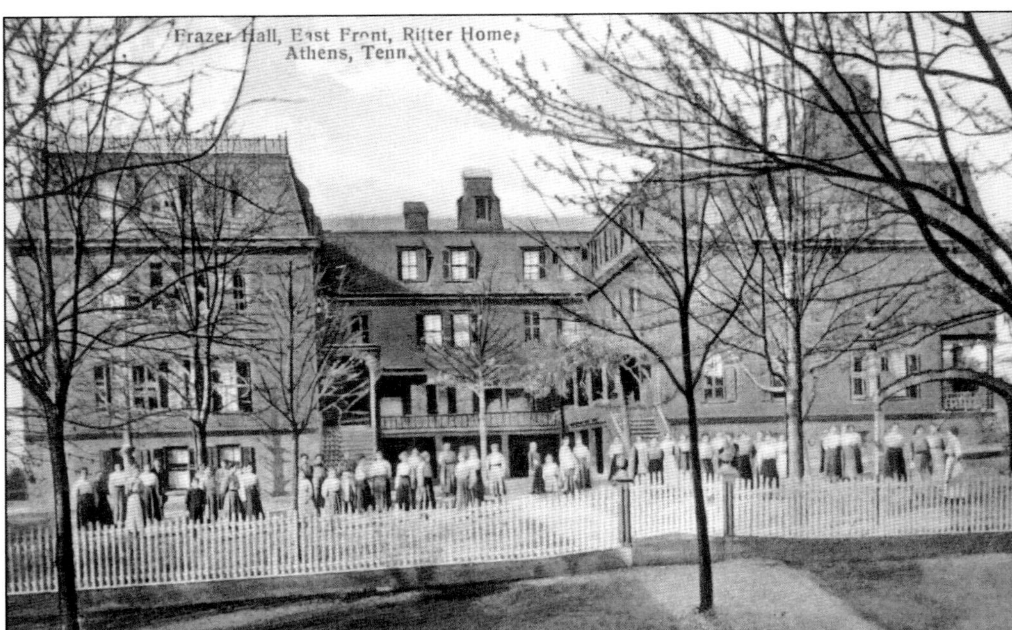


A 1910 postcard shows the open courtyard of Ritter as it faced west, with many of its female residents out front. With the construction of newer brick residence halls, Ritter was torn down, and the site is now a parking lot.

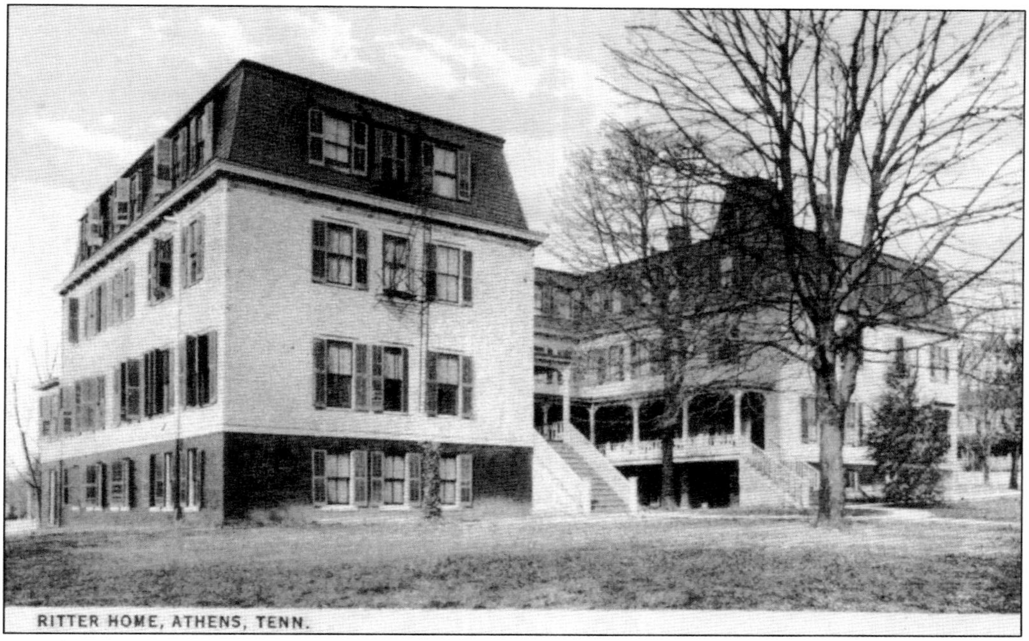


Another view of Ritter Hall shows the two wings enclosing a courtyard between two staircases. The initial purpose of Ritter was to train young women in the "domestic economy" of sewing, cooking, and marketing their own products. The building initially held about 50 students. Many older alumni recall fond memories of their time living in Ritter, which was demolished in 1968.

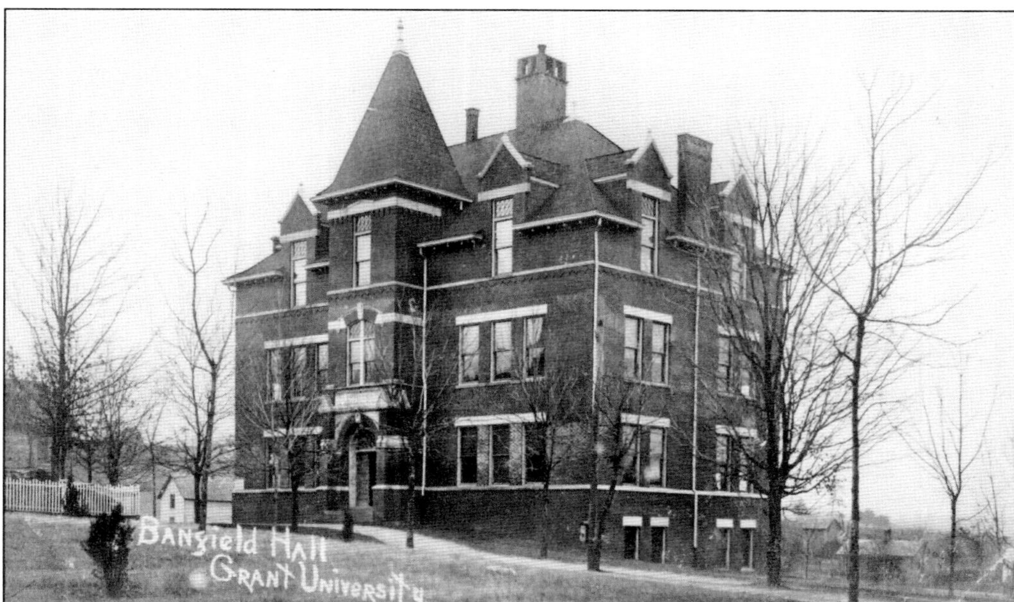


A close-up picture of Banfield Hall is shown with a view to the northeast. Built in 1902, the building was funded largely by a donation by Pennsylvania industrialist William Banfield in memory of his deceased son. It initially provided science classes and laboratories on the lower floors and held the library on the top floor.

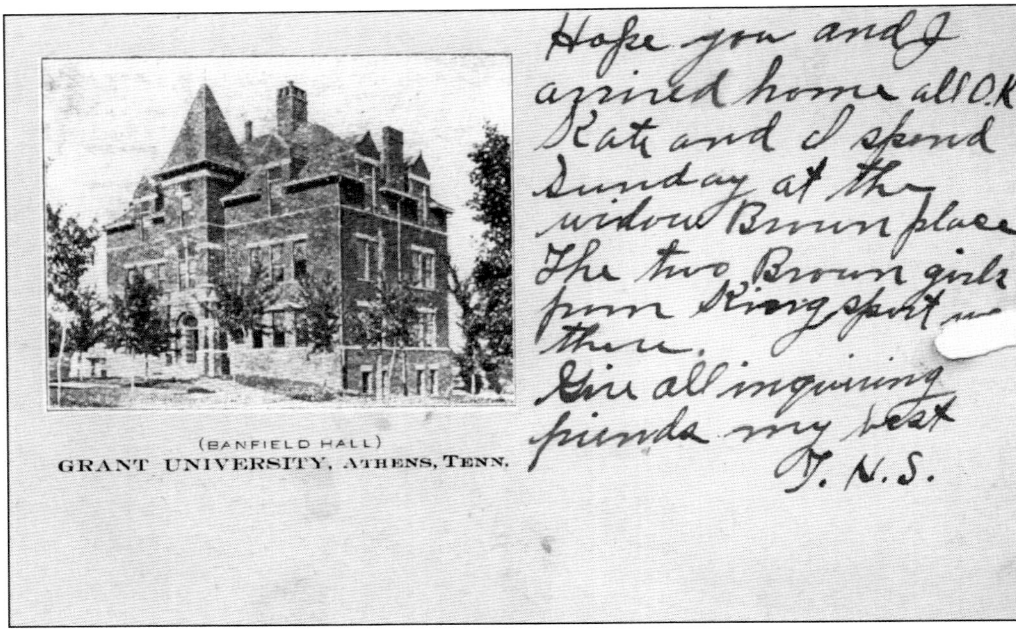


This 1906 postcard features a small picture of Banfield Hall when the school was known as Grant University. It was remodeled in 1968 and renamed Durham Hall.

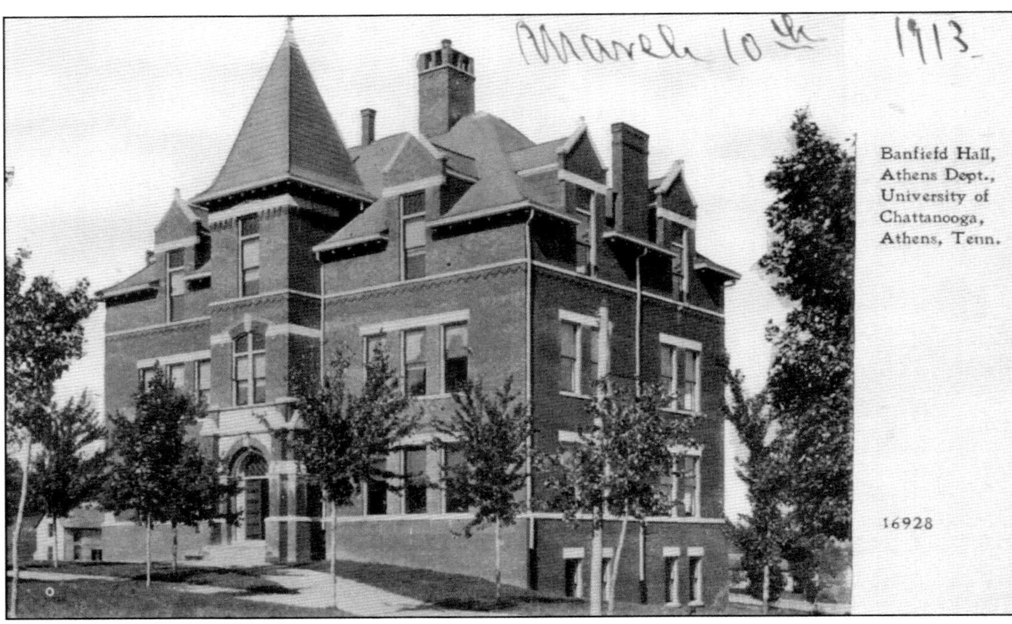


This postcard, sent on March 10, 1913, is another view of Banfield, then part of the Athens Department of the University of Chattanooga.

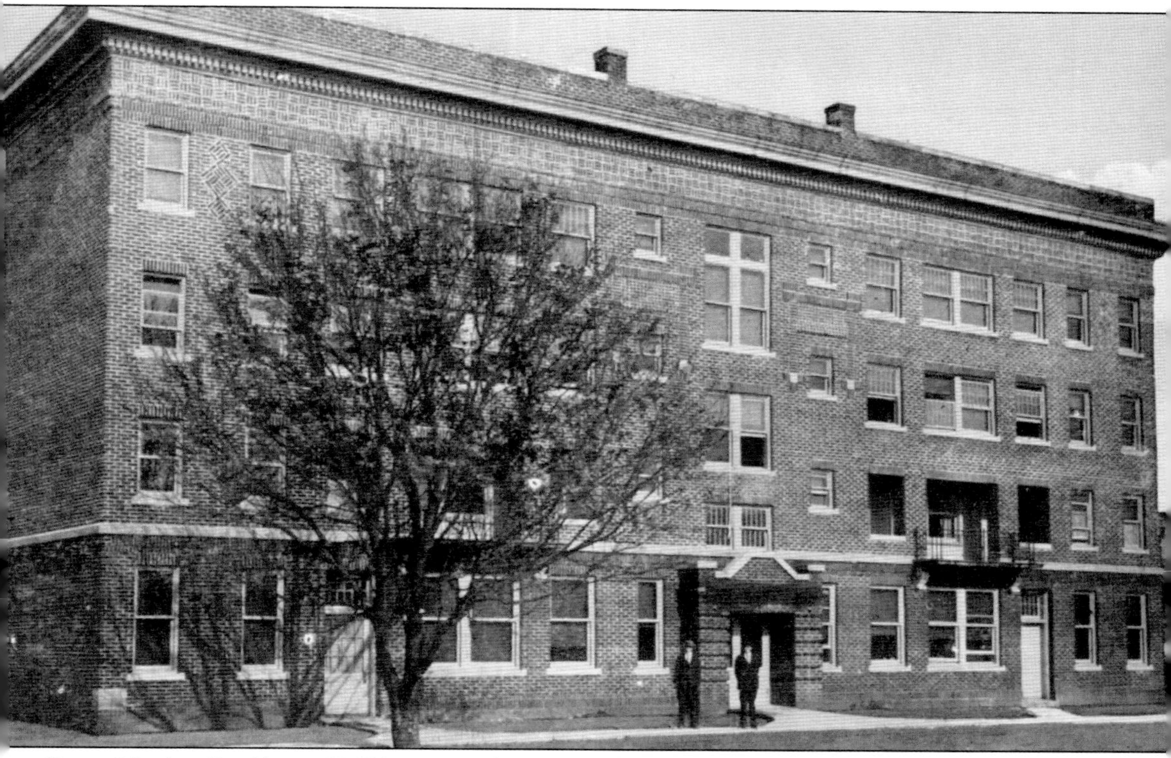

Petty-Manker Residence Hall is seen in this postcard, dated 1931. Built in 1913, it was located on the north end of campus along Green Street, but after falling into disrepair, it was torn down for a parking lot. The card's message seems to relate a Michiganer's encounter with one of McMinn County's finer products: "Dear Francis: Held up in this burg for one hour for my brakes, crossing main street, cops and everybody running, I start to, find young kid with 15 gals of Moon in a Chevrolet Roadster, yum yum."

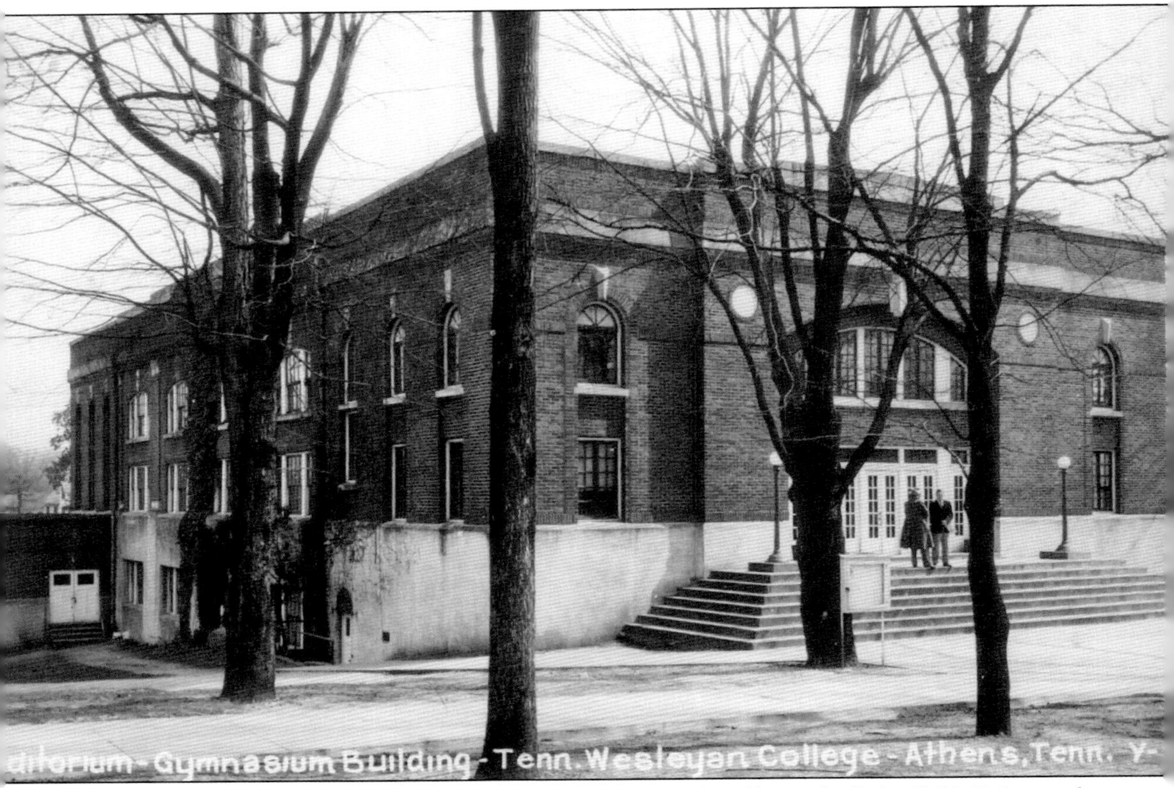


The auditorium/gymnasium, later known as Townsend Hall, was built in 1924. It is seen here in a postcard from 1937. Concerts, recitals, classes, and student body gatherings were held here, along with basketball and other sporting events in the basement gymnasium.

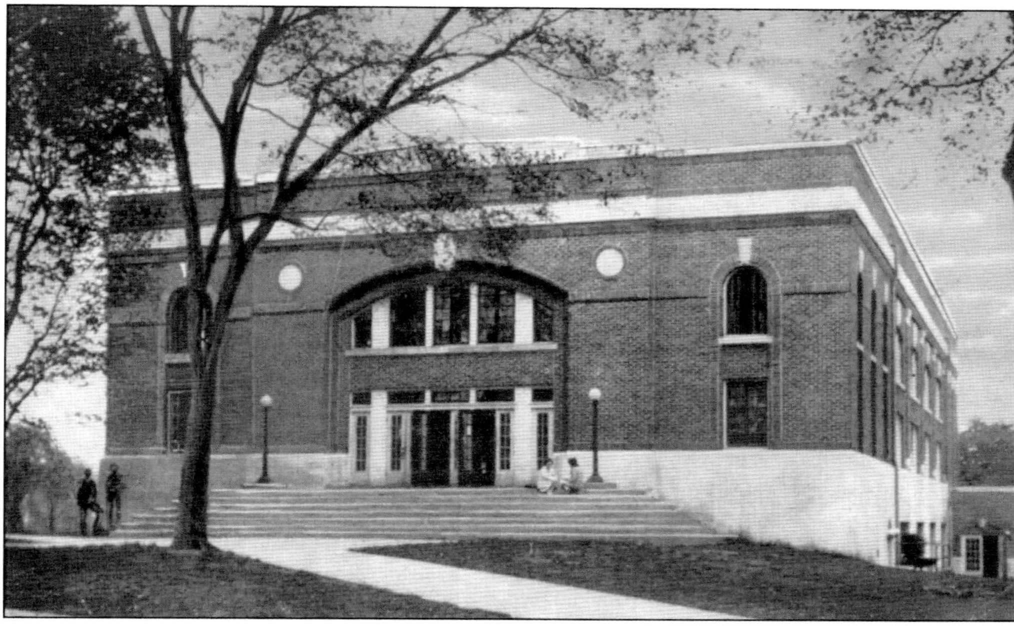

Another view of Townsend Hall is seen here. The building still serves as the college auditorium.

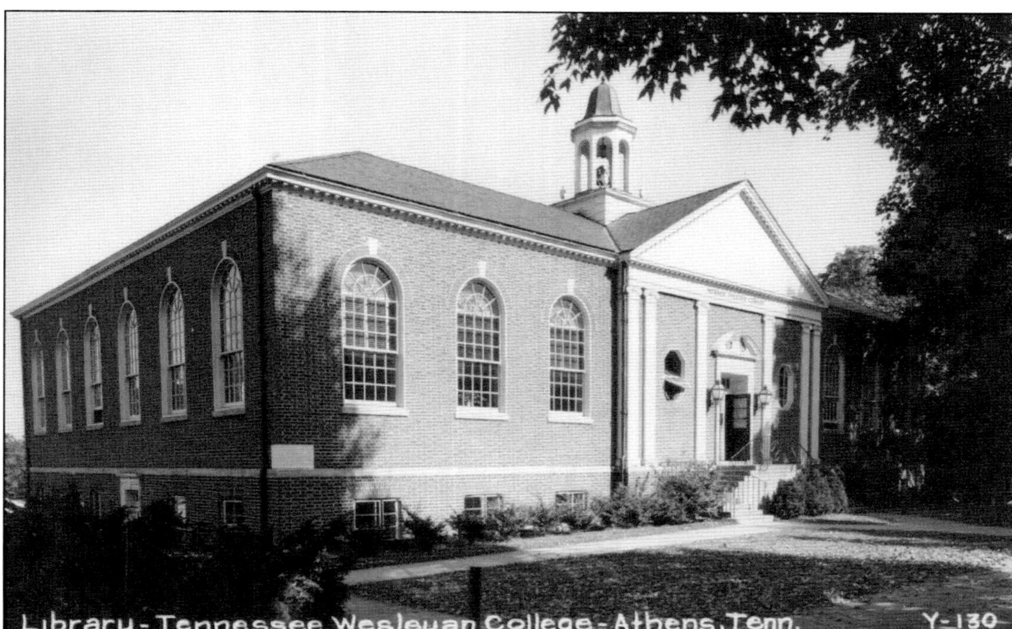


The Tennessee Wesleyan College Library, seen in this postcard, was built in 1941 with contributions from Annie Merner Pfiefer of New York. The new library provided a much-needed building dedicated entirely as a library and relieved the cramped space of Banfield Hall. The building sits near Banfield Hall and is still in use.

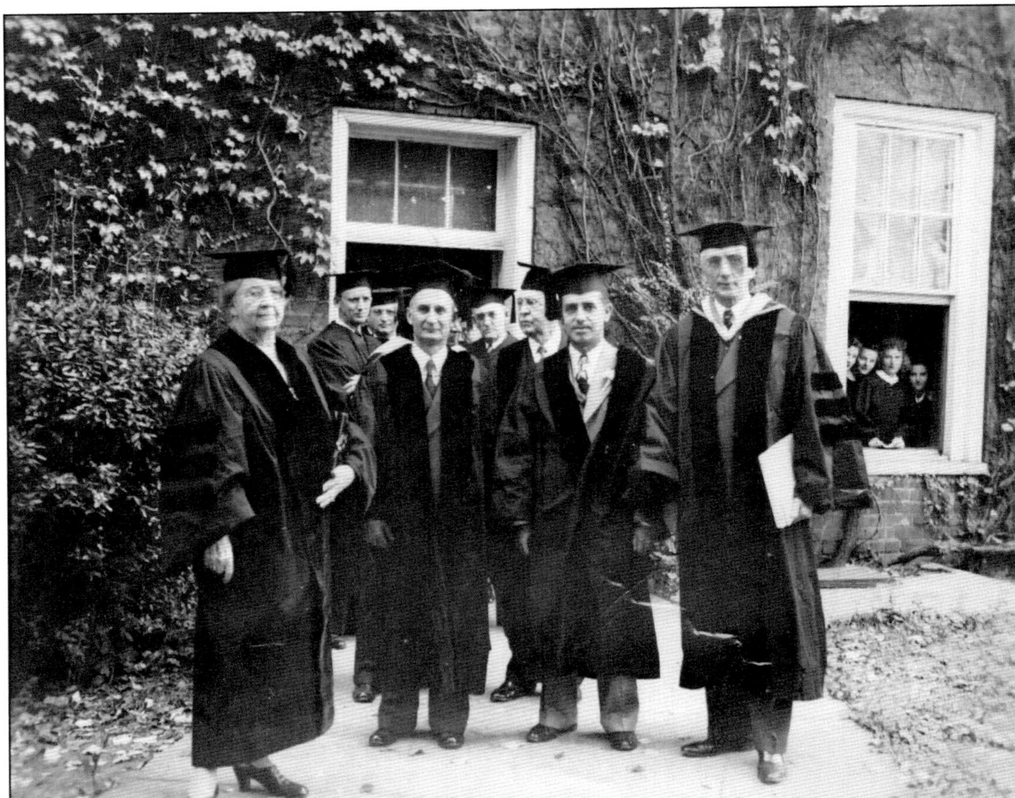

This photograph shows the dedication of Merner-Pfeifer Library. From left to right are Annie Merner Pfeifer, Bishop Paul Hern, Gov. Prentice Cooper, and TWC president James L. Robb.

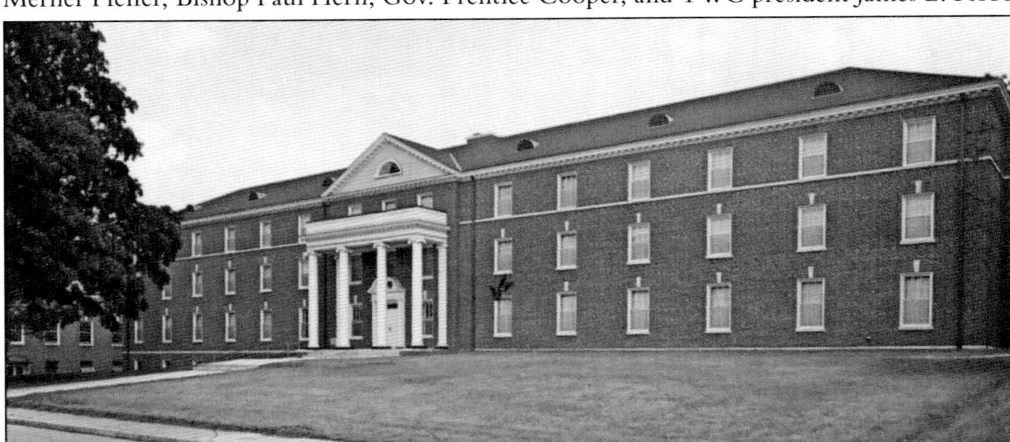

Lucy Hornsby Fowler Hall, built in 1961 to replace Ritter Hall, sits along Green Street and remains a residence hall at Tennessee Wesleyan College. The student who sent this postcard in 1964 indicated the location of her dorm room as well as her impression of dorm life: "Here's the prison. The arrow is pointing to my cell." She also admits to some rule breaking: "We aren't allowed to have pets in the dorm, but sometimes we sneak a little dog in with us. We feed him the food from the cafeteria since we can't eat it."

# *Four*

# Englewood and Etowah

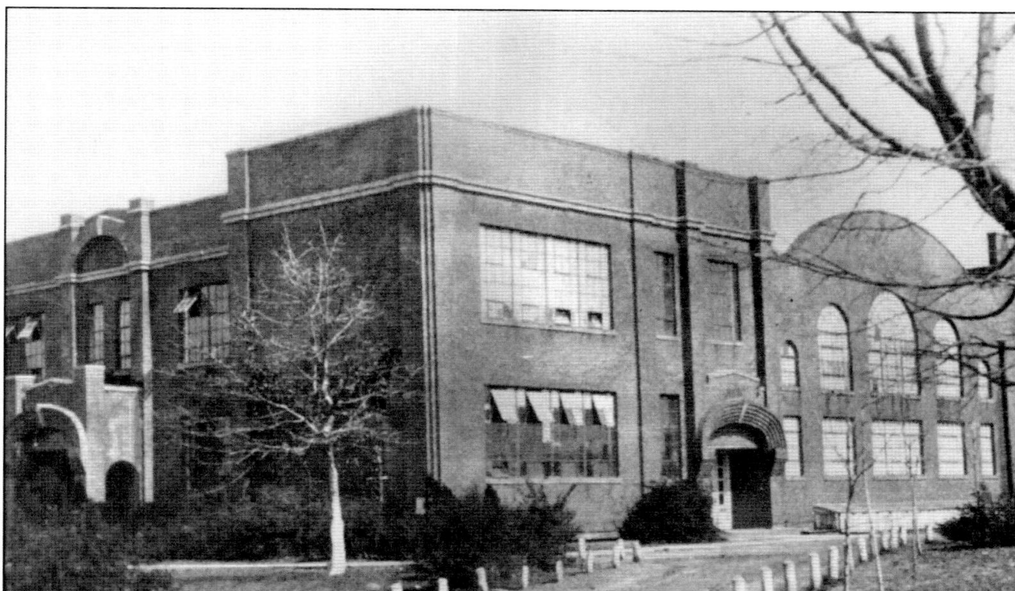

Englewood School has occupied the same location on College Street since 1906, when it was moved from a location on the west side of the railroad tracks across from First Baptist Church. The brick building shown here was constructed in 1925 to replace a wood-frame building that burned the year before. This building housed grades 1 through 12 and was used until it was destroyed by fire on December 23, 1965. A new elementary school was built here in 1966.

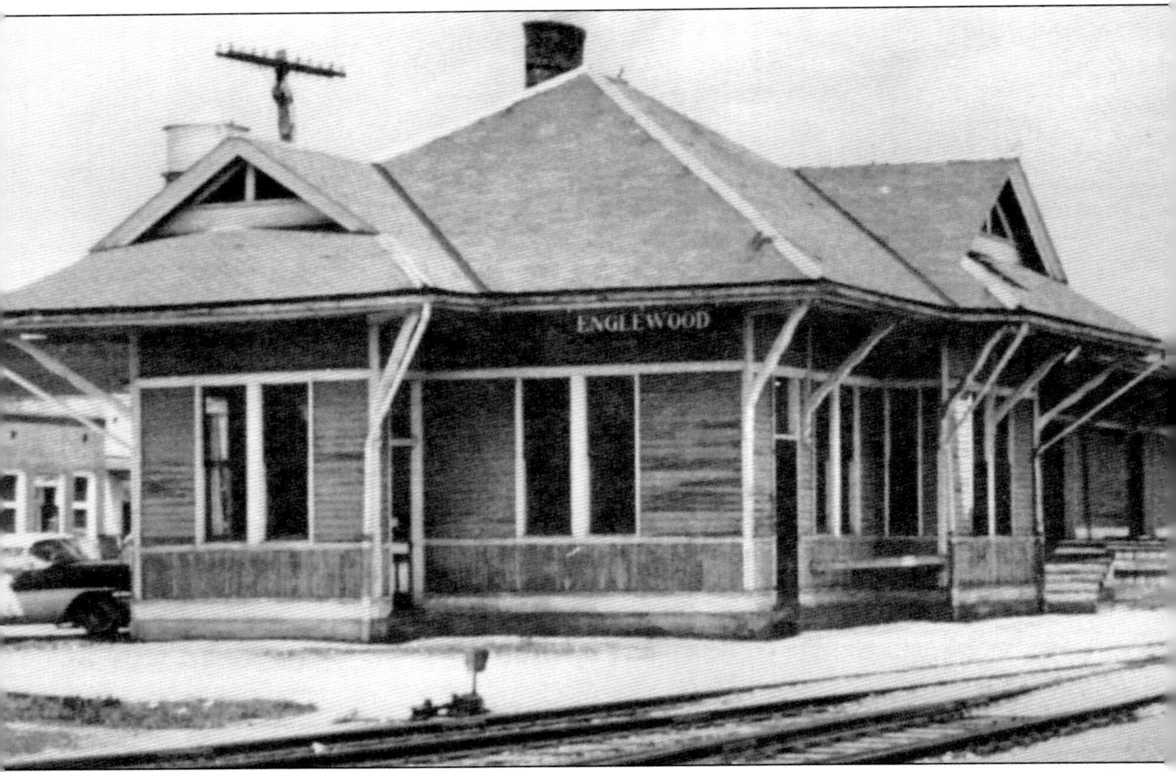


Englewood traces its origin from a community known as Eureka Mill, located 2 miles south of the present town. An east-west railroad line was constructed between Athens and Tellico in the late 1880s, followed by a north-south line built by Knoxville Southern Railroad around the same time. The place where the two lines crossed was called Tellico Junction, and soon a small community sprang up. Eureka moved its town and mill to along the line, making it easier to ship the mill's textiles. Additional mills were started, and the town grew. It has been known as Englewood since 1908. This postcard shows the old depot that once sat near the rail line junction.

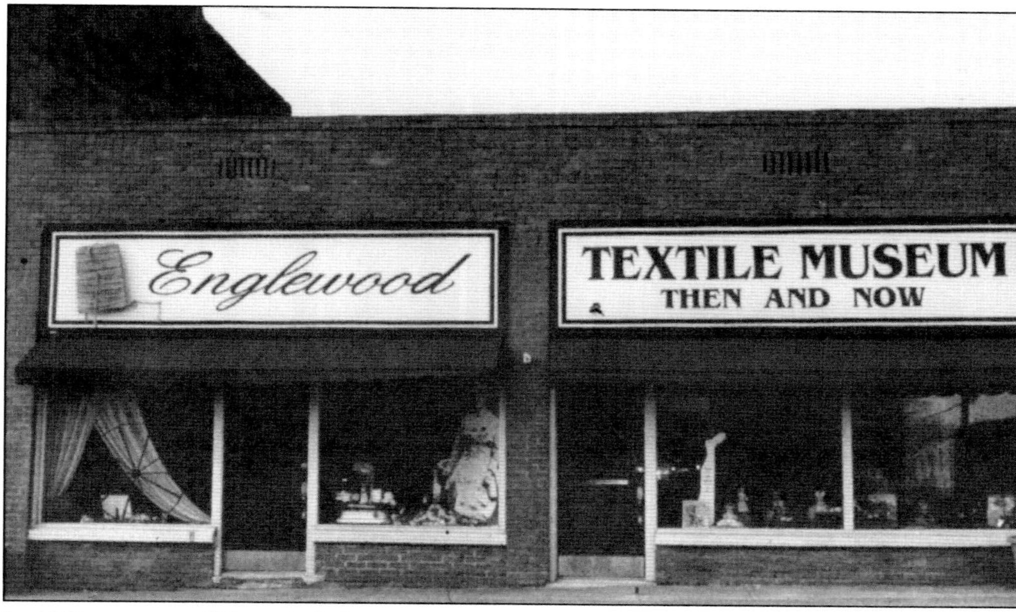


In 1987, a group of like-minded citizens formed the Community Action Group of Englewood (CAGE) as a grassroots movement to promote the town's mill heritage. The group's focal point is the Englewood Textile Museum, located near the center of town in the former site of Jim Basket's Café on Manila Road.

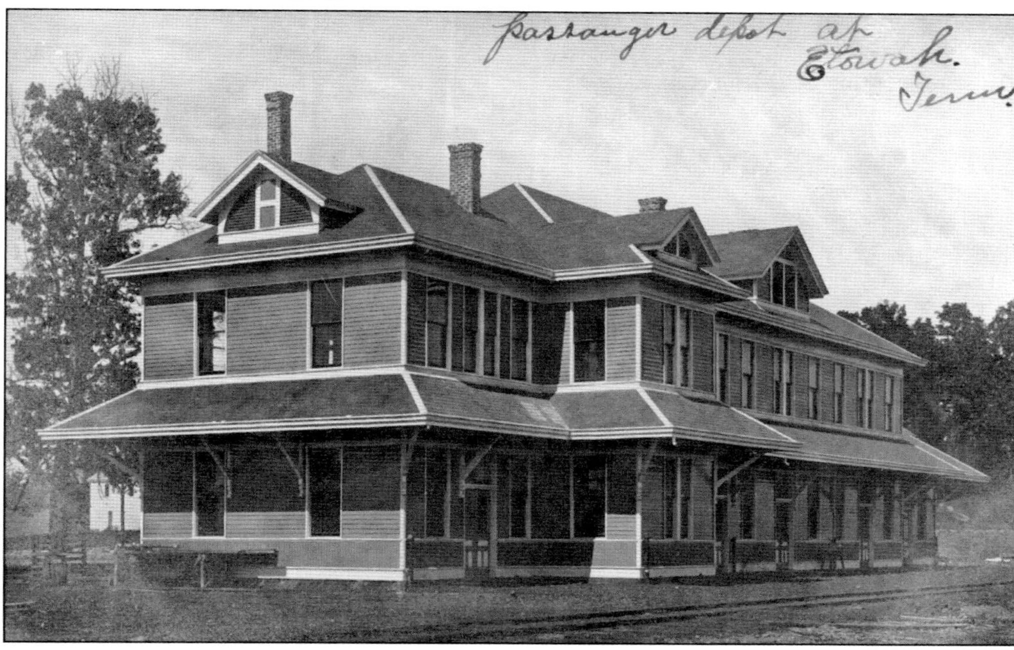


The Etowah Depot was built in 1906 as part of the Louisville and Nashville (L&N) Railroad's project to construct its shops and division headquarters at a central location between Knoxville and Atlanta. When the 1,400 acres of property was acquired by the L&N Railroad in 1904, the area was a low-lying wetland. Copper slag was hauled from the Ducktown Basin and dumped here in order to build up the land for the depot, shops, and rail yards.

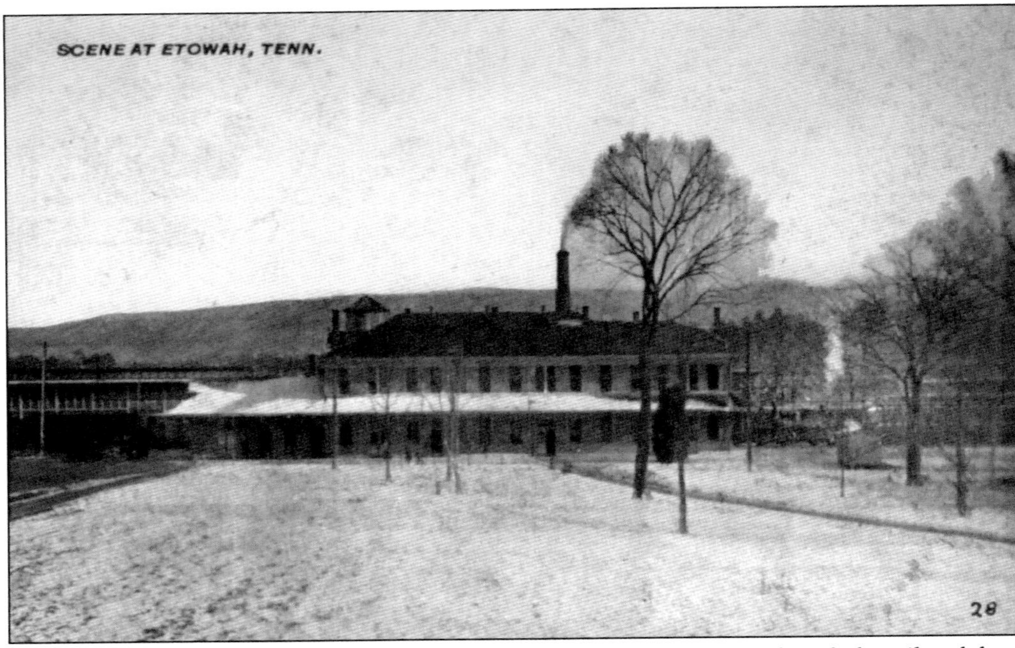


In this postcard, dated 1916, the depot is shown as it was initially constructed, with the railroad shops and yard behind and before the front portico room was added. The imposing depot held the central offices of the Atlanta, Knoxville, and Nashville Division of the L&N Railroad. It was the center point of the town that became known as Etowah and remains its most recognized building.

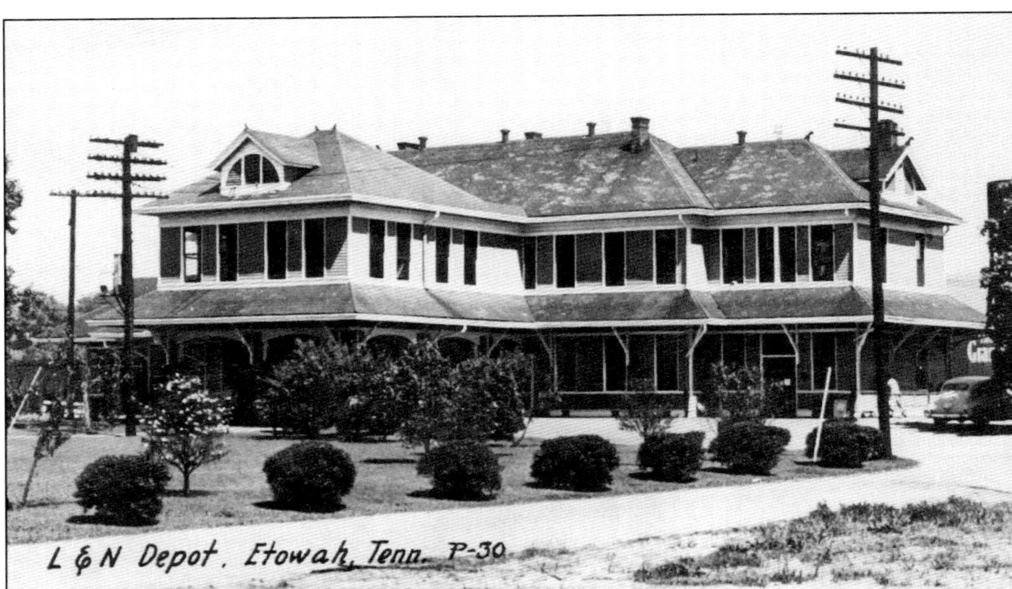


The Etowah Depot rivaled other terminals in larger cities such as Knoxville, Athens, and Cleveland. This trackside photograph shows the view as seen by passengers arriving by train from the south. Here troops left for World War I, World War II, the Korean War, and Vietnam. Travelers could buy tickets to destinations as close as Englewood and Cleveland or as far away as the rail could take them.

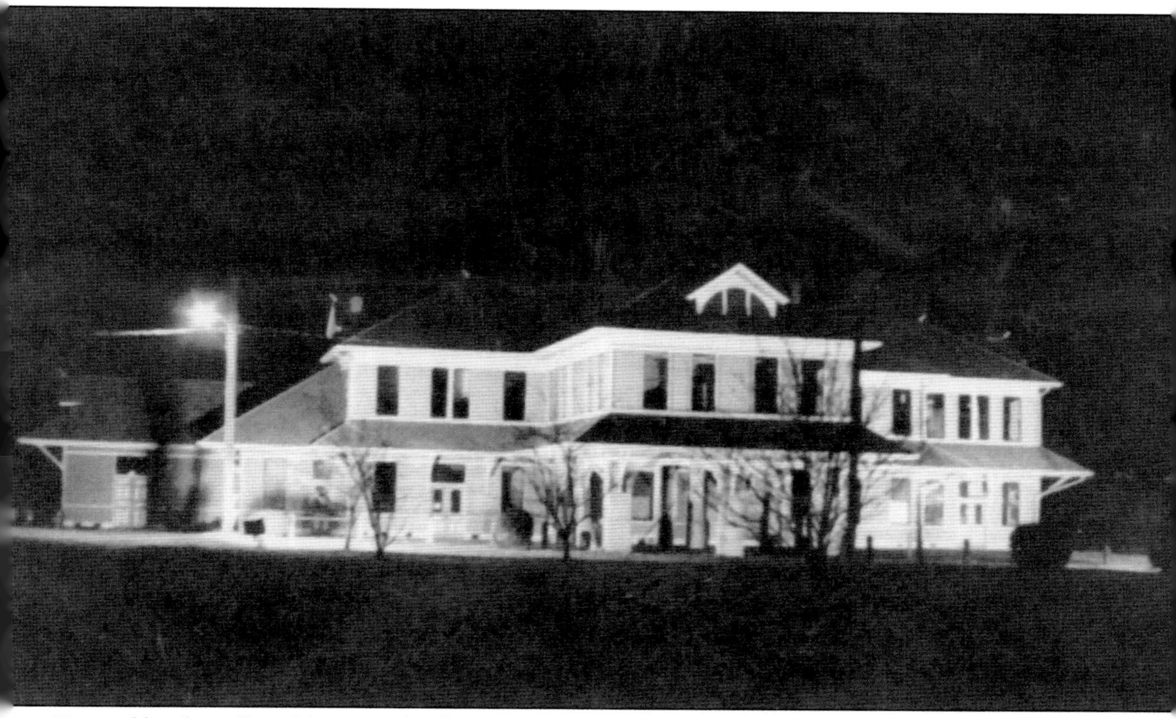

Vacated by the railroad in 1974, the depot was purchased by the City of Etowah in 1981 and was renovated with a groundswell of public support. It houses the L&N Railroad Museum, Etowah Chamber of Commerce, and the offices of the Tennessee Overhill Heritage Association. This postcard shows a modern view of the proud symbol of Etowah's railroad heritage.

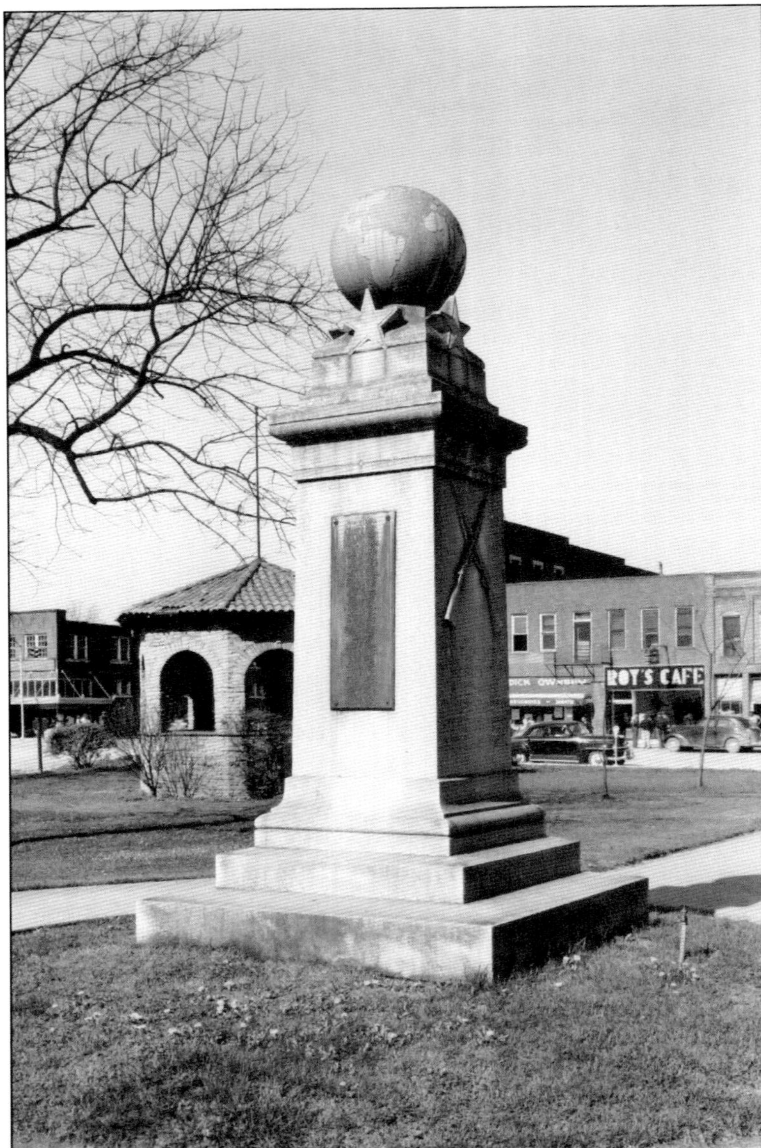


A memorial standing on the grounds of the Etowah Depot, constructed just after the end of World War 1 in 1918, recognizes the heroism of the men and officers of the 117th Infantry, made up almost entirely of Etowah men, who fought throughout France against the German army. In the background is the stone bandstand, built in 1931 of Crab Orchard Stone from Crossville, Tennessee. A gift to the town from Augustus McClary, the bandstand served local citizens with music performances and orations for several decades. It was enclosed in 1961 and was used as the office for the Etowah Chamber of Commerce until 1983. Since that time, it has been renovated and returned back to its original purpose. Etowah, known as the "one-sided town" is viewed at the rear of the photograph. The entire town was built on the west side of its main street, Tennessee Avenue. The railroad occupied the east side.

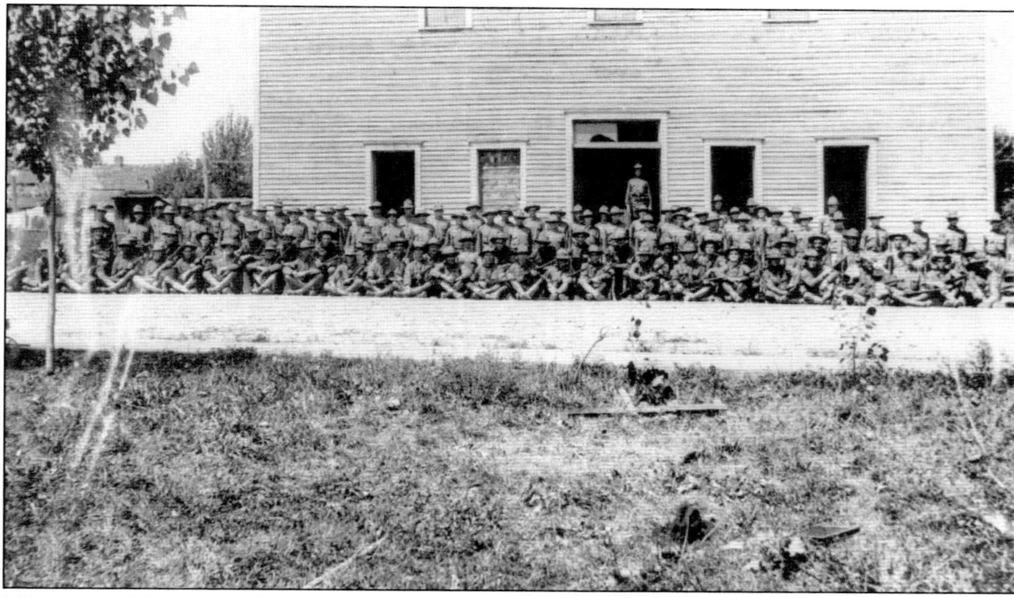

The men of Co L, 117th Tennessee Infantry, are shown as they muster on August 25, 1917, in front of the Etowah Armory near the corner of Ohio Avenue and Ninth Street, just prior to shipping out for service in World War I. These are the men whom the depot memorial honors. (Courtesy McMinn County Historical Society.)

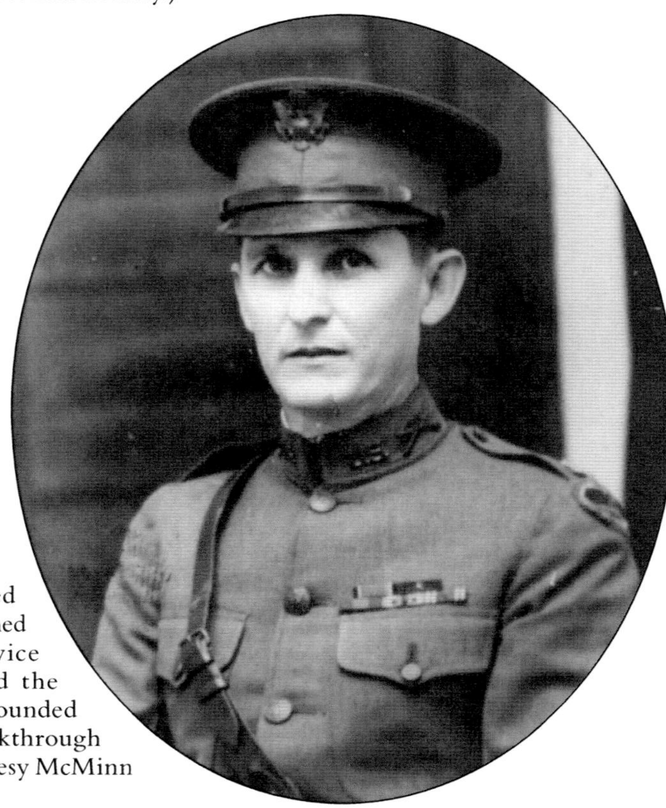

Capt. David Lillard commanded Co L. He received the Distinguished Service Cross for heroic service during the war. He survived the conflict after being severely wounded while participating in the breakthrough of the Hindenburg Line. (Courtesy McMinn County Historical Society.)

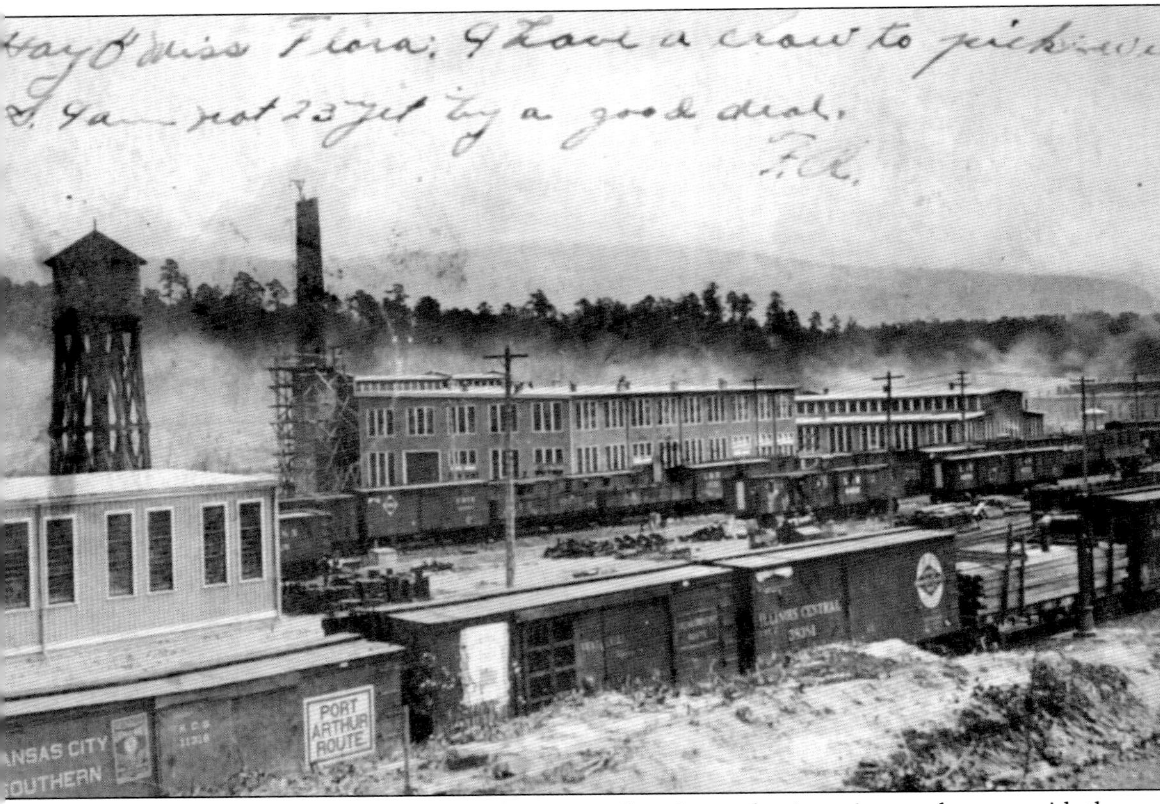


This 1907 postcard shows the Etowah L&N Railroad complex in a view to the east, with the water tank to the left and construction still going on at the shop building. The train cars in the foreground sit on the main line, and the cars behind sit in the rail yard. The water tower that filled steam locomotives is at left center, and the roundhouse is visible on the far right. When the L&N shops were completed and operating at full capacity, the L&N operation was the largest employer in McMinn County, providing more than 2,000 jobs in the shops and on the rails. Etowah provided the L&N Railroad with a centrally located site for passenger service and engine and car repair. Workers labored around the clock to repair engine boilers or to rebuild wooden boxcars. The shops thrived until they were relocated to Knoxville in 1929. During the next 40 years, the town lost the main railroad offices, shops, and passenger service.

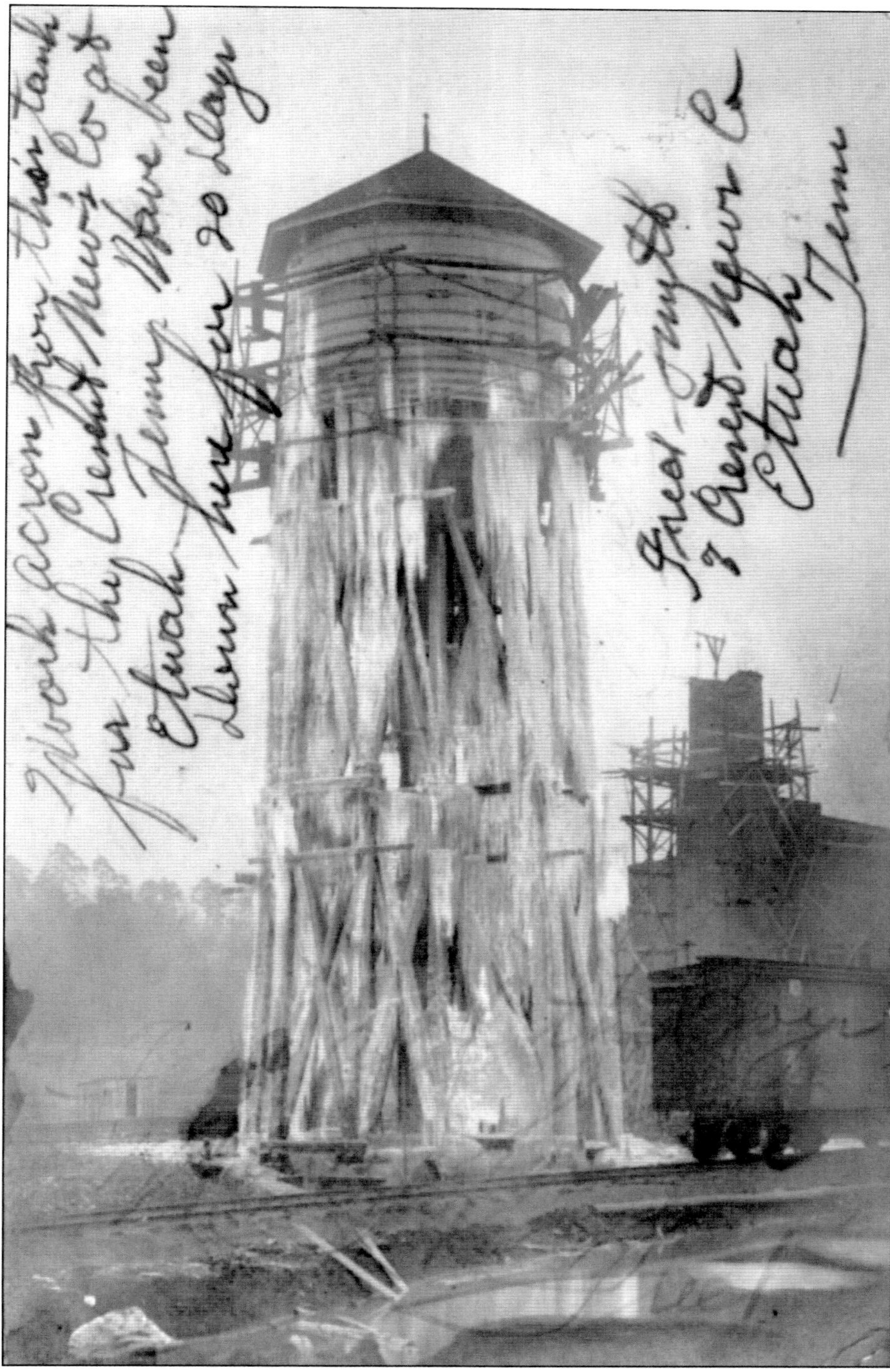

In this early postcard, one of two water tanks in the Etowah yard is shown. Ice is visible clinging to the sides and understructure, frozen from the water that habitually leaked from the tank and cascaded onto the track below. To the right is part of the smokestack from the engine shops, which was still under construction.

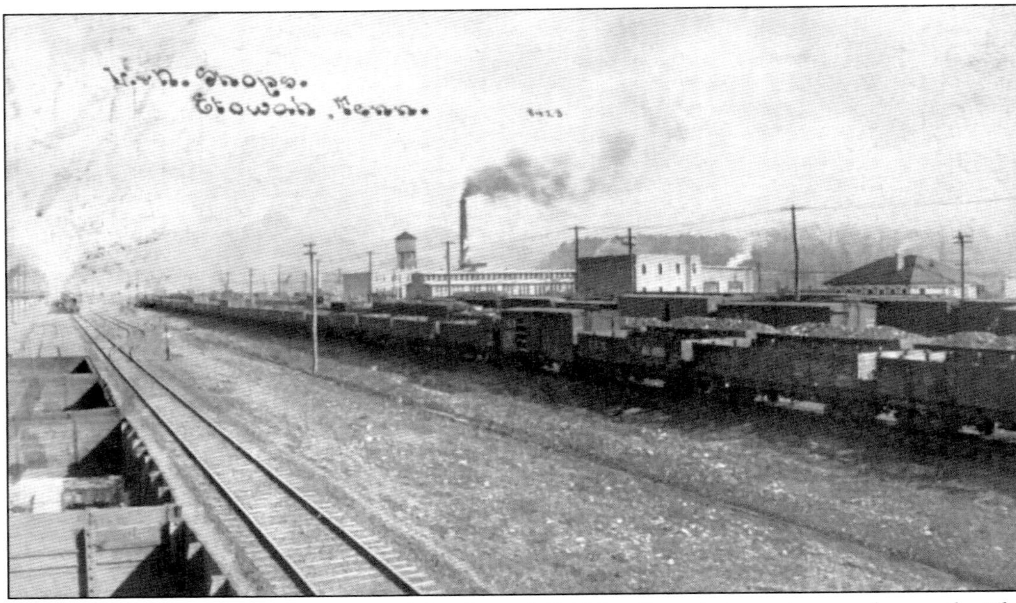


In a postcard dated 1914 is a view of the Etowah L&N rail yards in a view to the north. The depot is barely visible at extreme left center, with the shops, roundhouse, and freight depots on the right.

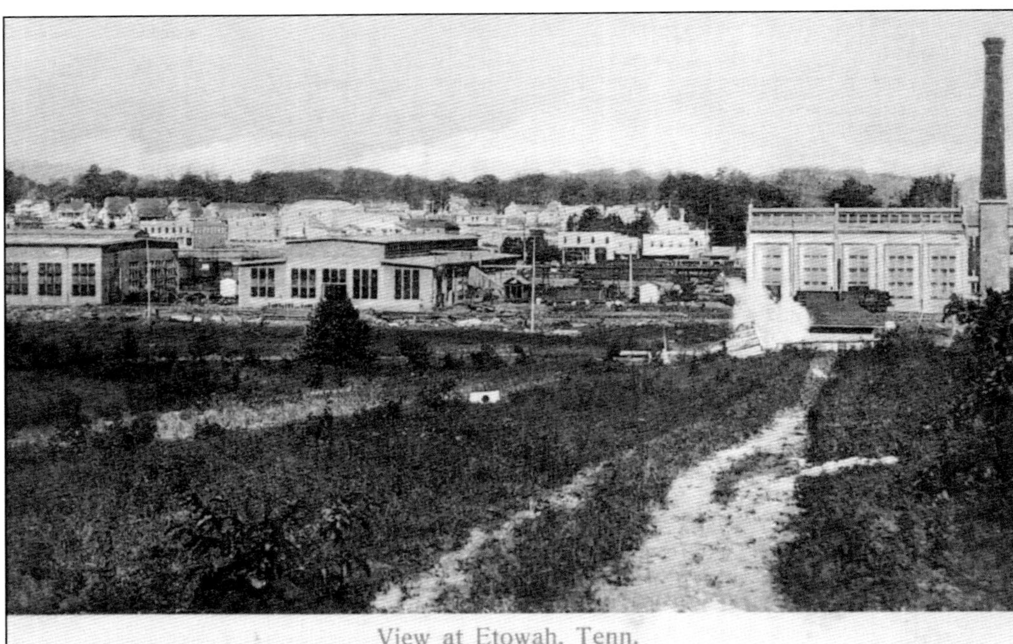


Only two years had passed when, in 1908, this postcard was mailed, showing the L&N engine shops and freight depots in a view to the west. In the background, the storefronts of Tennessee Avenue are visible, as are residences that have begun to spring up on the streets behind. A true boomtown, Etowah came to life in only a few years, rivaling the county seat at Athens in wealth and influence.

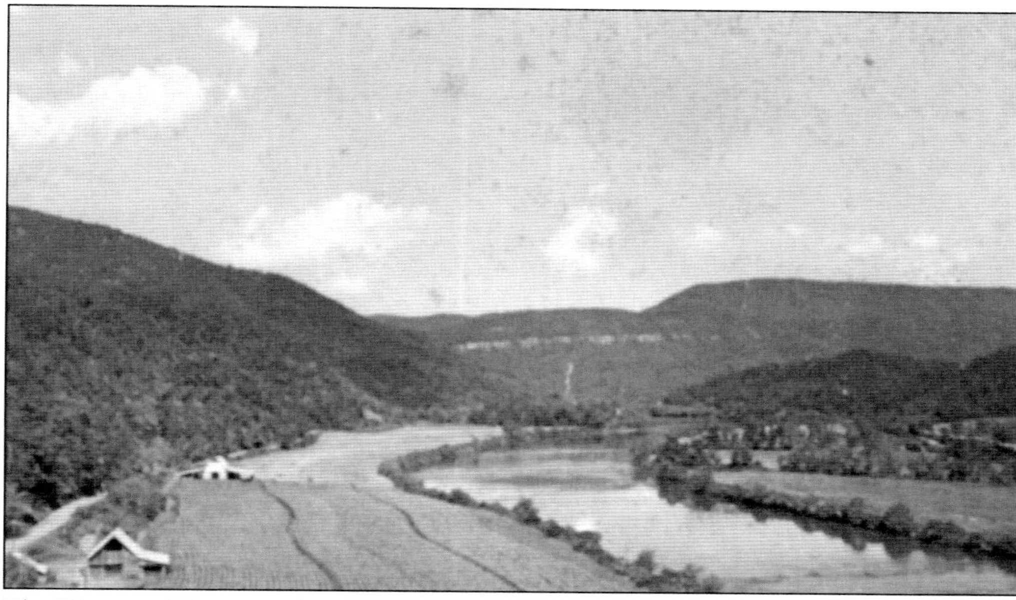

The Hiwassee River at Reliance, Tennessee, is shown in a view to the west. The old Joseph Dallas Vaughn farm is on the left, with the River Road visible at the extreme left. The old line railroad runs along the foot of the hills to the right before crossing the river upstream behind the photographer. The Hiwassee Bluffs are in the distance, skirting Iron Mountain. Reliance is just inside Polk County.

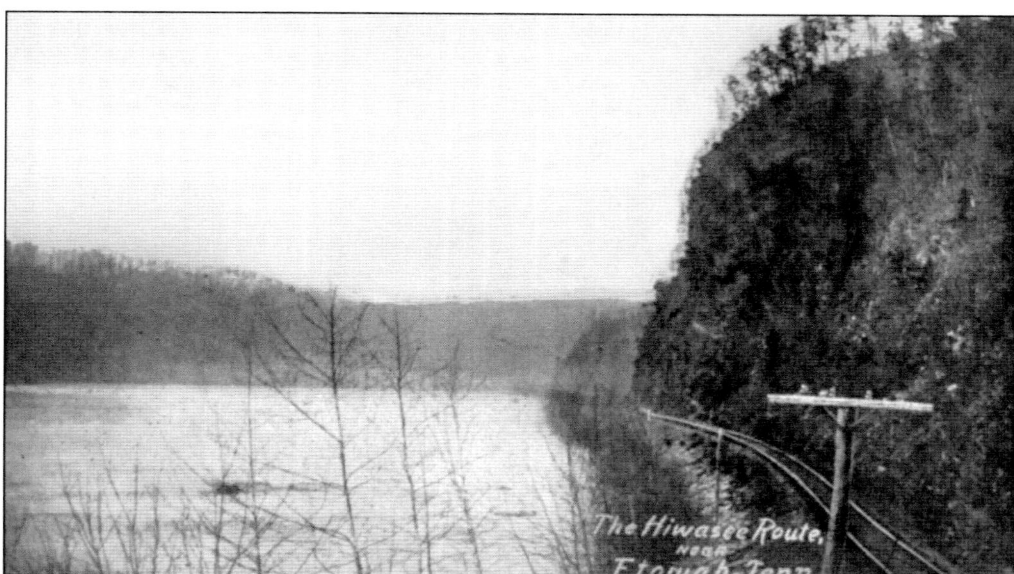


In this 1929 postcard, the Old Line Railroad is seen hugging the Hiwassee Riverbank upriver from Reliance. Now contained within the Cherokee National Forest, little has changed along the tracks up the river.

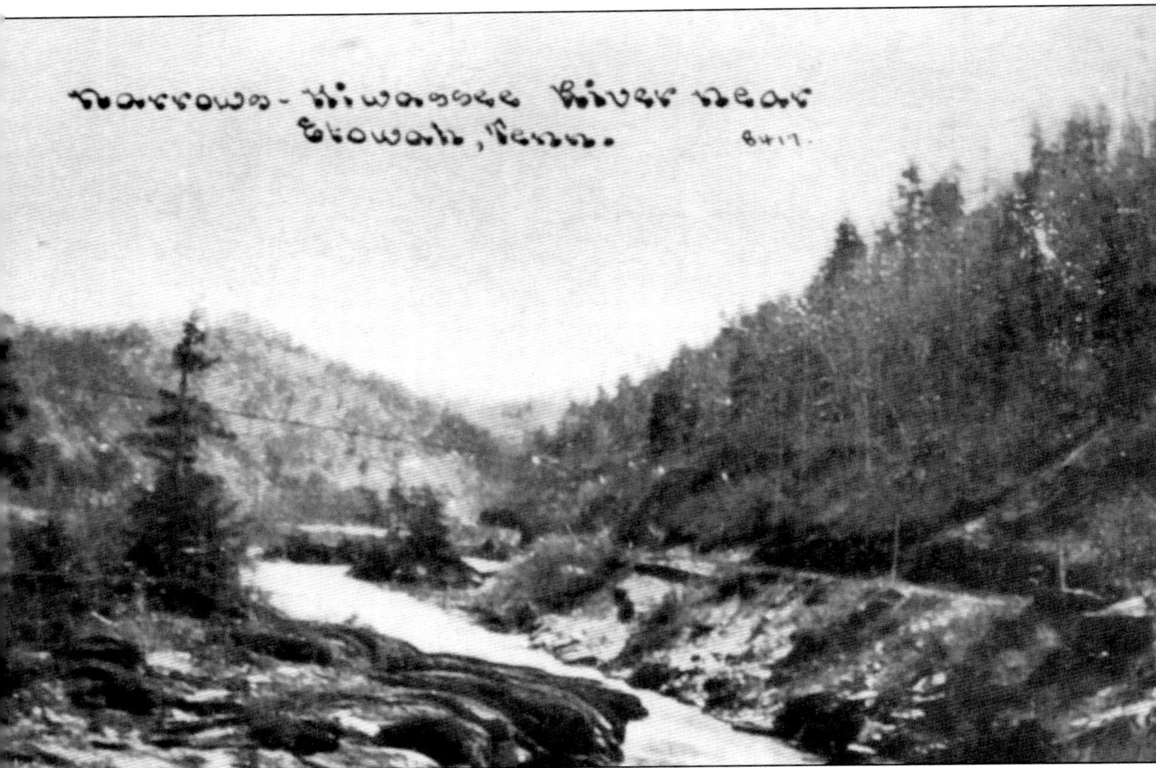


Nearing the Bald Mountain Loop, the Old Line Railroad follows the Hiwassee River through what is known as "the Narrows." This rugged section of the river gorge brought serious difficulties to the railroad construction in 1889, requiring much of the work to be done by construction crews working by hand, with some inmate labor leased from the State of Georgia. Crews worked north from McCaysville, Georgia, and south from Reliance, and the rails were joined near Appalachia on June 30, 1890.

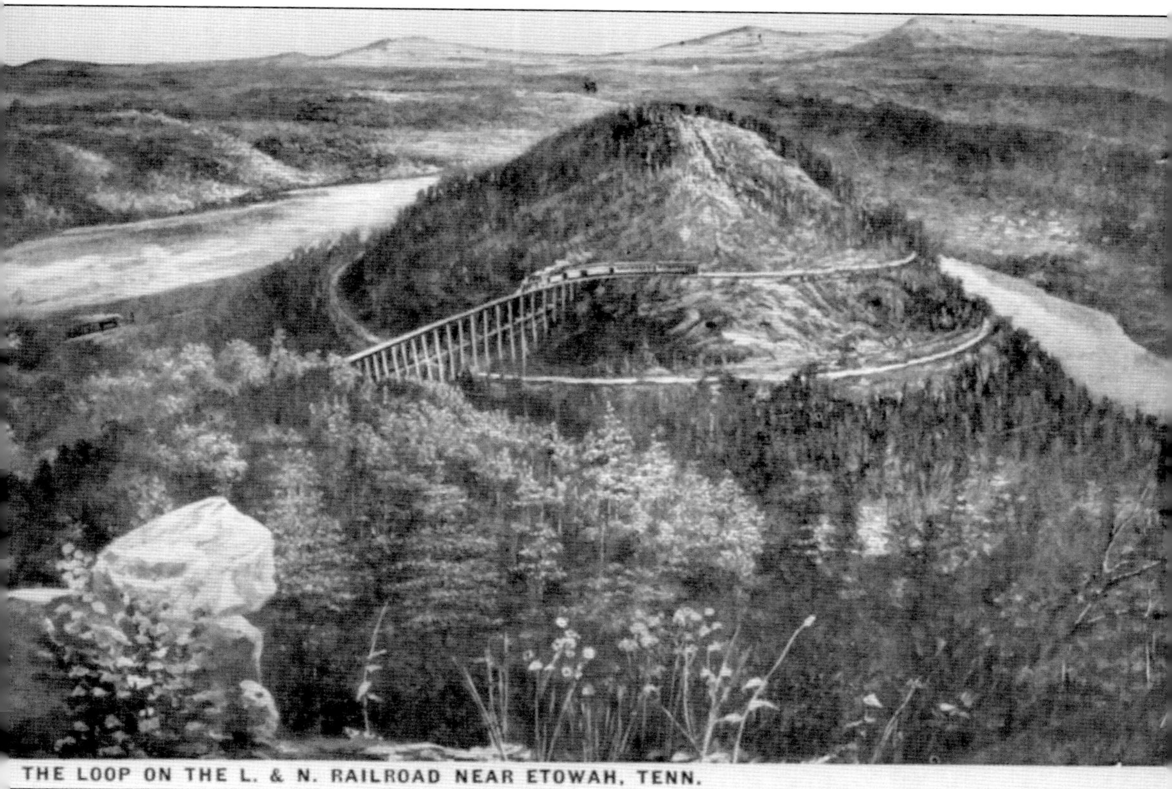


Completed in 1898, the Hiwassee Loop was an engineering feat that encircled Bald Mountain to connect East Tennessee and Etowah with the copper mines in Copper Hill and North Georgia. The loop replaced a series of switchbacks built in the 1890 construction that demanded small trains to back uphill for a running shot up the mountain grade. On long trains, the engineer could pass over the bridge and see the end of his train passing underneath him 62 feet below. The loop today is the featured attraction on the Old Line Railroad.

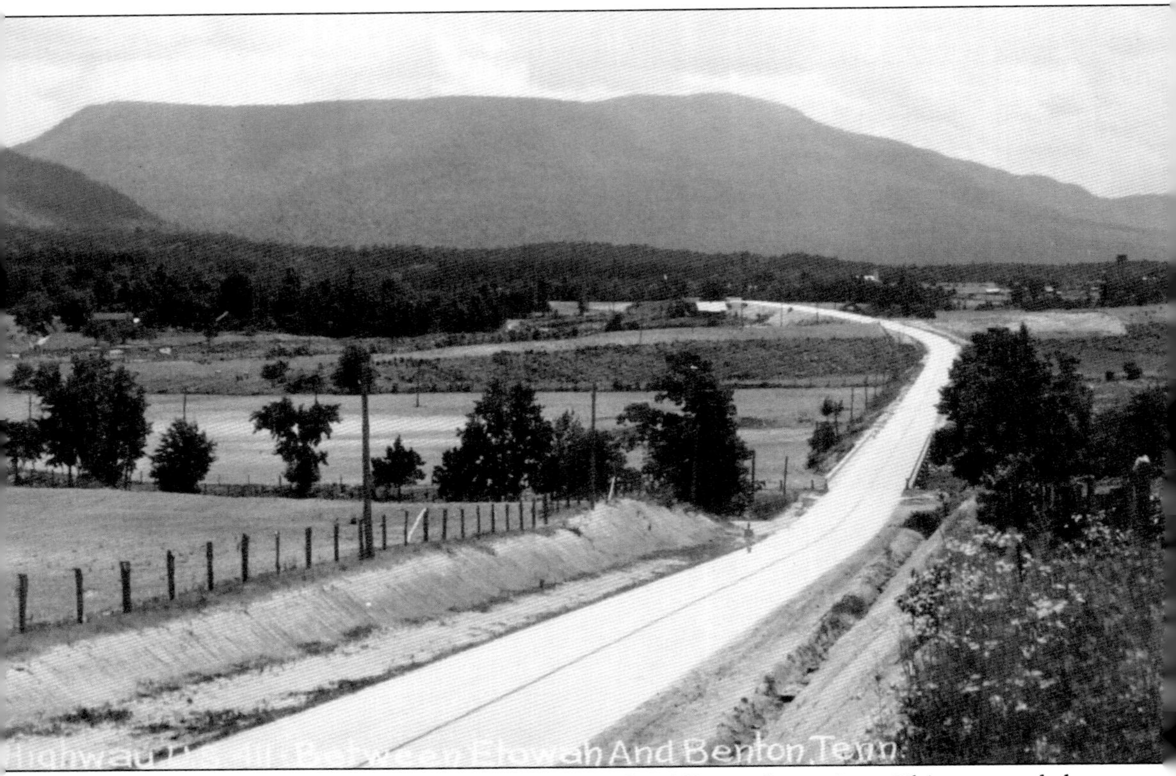


Highway 411 was built in 1933 as a New Deal public works project. This postcard shows Highway 411 south of Etowah with the Hiwassee River Gorge and Polk County in the distance. Conasuga Creek flows under the bridge in the center. The Old Line Railroad passed near the foot of Starr Mountain and through the river gorge. The New Line, constructed in 1906, bypassed the River Gorge on a more southerly route to reconnect with the line in Marietta. This portion of Highway 411 follows the route of the Old Federal Road and the Great Indian Warpath into Georgia.

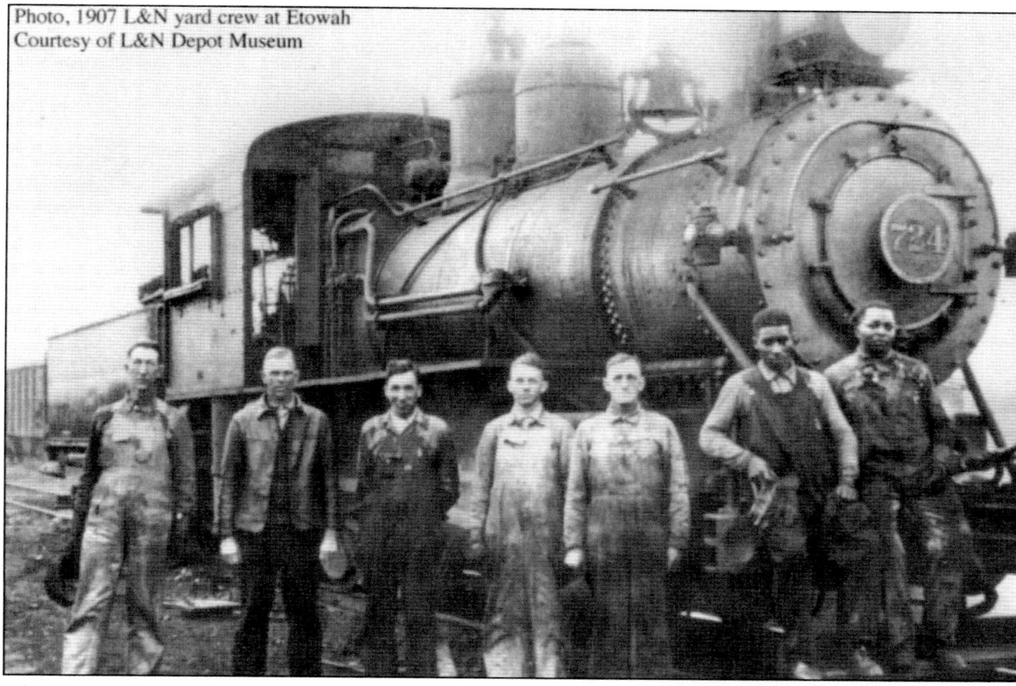


This postcard shows an old photograph of some railroad employees in the Etowah yard in 1907. The engine pictured above was a small "switch engine" used to build trains in the rail yard that would be pulled on the main line by larger engines. As the men's clothing suggests, railroading was a hot and dirty business. During the past 100 years, several generations of Etowah families have worked as track crews, mechanics, and train crews.

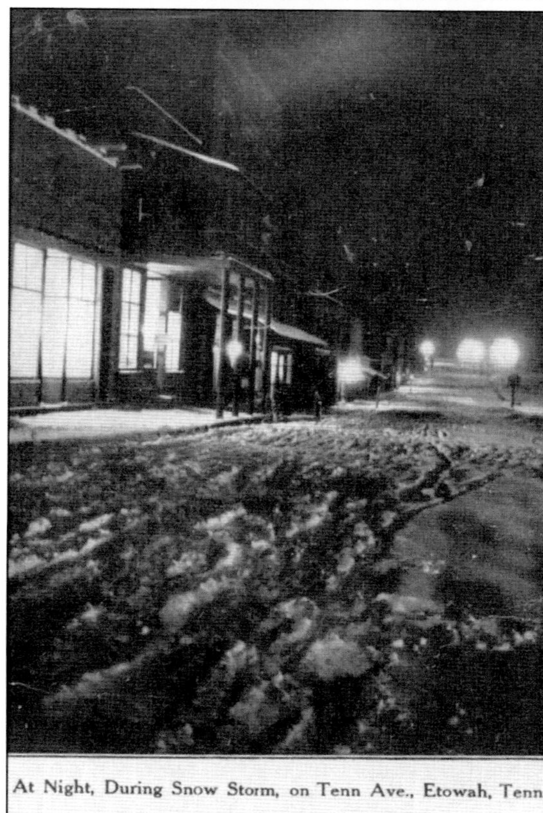


Etowah is shown in this nighttime view after a wet snowfall on Tennessee Avenue. Within four years of its founding, Etowah had its own electric service. Being a railroad boomtown certainly had its advantages.

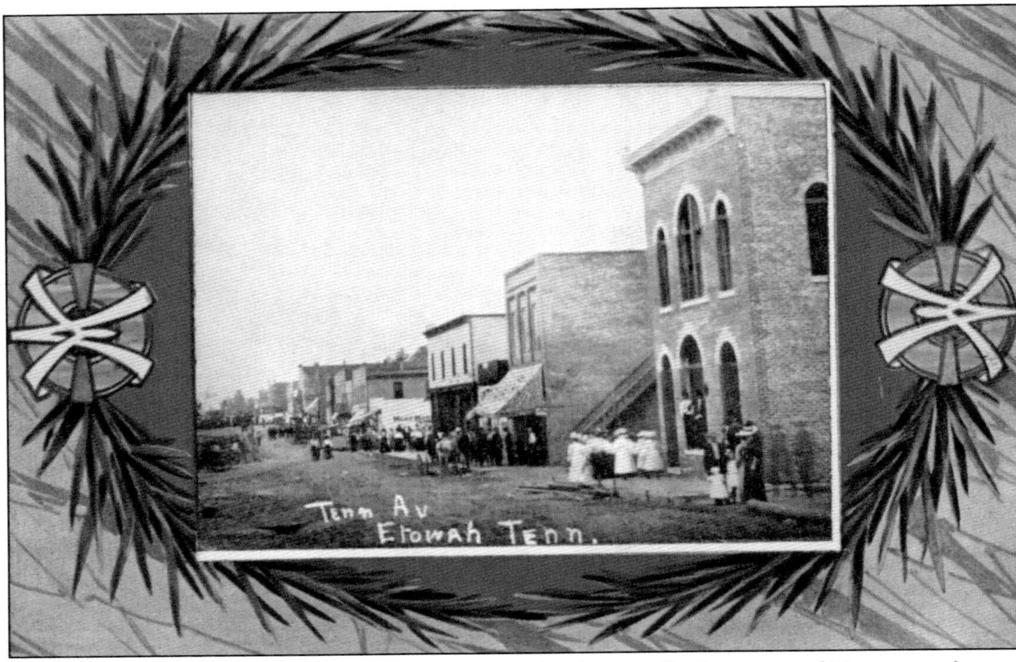


This old Christmas-themed postcard shows an early picture of a dirt-covered Tennessee Avenue in Etowah with a view to the south. Ladies mill around the First National Bank's grand opening at the far right, and just left of center is the intersection with Eighth Street. Etowah grew quickly, and its wood-frame storefronts quickly gave way to ones of brick.

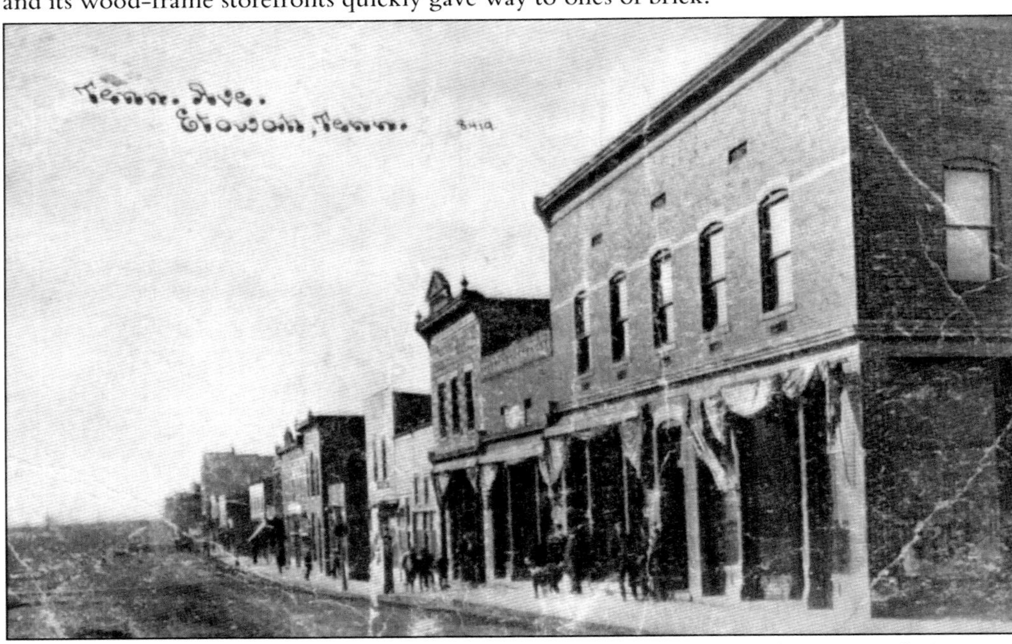


About 1907, C. L. Davis built the brick duplex on the corner of Seventh Street and Tennessee Avenue. Davis operated a store on the corner. Other stores came and went until 1929, when Bill Murphy opened Gem Drug Company here beside the Gem Theatre, which had opened two years earlier next door.

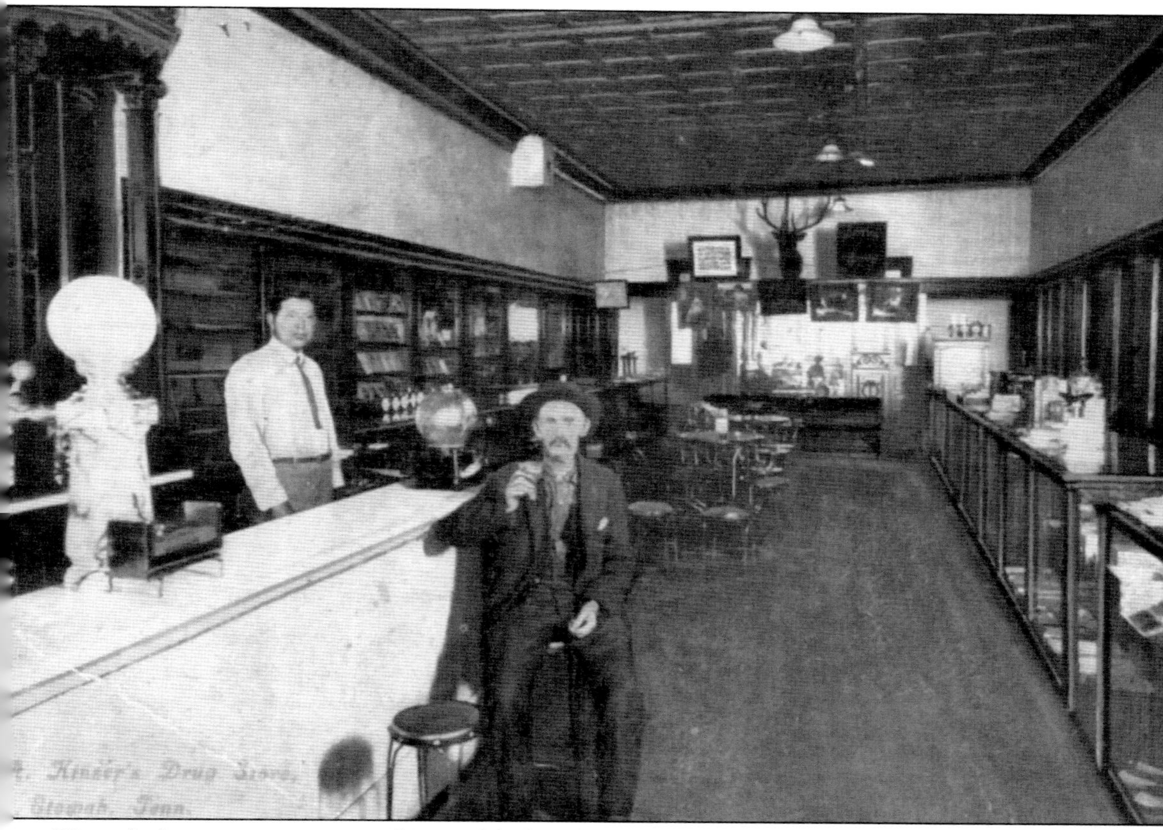


Kinser's drugstore was one of Etowah's first businesses, opening in 1908 and located at 207 South Tennessee Avenue. It was owned by P. A. and L. N. Kinser, who operated it until 1924, when the business passed to a son, J. M. Kinser, and J. M. McCampbell. The business went bankrupt during the Depression and was bought by M. Tallent in 1931. Upstairs was the office of Dr. L. C. Ogle, who would broadcast the World Series from his radio through a megaphone to listeners gathered on the street below. In 1931, O. A. Rule bought the building and operated a furniture store, which passed through three Rule generations until it was lost to fire. The building was refurbished as a general store in 2008.

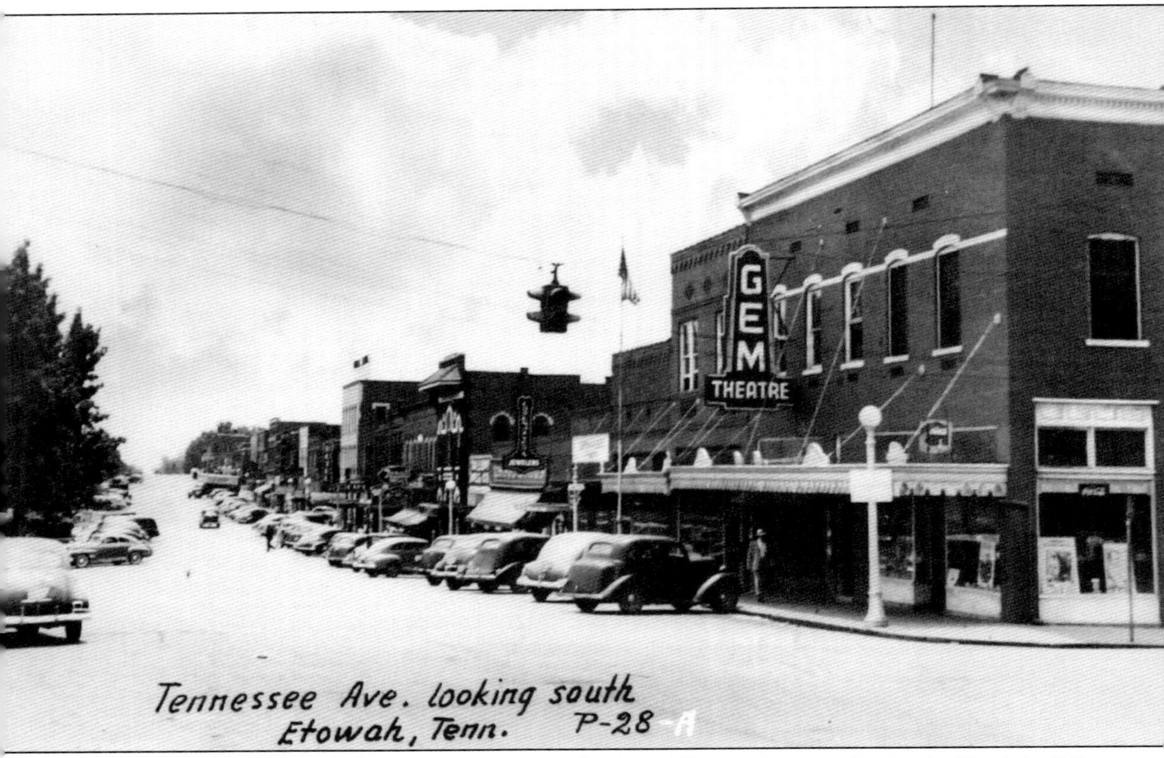


In this postcard photograph from the 1940s, the Gem Theatre is operating in the Davis building, with Murphy's Gem Drug Company on the corner of Seventh Street and Tennessee Avenue. The Gem Theatre opened in 1927, when Hugh V. Manning renovated the front of the building for a lobby and the back of the building to accommodate a theater. The Gem was part of a chain of theaters owned by Manning. It was both a live venue as well as a movie house, and upon the completion of Highway 411 in 1934, the Gem was one of the finest theaters between Knoxville and Atlanta. During the 1940s, Gem Drug Company remained on the corner, with the Etowah Post Office down the street next door to the Gem, Rule Furniture in the next building, which was followed by Copenhaver Jewelry, Etowah Five and Dime, and First National Bank in the distance.

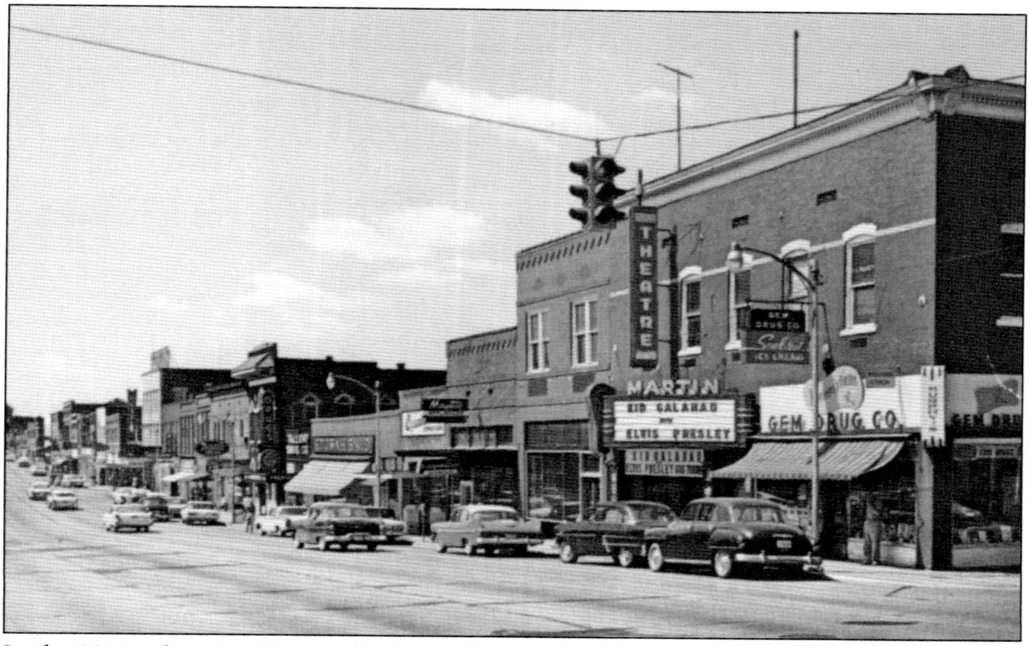


In the 1950s, the Gem Theatre had been decorated with a proper marquis, and this postcard advertises *Kid Galahad*, starring Elvis Presley. Hugh V. Manning sold the Gem to Martin Theatres in 1960, which operated the Gem until it was closed in 1979. Later purchased and renovated by the City of Etowah, the historic Gem Theatre remains a venue for live music, plays, and storytelling events.

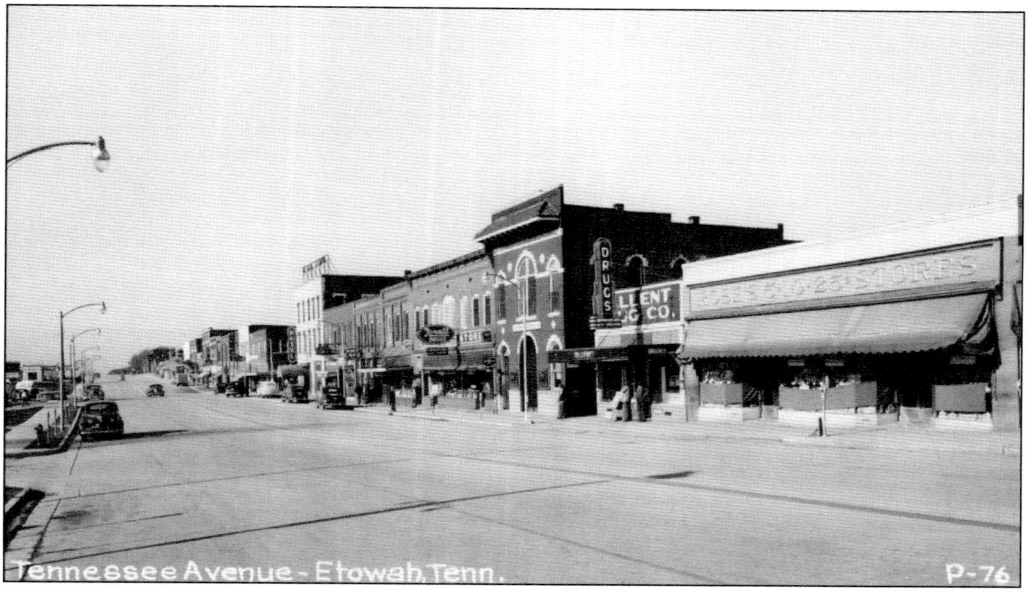


This 1949 postcard shows another view south down Tennessee Avenue. Rose's Five, Ten, an Twenty-five Cent Store is at the far right, with Tallent Drug Company, the First National Bank, Charles McConkey's Etowah Rexall Drugs, Roy's Café, and the white front of the Glenora Hotel on the corner of Eighth Street. The message on the back reveals the character of its rural author, writing from Reliance in Polk County: "Here is a view card of the town closest to me."

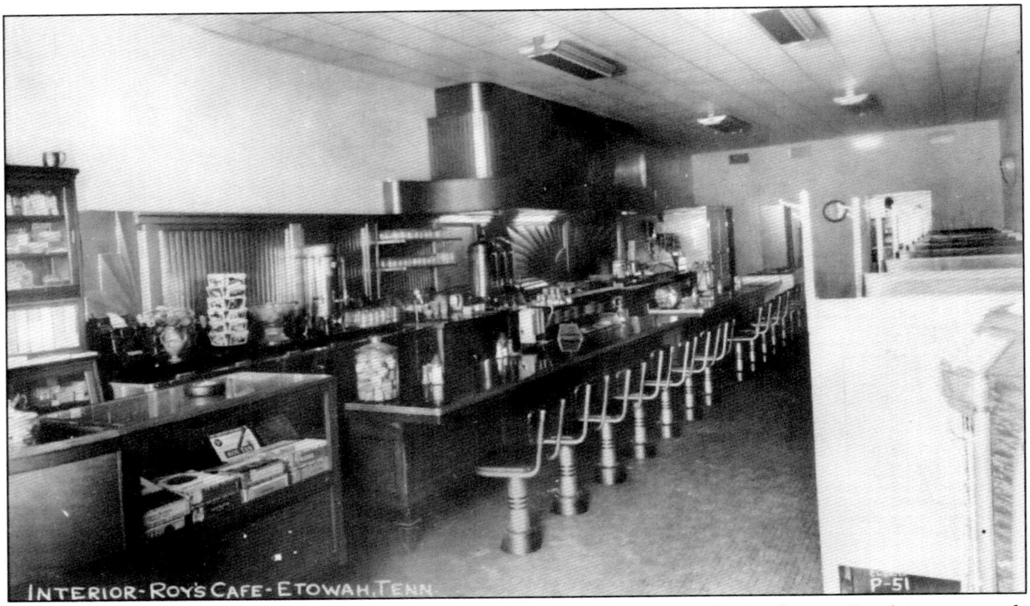

A later view of the interior of Roy's Café, operated by Roy Rule, is shown in this postcard. Rule remained the owner until he sold the business to M. L. Stone in 1964.

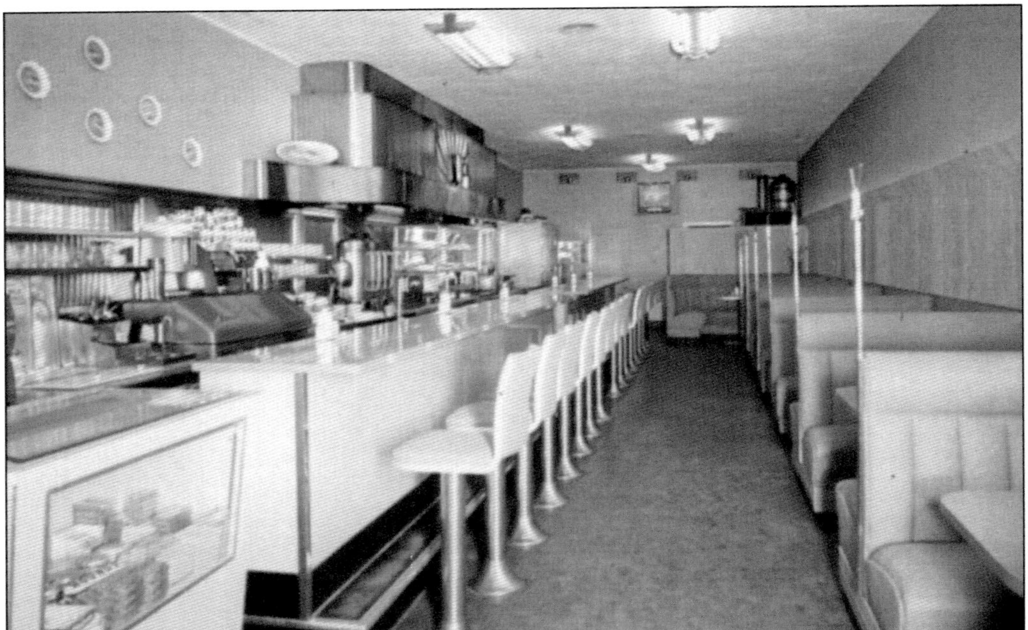
Roy's Café served hot meals to residents and visitors to Etowah for more than three decades. Whether at the bar or in a booth or table, Roy's provided convenient service and good food.

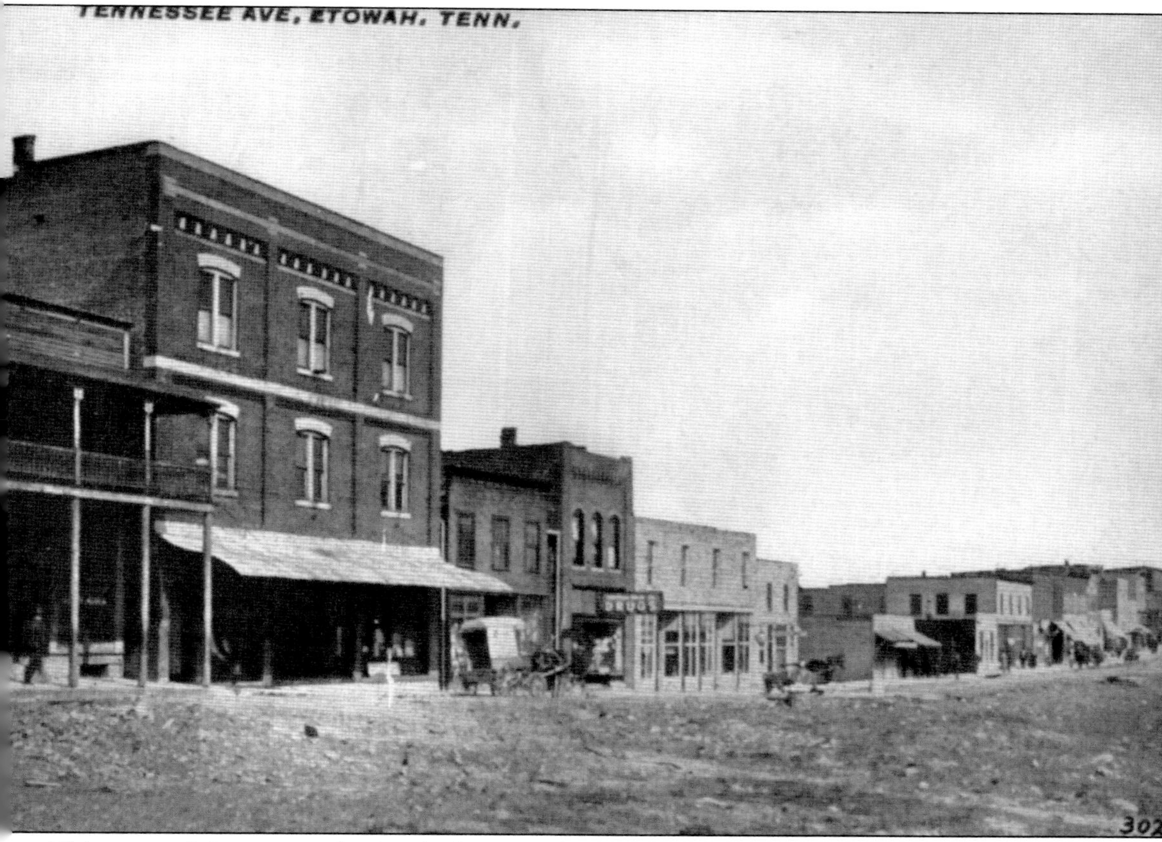


This postcard shows an early view looking north on Tennessee Avenue. From the left is a closer view of Schnieder's Meat Market. The three-story Christian building, built about 1909, was, at the time, Etowah's tallest building until a 1925 fire reduced its floors from three to two. Next are Center and Powell Hardware and Furniture, a drugstore, and then the Grey Goose Café and Buck's Cleaners, then on to the corner of Eighth Street. Beginning the next block is the Carlock Hotel, later the site of the Glenora Hotel.

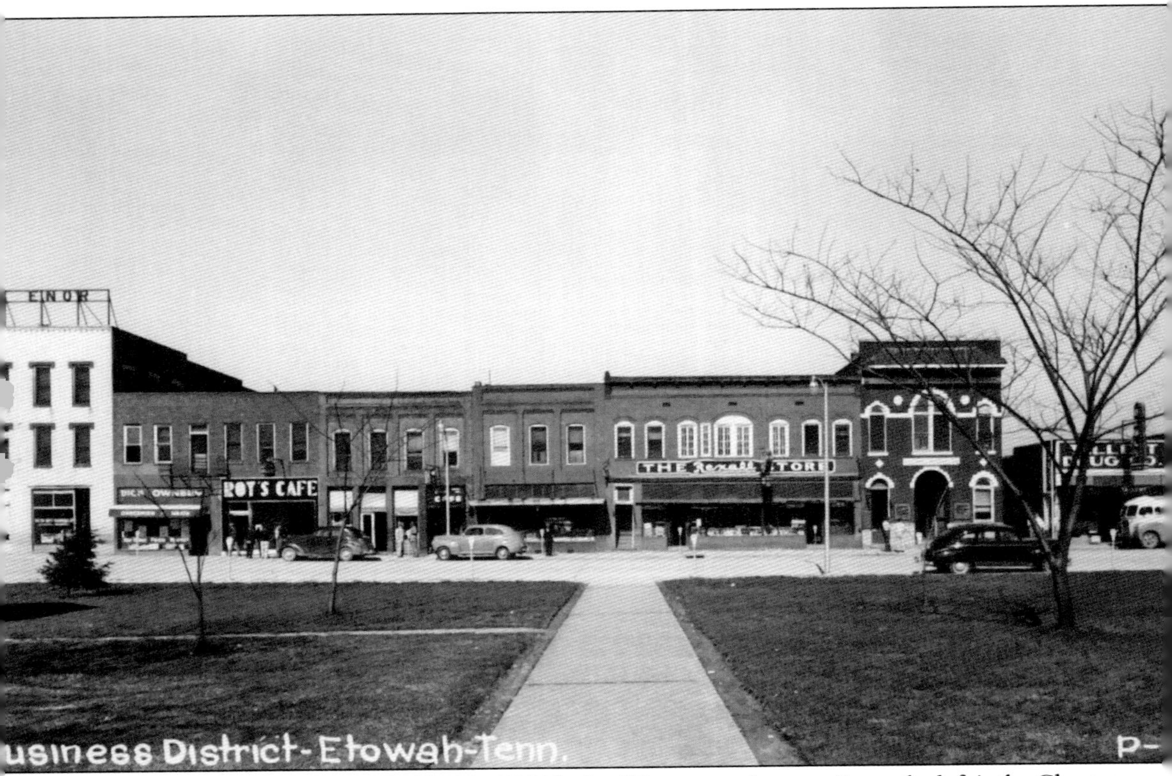


Shown here is the southern half of the 700 block of Tennessee Avenue. From the left is the Glenora Hotel, built in 1916 by two doctors, W. R. Fronenberger and J. O. Nichols, and named for their two daughters, Glenn and Ora. The hotel operated for some 40 years before being converted to retail and office space. It was razed in 1985. Next are Dick Owenby's Grocery Store, Roy Rule's Café, the First City Café, the City Food Market, the Charles McConkey Rexall Store, and the First National Bank. Somewhat hidden behind the tree is Tallent Drug Company. The building holding Owenby's and Roy's was destroyed by fire in 1975.

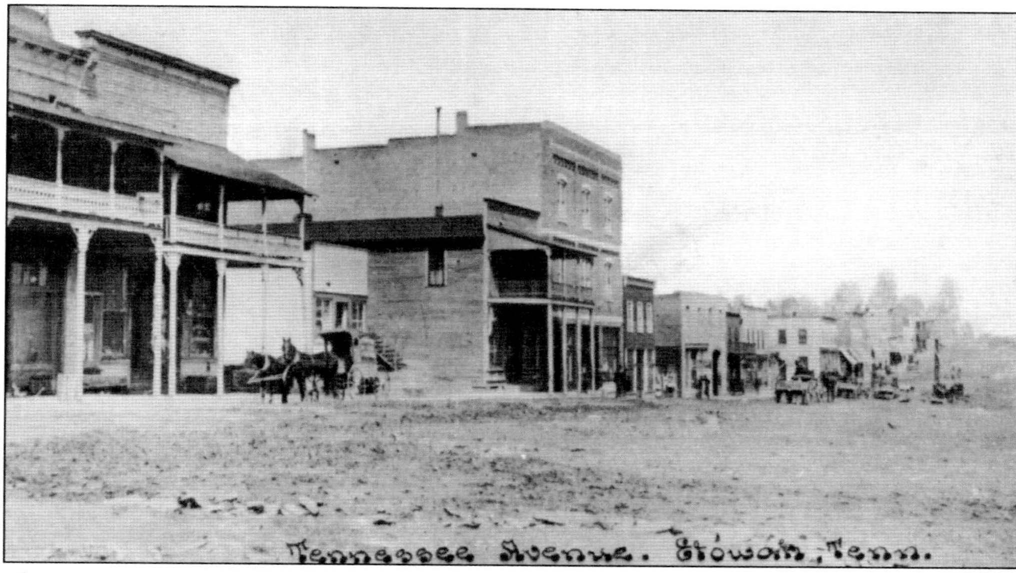


This postcard shows an early view looking north up the 800 block of Tennessee Avenue. Nothing is known of the two frame storefronts on the left, but the two-story frame building with the large porch at center is the J. C. Schneider Meat Market and later John Rule's store. The large Christian building is next. Tennessee Avenue was still a dirt street occupied by wagons and buggies like those pictured.

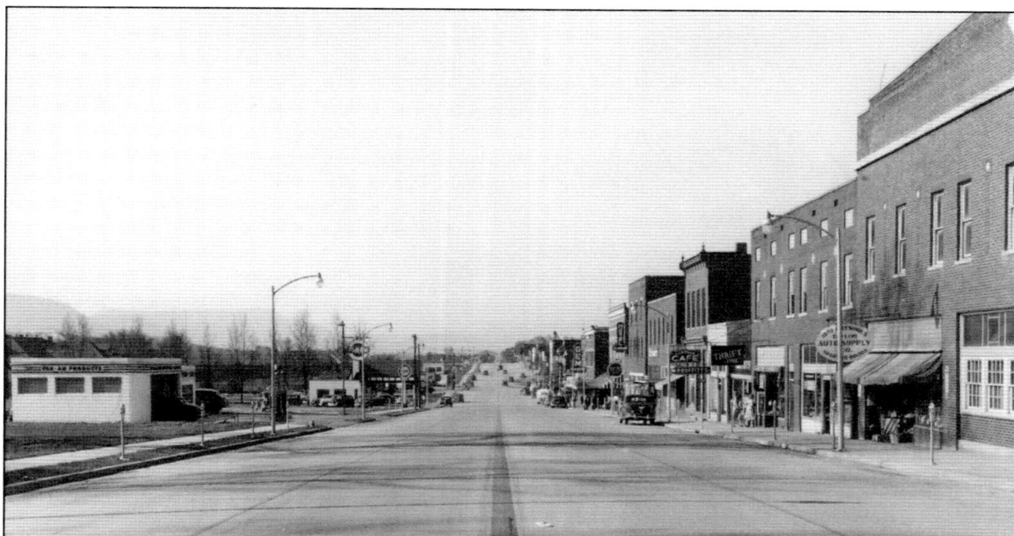

This postcard shows a picture of the 600 block of Tennessee Avenue in the 1940s. In the distance, just this side of the Gem Theatre, is the Rains Building, constructed in 1913. About the time of this photograph, the building housed the Dixie Plunge, a swimming pool operated by Stella Shearer. Next is the Stafford Hotel, perhaps Etowah's oldest building, constructed in 1907. It was remodeled with a brick facade in the 1940s and remained an active business until the mid-1980s. Still closer is Western Auto, operating about the middle of the block, and next is Munger's Café and Proffits Dress Store. Taylor Auto Supply and Sporting Goods is visible in the foreground, with a bowling alley operating upstairs.

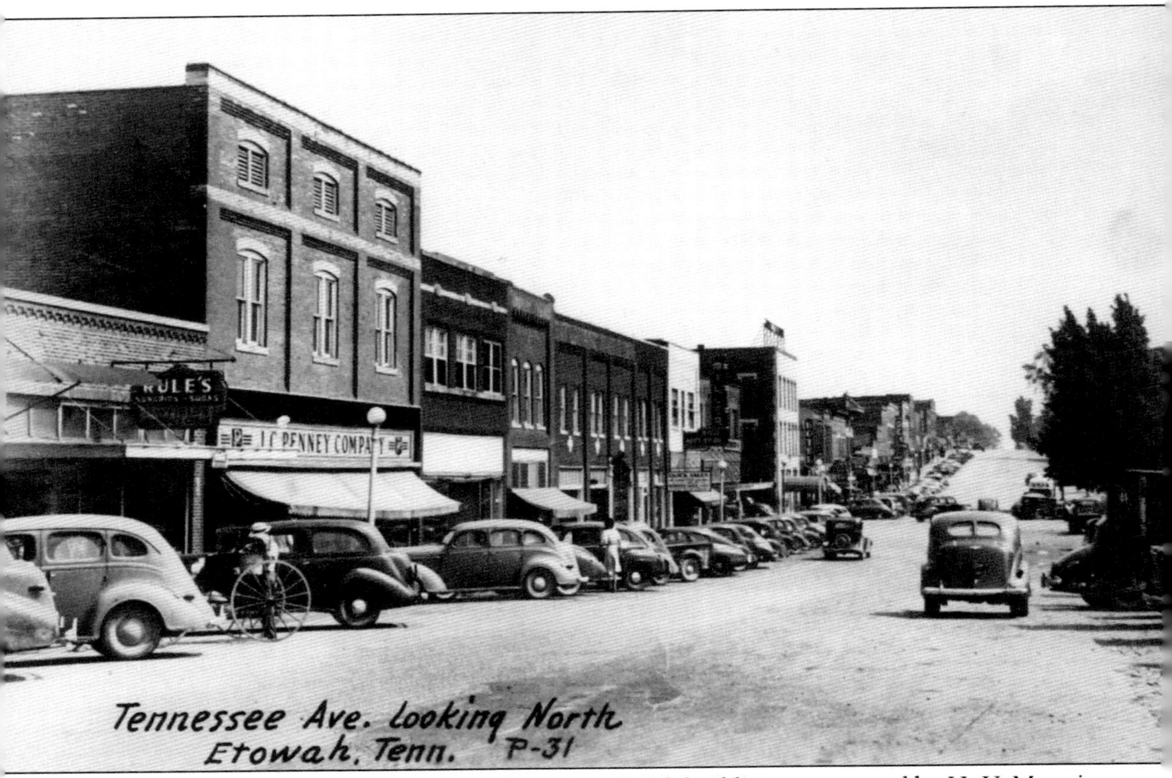


In a postcard photograph from the early 1940s, a brick building constructed by H. V. Manning, which housed Donald Rule's store, has replaced the old frame structure from 1909. J. C. Penney is operating in the Christian building, with Ed Johnson's store next door. Down the block are Miller's Department Store and the U.S. Five and Ten Cent Store. The K. C. Robinson store is on the corner in the Tom Sherman building. Tennessee Avenue is, by this time, a paved street. A lone buggy sits among the modern automobiles parked on the street.

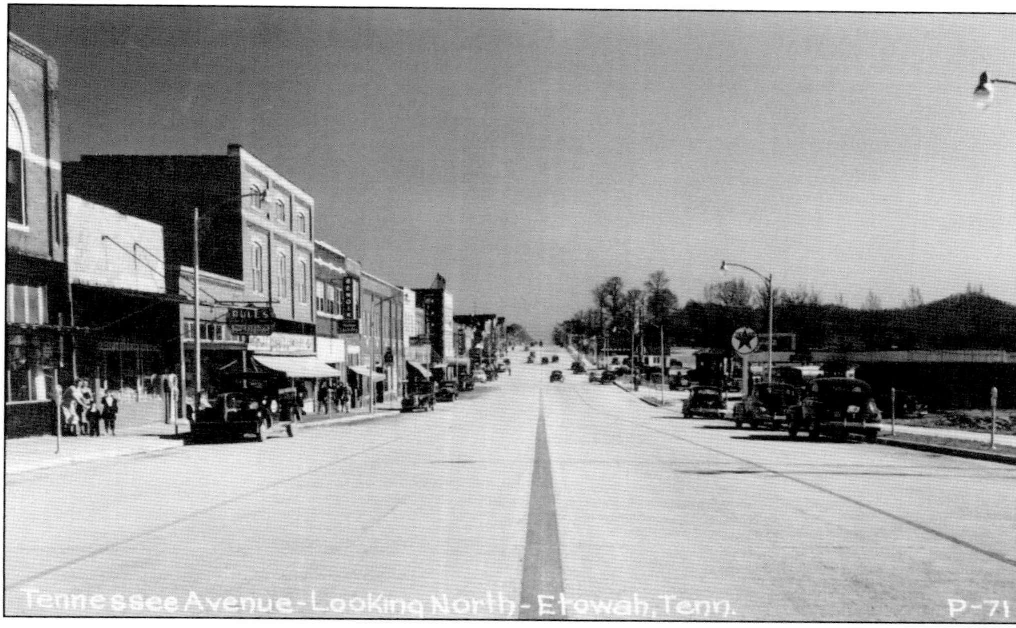

Here Tennessee Avenue/U.S. Highway 33/411 is a broad, paved street with newly installed parking meters. Most of the businesses mentioned in the previous photograph remain on the left, and the Texaco is shown on the right.

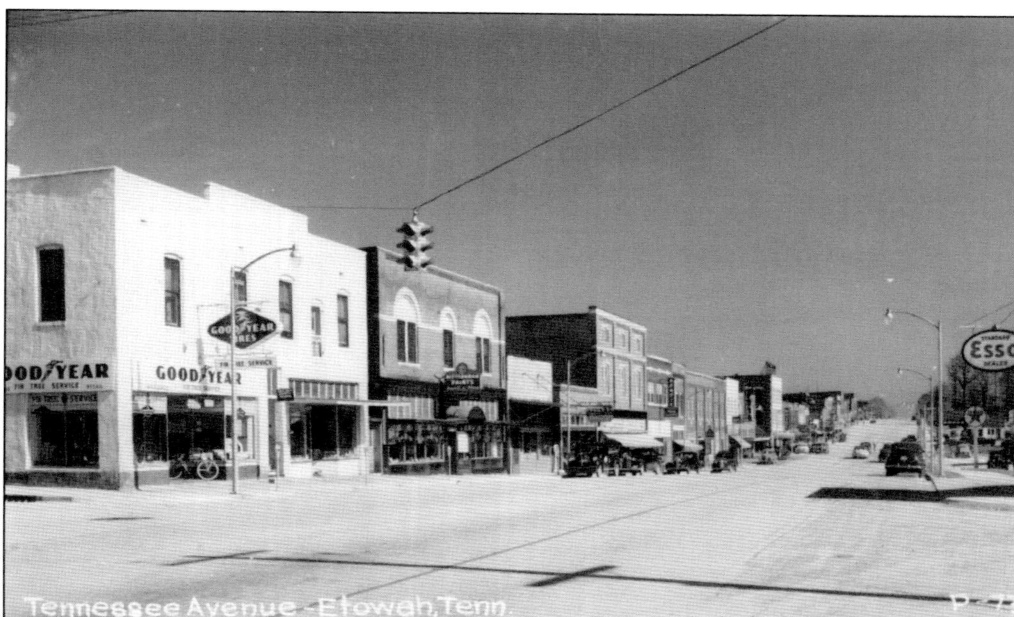

The southern end of Tennessee Avenue's 800 block is shown in this photograph, which is simply a more distant view of the one shown in the previous photograph. The Goodyear Store is shown on the near corner, with Powell Furniture next door. Both the Esso and Texaco signs show the gas stations on the west side of Tennessee Avenue, away from the businesses on the right side.

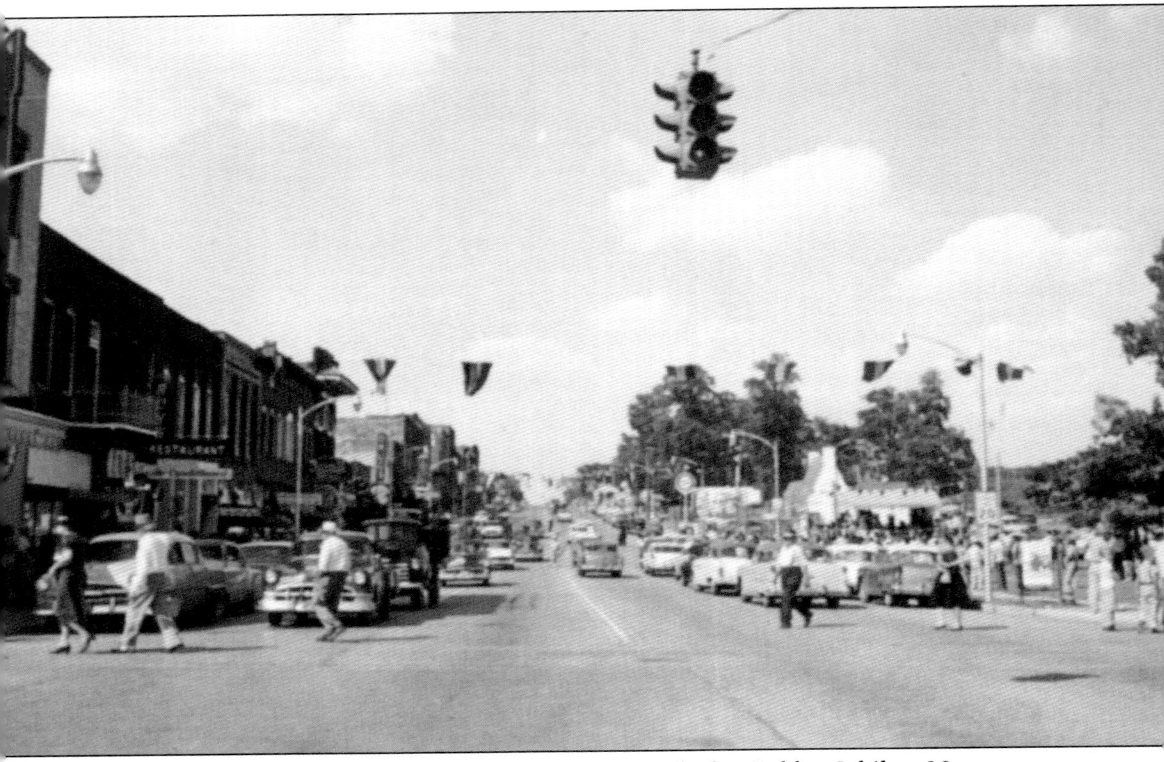

In 1957, Etowah celebrated its 50th anniversary with the Golden Jubilee. Numerous events and a parade were held to commemorate the town's birthday. This postcard shows the town as citizens and visitors enjoy the Fourth of July celebration. This view looks north up Tennessee Avenue at the Eighth Street red light. The Glenora Hotel is at left, with Roy's Restaurant and Tallent Drug Company visible down the block. Now past its 100 year mark, Etowah continues to celebrate its annual Fourth of July homecoming at the L&N Depot.

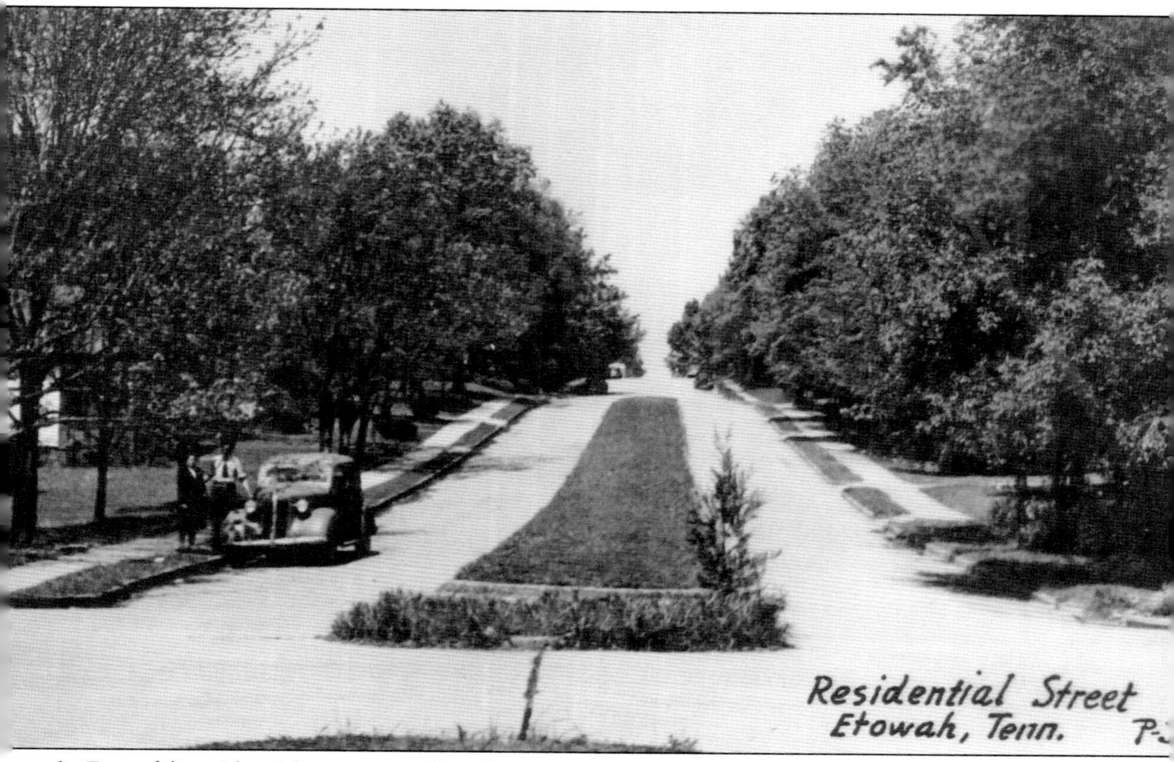


As Etowah's residential areas grew, broad streets with grassy medians were built in the affluent neighborhood known as Todd's Park. These back streets had a "park-like" atmosphere. This postcard from the 1940s shows the intersection of Tenth Street and Washington Avenue, with the Donald Rule family standing at left. The attractive medians were removed overnight by city workers in the 1970s, much to the chagrin of Etowah's citizens.

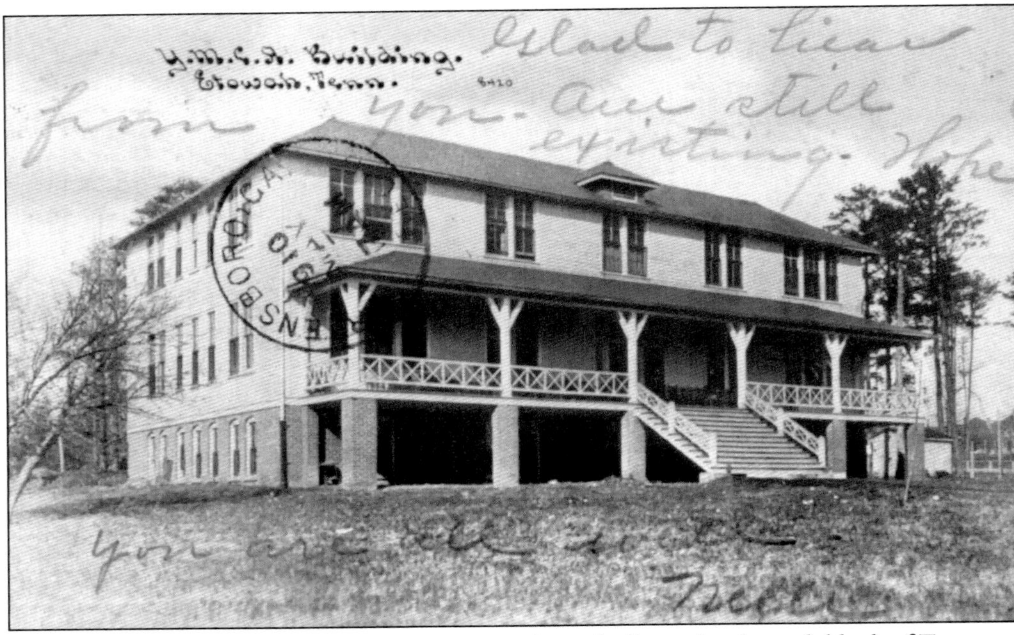


The Etowah YMCA, shown in this 1910 postcard, was built on the eleventh block of Tennessee Avenue soon after the town was founded. This two-story frame building was a home away from home for weary train crews, shop workers, and rail crews.

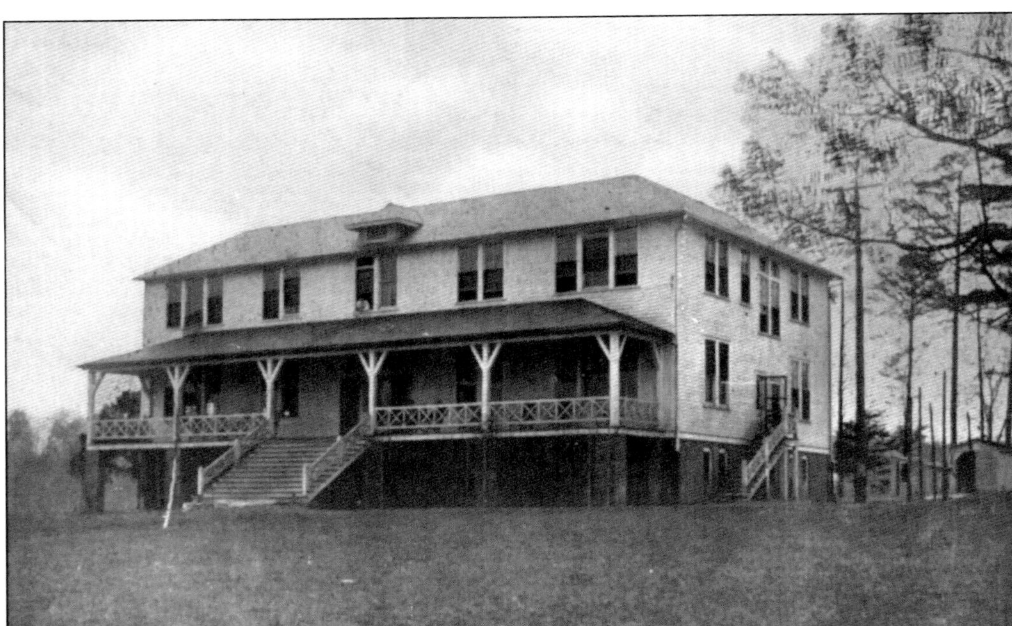


Another view of the YMCA shows its side entrance. More than 50 rooms provided lodging for itinerant laborers as well as those simply traveling through Etowah. The building also functioned as somewhat of a community center.

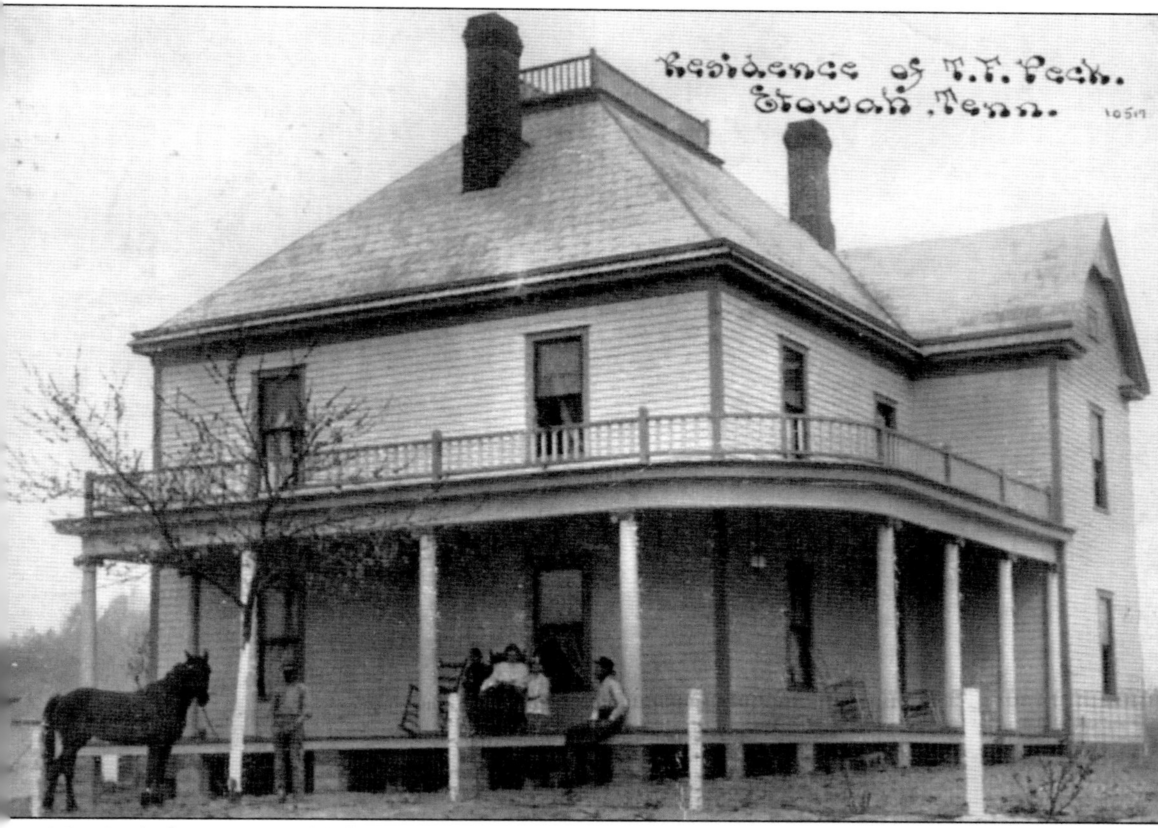


The Peck farm was established in the vicinity of the future town of Etowah before the Civil War. When the L&N Railroad began buying up property for its yards and shops, T. F. Peck, a businessman and Spanish-American War veteran, sold hundreds of acres of his family farm to the railroad. Buying certain tracts back, Peck speculated on the new town and became quite wealthy. In January 1907, he established the first newspaper, the *Etowah Enterprise*, which he operated until 1911, when he became the Tennessee commissioner of agriculture. Later he was active in Etowah banking and its early utilities. The home remains in East Etowah, overlooking the rail yard.

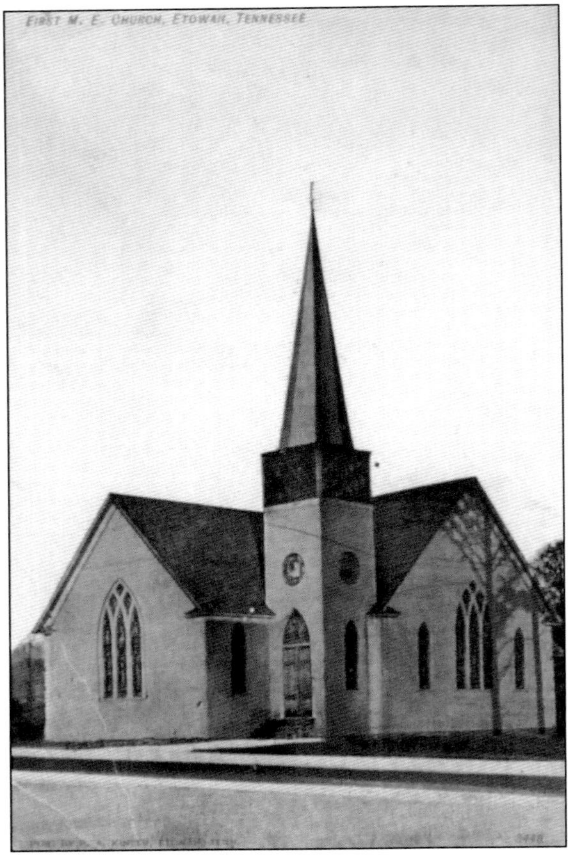


The Methodist Church in Etowah began in 1907, meeting in a storefront on Tennessee Avenue. This frame church building was located on Pennsylvania Avenue. A new building was needed in the 1920s to hold the growing congregation, and a Gothic-style building was completed on Eighth Street in 1927.

With the unification of three area Methodist congregations in 1939, St. Paul's United Methodist Church was born. The church remains at its Eighth Street location.

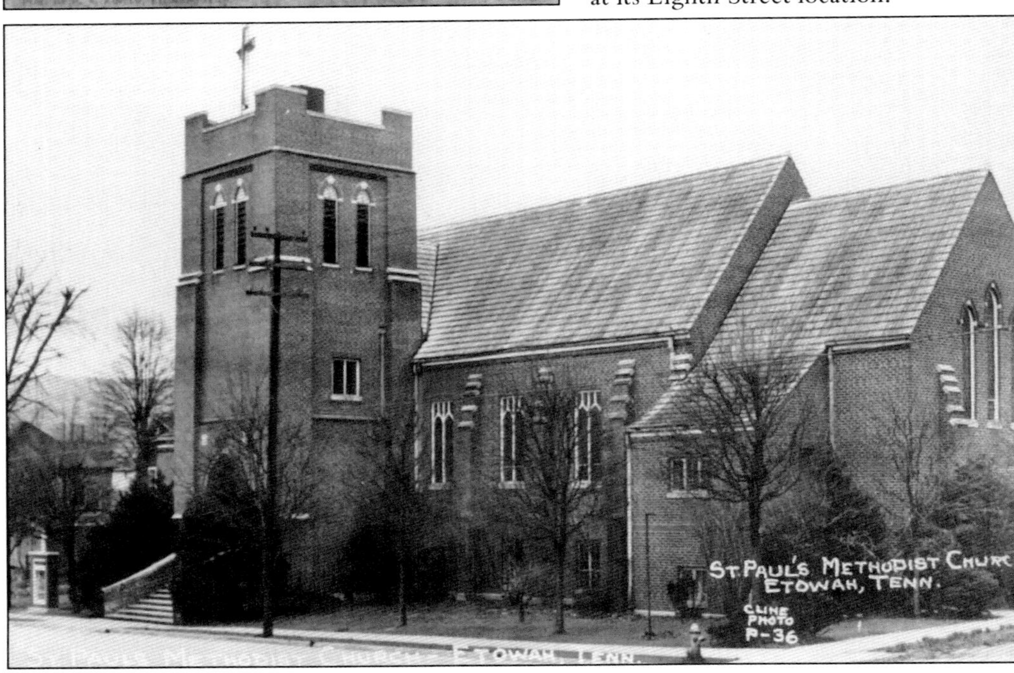

M. E. Church South is believed to be Etowah's oldest denomination. It was started in 1906 in a frame building on the corner of Ohio Avenue and Tenth Street. The building had a tall steeple bell tower and was used until the new building was constructed across the street in 1910.

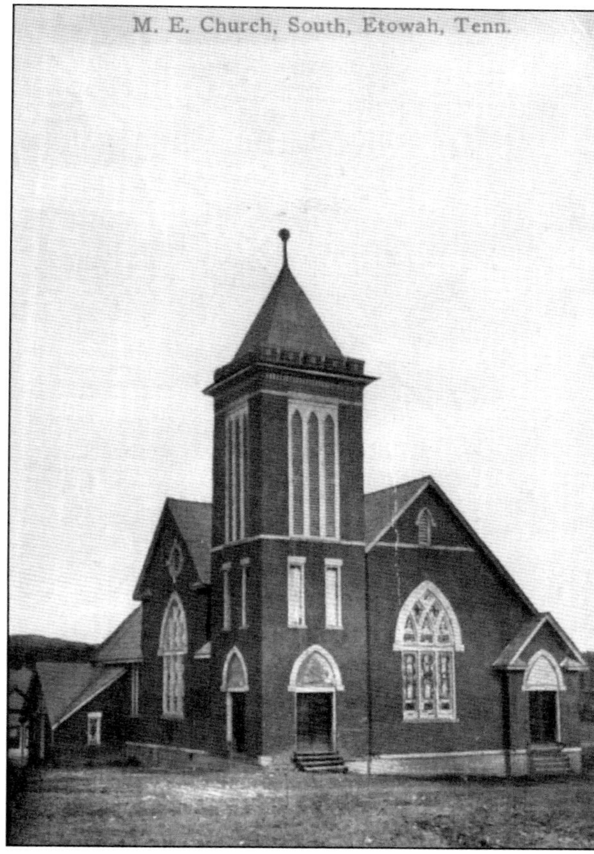


Wesley Memorial United Methodist Church, formerly Methodist Episcopal South and Tenth Street Methodist, has occupied this brick building since 1910. The imposing brick bell tower was removed around 1980, and the church bell was displayed outside.

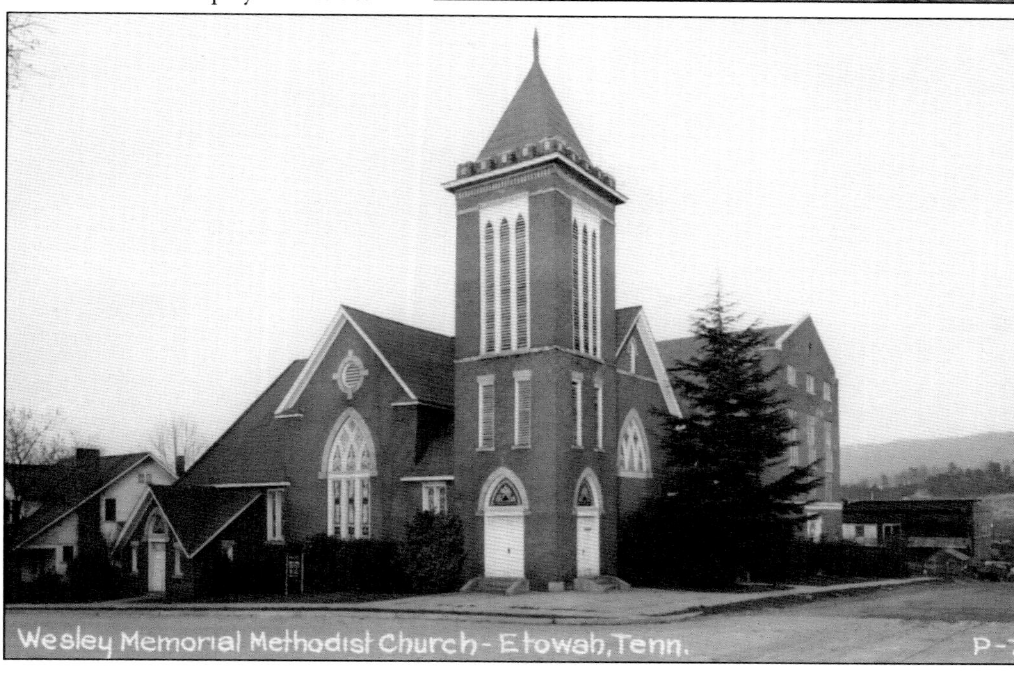

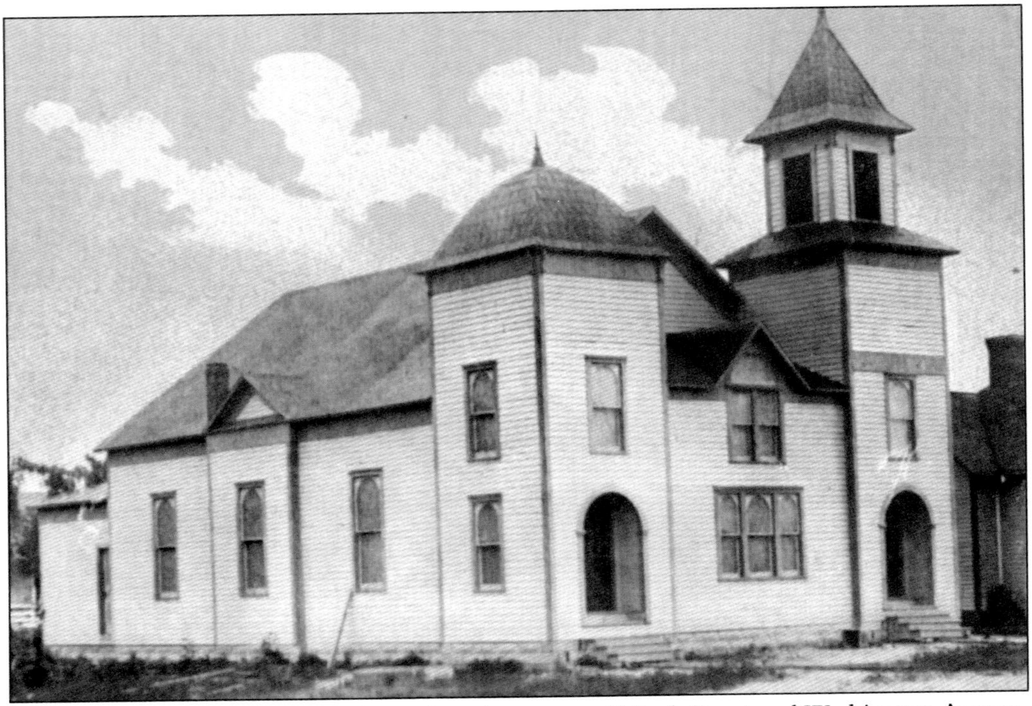

The original Baptist church was located on the corner of Ninth Street and Washington Avenue, with a busy Texaco Station anchoring the back corner of the block. When the Baptists built a new church next door of brick, this site became a parking lot.

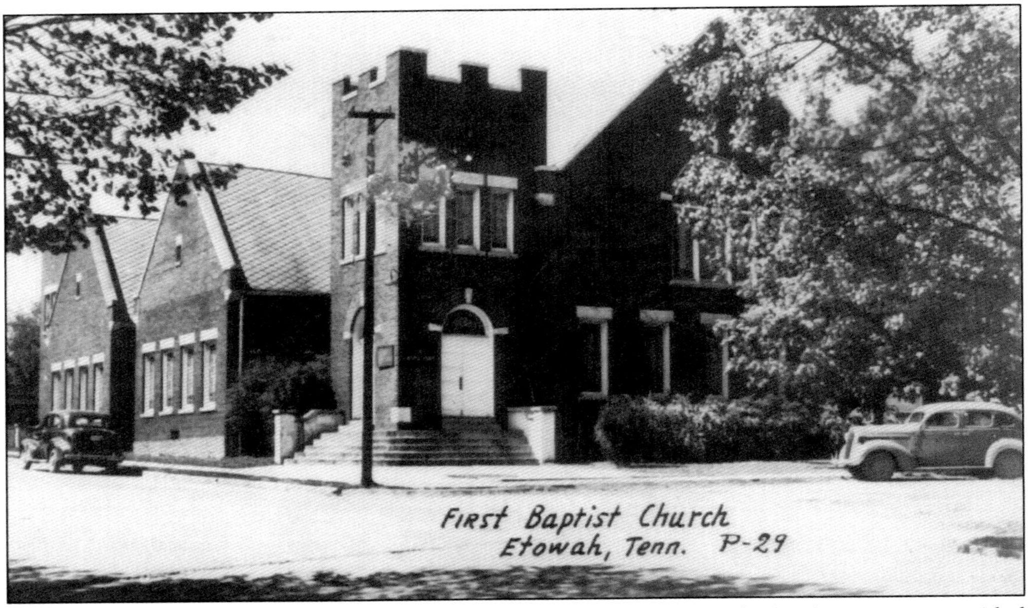


First Baptist Church replaced the old frame Baptist church building. The brick structure provided a larger sanctuary and an imposing tower. But within a few decades, the Etowah Baptists had outgrown this building.

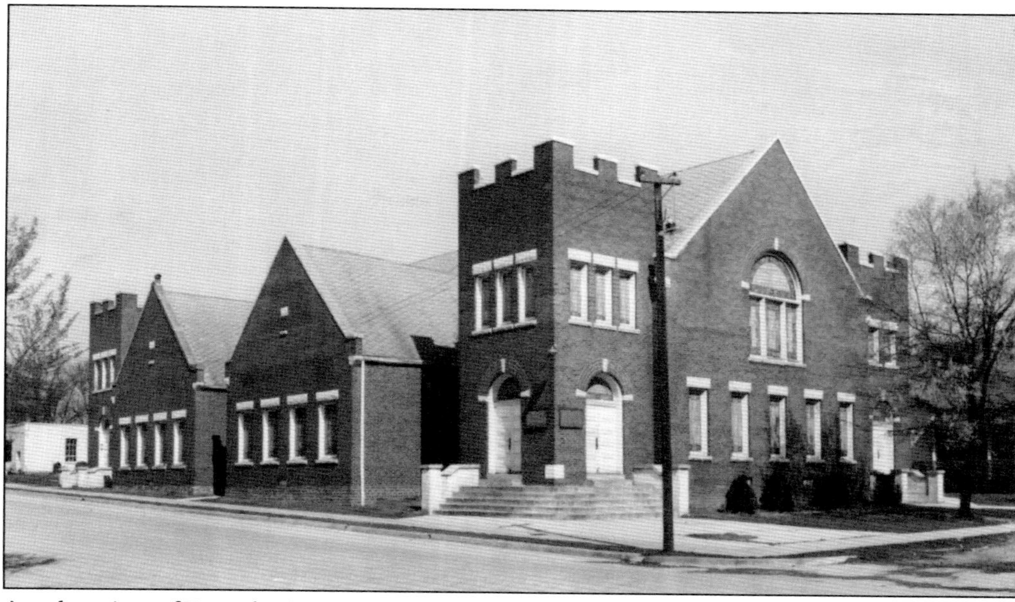

Another view of Etowah First Baptist Church is shown here. Its castle-like bell tower was unlike any other house of worship in town.

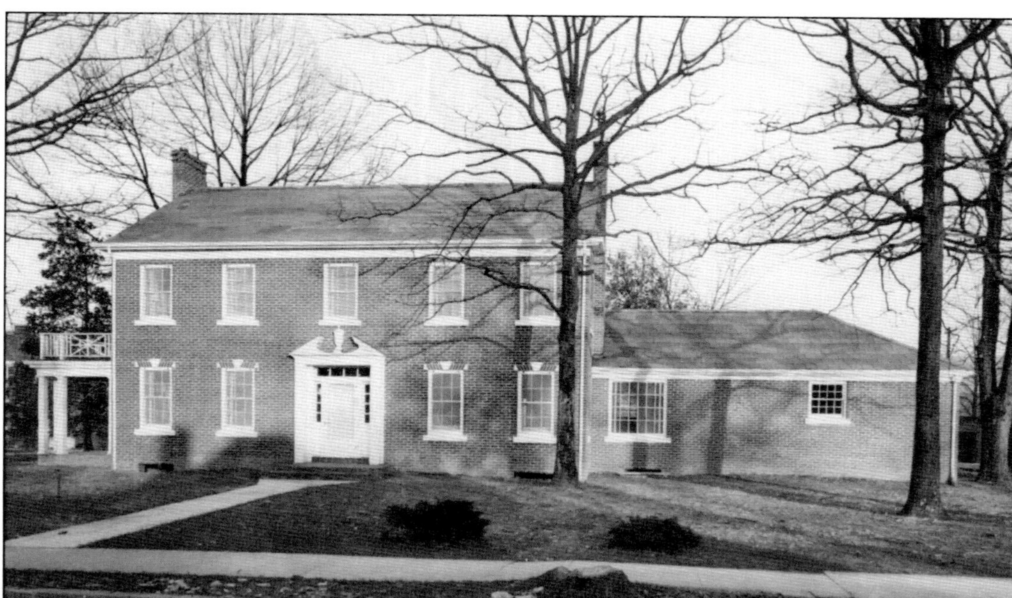


The First Baptist Church provided this parsonage for its ministers just across Pennsylvania Avenue from the church building. It is now a private residence.

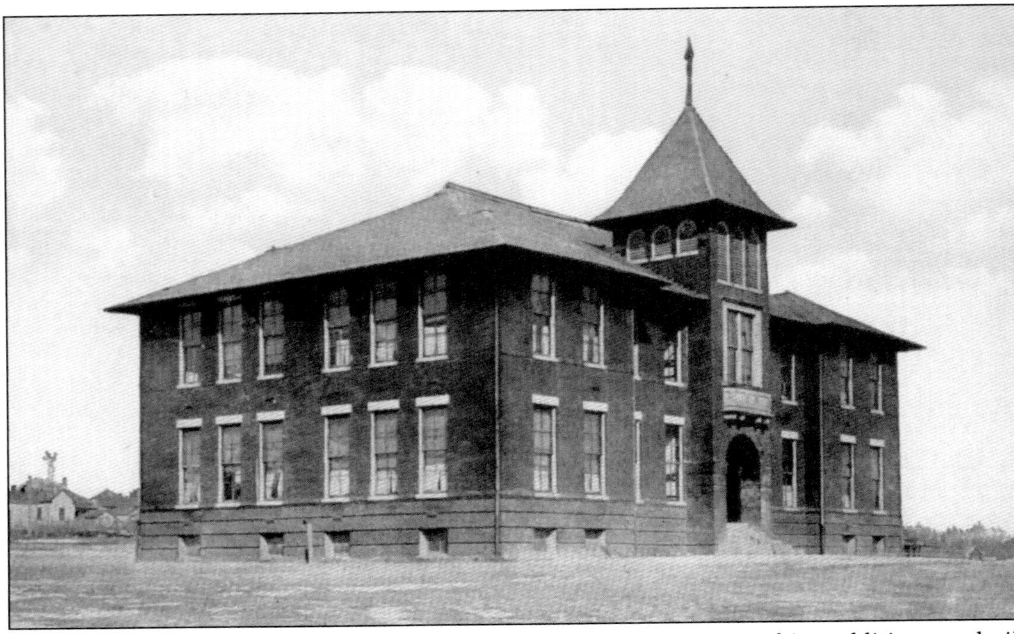

The old Etowah school building was constructed in 1915. Later a matching addition was built just to the left of this structure, which still stands on the 500 block of Indiana Avenue, now part of an adjacent park. The building pictured here was demolished in the 1970s upon completion of the present Etowah Grammar School on Eighth Street, and tennis courts now occupy the site.

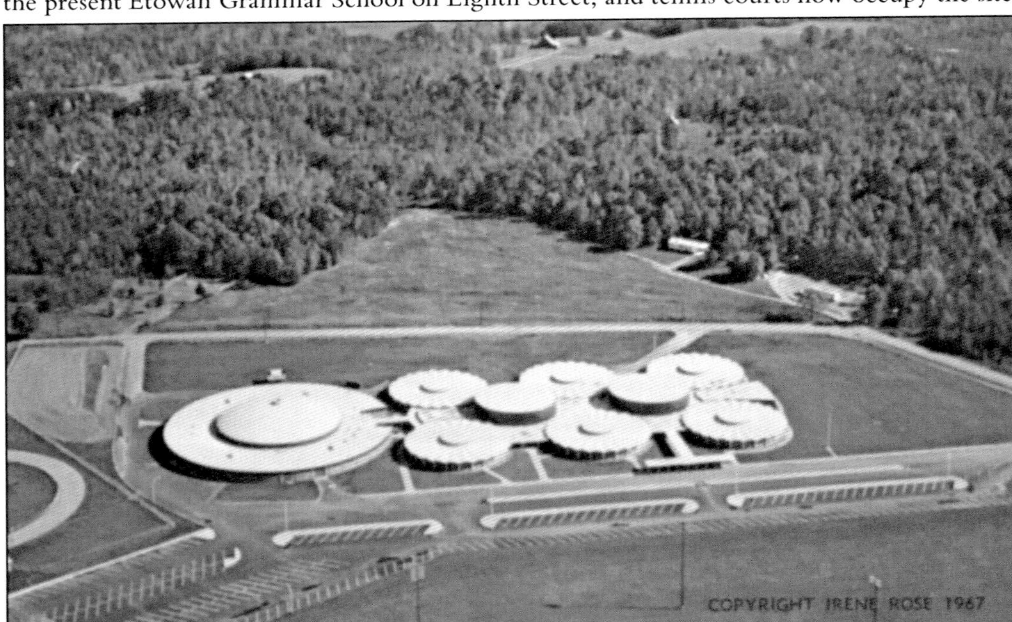


Central High School was completed and opened in 1966. It combined the students of Etowah High School and Englewood High School, which had, a few years earlier, been lost to fire. Built in round pods, as was the style in the late 1960s, Central has confused many lost freshmen trying to navigate its circular hallways. Central High remains one of McMinn County's two high schools, along with McMinn County High School in Athens.

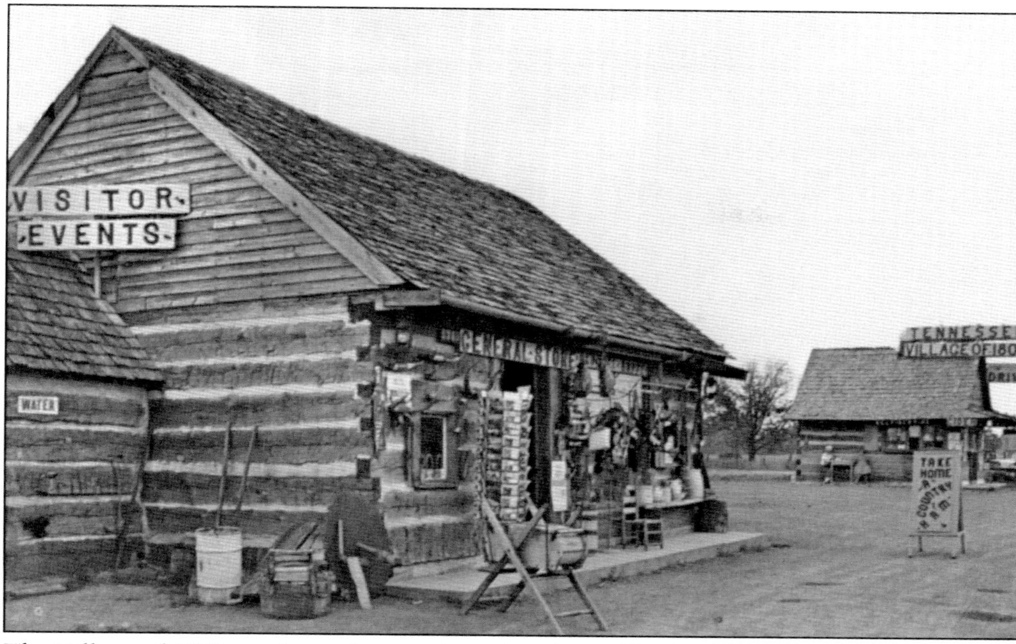


The Village of 1800 was located on a triangular piece of land where old Etowah-Englewood Highway intersected with Highway 411 just north of Etowah. Jim Owenby bought the antique cabins and buildings from an attraction in Pigeon Forge, Tennessee, and moved the "village" to Etowah. One of the highlights was the general store.

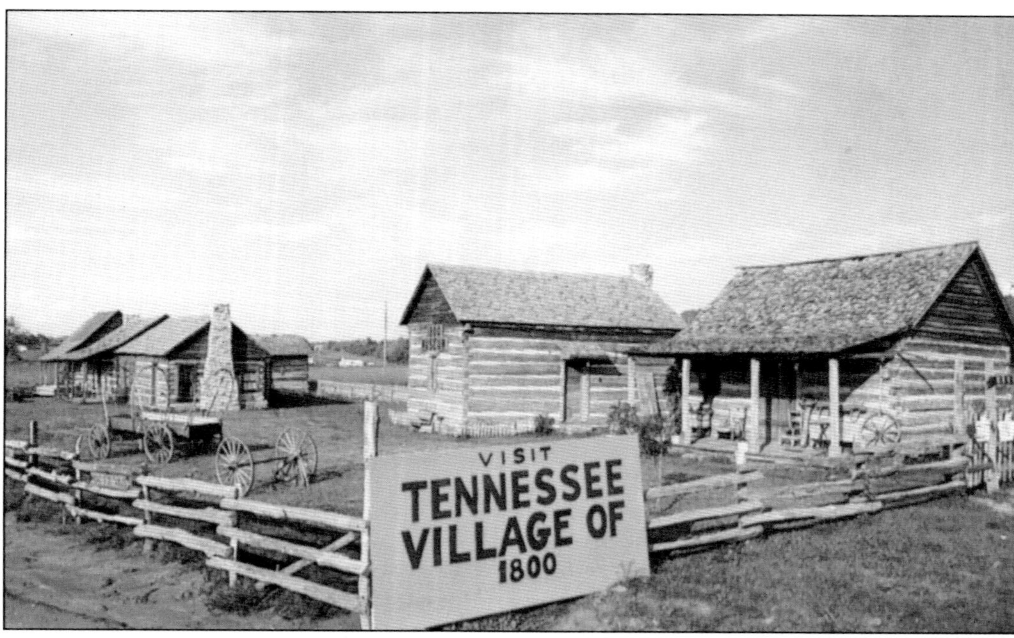


Another view of the Village of 1800 shows the "farmstead," complete with wagons and split-rail fence. The tourist attraction operated for several years before closing in the early 1970s. The buildings were sold off, and the site is now occupied by a McMinn County 911 ambulance station.

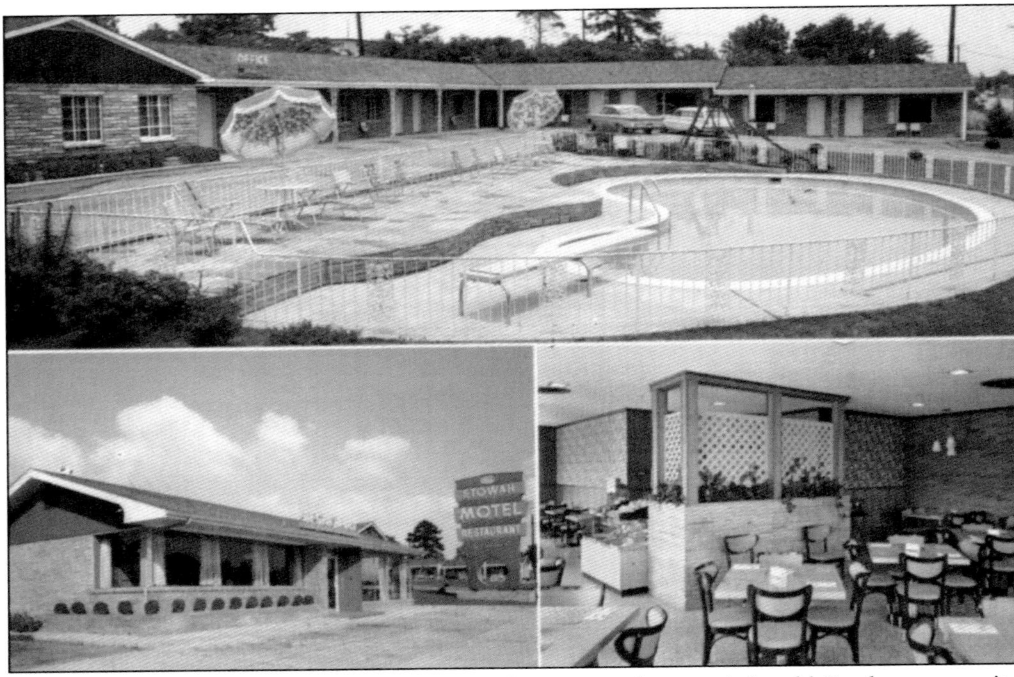


With the construction of Highway 411, Etowah grew north toward the old Grady community. This open area allowed for the building of more modern motor courts, such as the Etowah Motel. Rooms were connected to a central office, with parking right outside the patron's door. The hotel also featured an aptly named Etowah Restaurant.

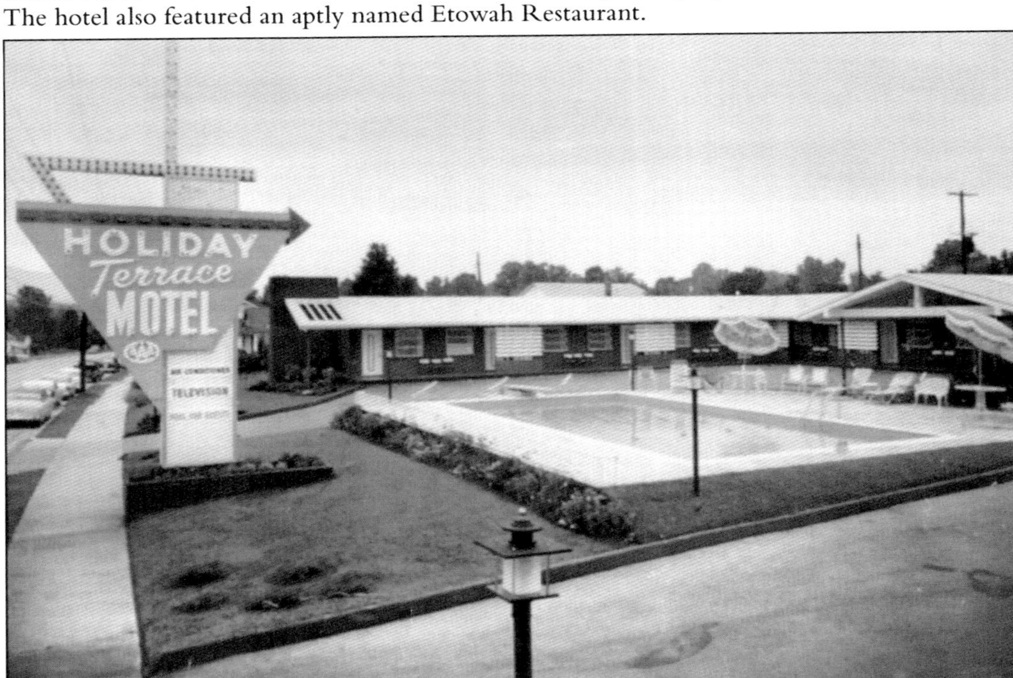


Holiday Terrace Motel was also a hotel that sprang up on Highway 411, right next door to the Etowah Motel. It featured a modern swimming pool as well.

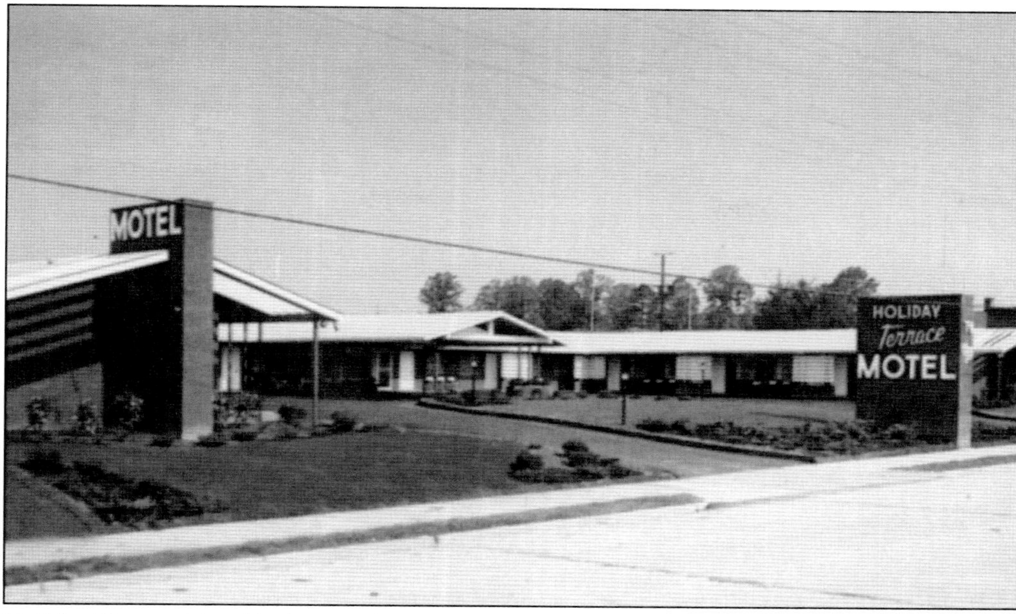


Holiday Terrace Motel is shown after some renovations to its sign on Highway 411. As Etowah continued to grow northward, a hospital was built on the site of the old Grady School, and soon Dunn's Hardware and several beer joints marked the coming of additional progress. Etowah's city limits would spell the end of the beer joints but allowed for the construction of a four-lane intersection of Highway 411 to State Highway 30, establishing a direct highway to Athens.

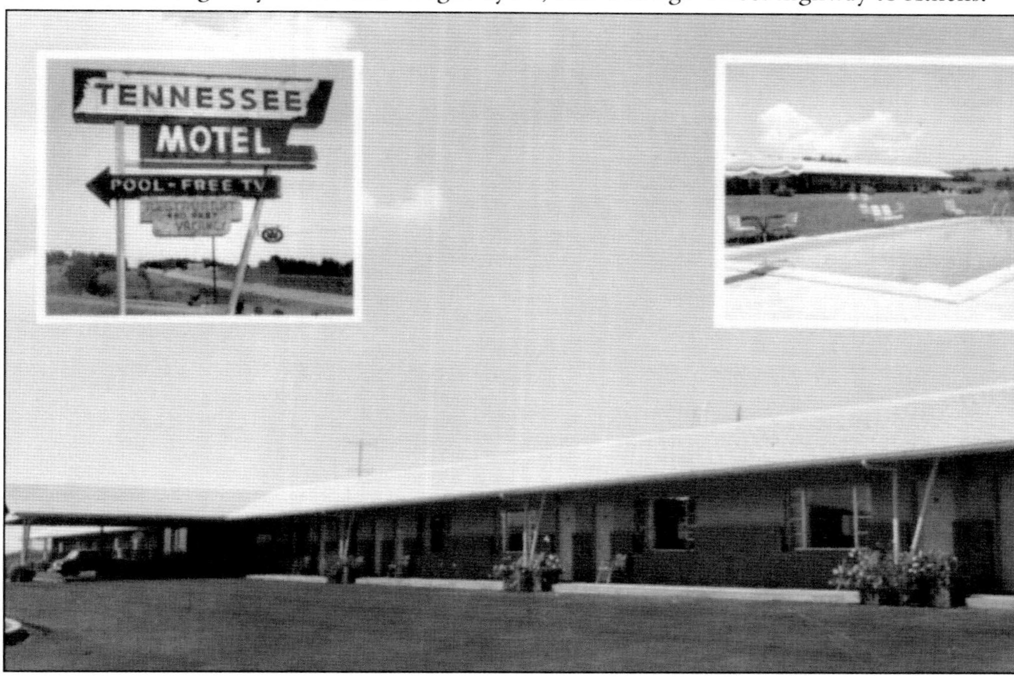


Still farther north on Highway 411 was the Tennessee Motel, owned and operated by Sam Waters. This place of lodging remained in business through the 1980s, until a fire swept through the derelict building. Portions of the complex have remained as a private night club.

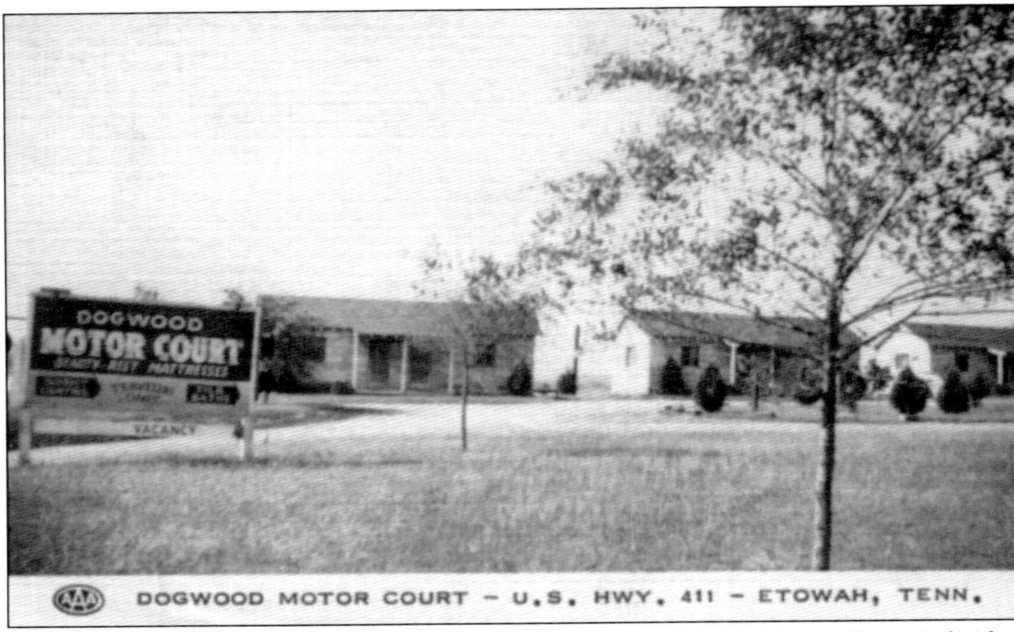


A little closer to Etowah, along Highway 411, was the Dogwood Motor Court. Offering individual cabins, the Dogwood provided its patrons with a picturesque setting among its namesake dogwood trees. It is shown in this postcard, dated 1953.

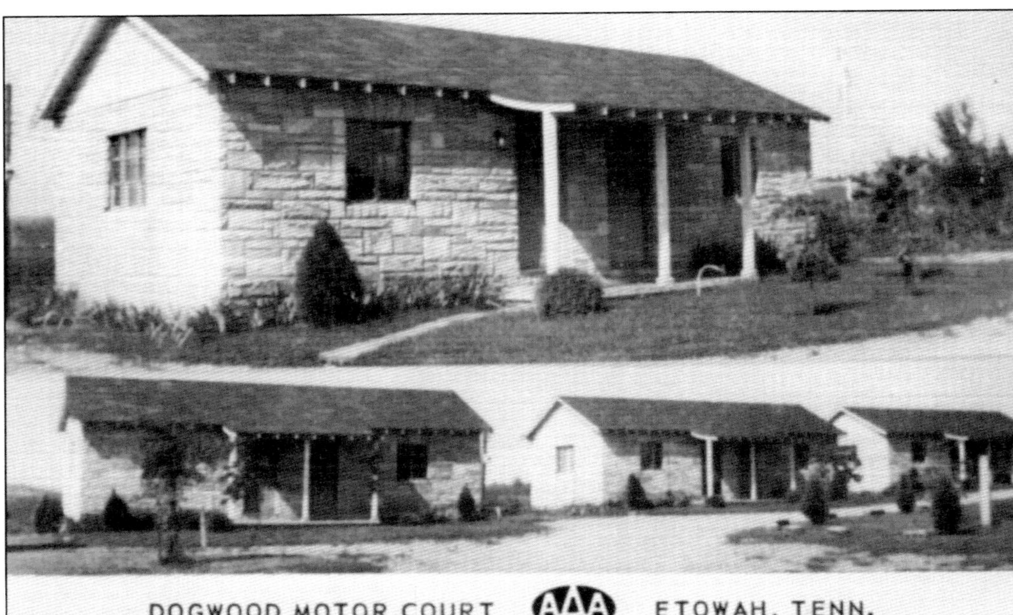


Dogwood Motor Court sat almost directly across Highway 411 from the Village of 1800, providing tourists a place to stay if their visit to the "historic homestead" ran late. Dinner was only a 3-mile drive south to Etowah. With the eventual closing of the Village of 1800, the Dogwood also declined.

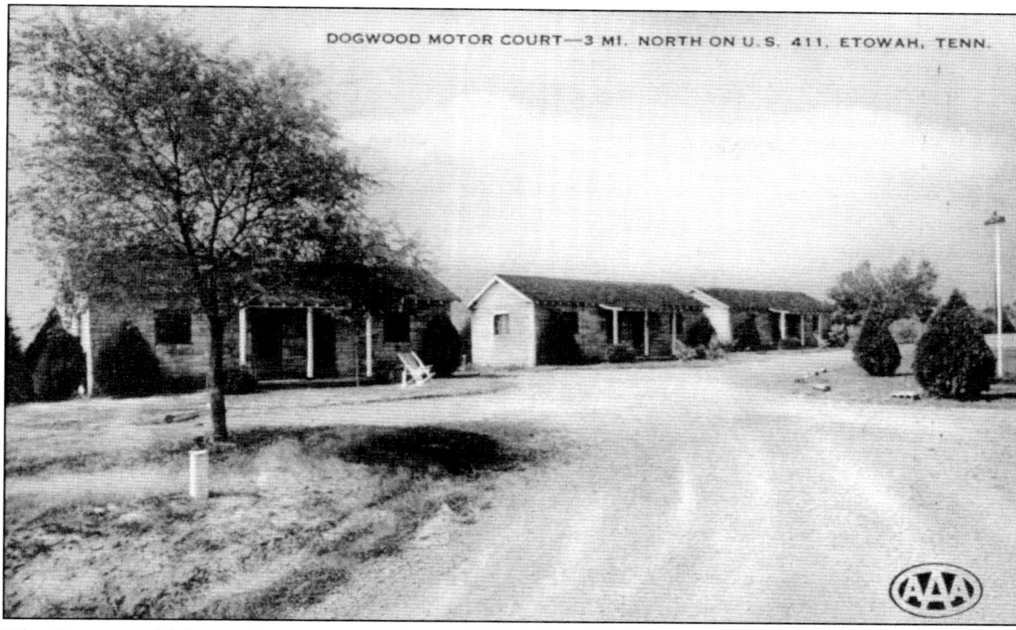


The Dogwood Motor Court eventually became the Dogwood Motel and remained a landmark along Highway 411 until the 1980s. Nearly all of its buildings still remain and operate as privately owned apartments.

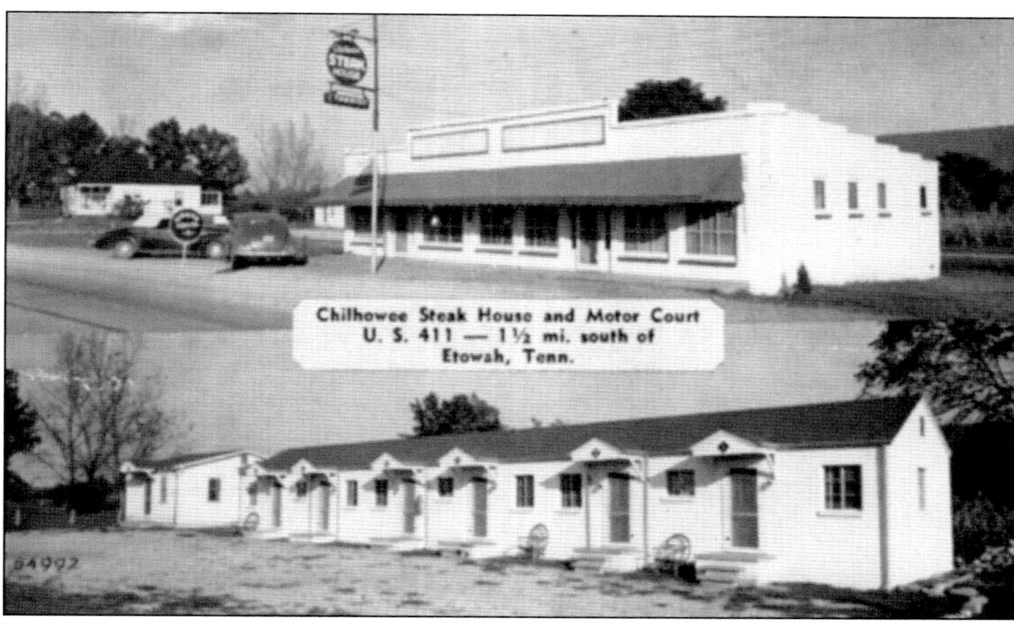


South of Etowah, Bo Dunn built the Chilhowee Steakhouse in the early 1940s, not long after the completion of Highway 411. The diner provided food and entertainment to the automobile travelers who rolled up and down the new highway, and soon hotel rooms were added to the rear of the building. By the 1970s, the steakhouse had evolved into an old-fashioned beer joint and its motel rooms into cheap apartments. Frequently under the eyes of local law enforcement, the business disappeared forever with the widening of Highway 411 in 2002.